AF411814

Kiln to Kitchen

ALSO BY JEAN ANDERSON

The Doubleday Cookbook (with Elaine Hanna, all editions), winner,
R. T. French Tastemaker Award, Best Basic Cookbook (1975), and
Cookbook of the Year (1975)

The Family Circle Cookbook (with the Food Editors of *Family Circle*)

Half a Can of Tomato Paste & Other Culinary Dilemmas (with Ruth Buchan),
winner, Seagram/International Association of Culinary Professionals
Award, Best Specialty Cookbook of the Year (1980)

The Food of Portugal, winner, Seagram/International Association of Culinary
Professionals Award, Best Foreign Cookbook of the Year (1986)

The New German Cookbook (with Hedy Würz)

The American Century Cookbook

The Good Morning America Cut the Calories Cookbook (coedited with
Sara Moulton)

Process This!, winner, James Beard Cookbook Awards, Best Cookbook,
Tools & Techniques Category (2003)

A Love Affair with Southern Cooking: Recipes and Recollections, winner,
James Beard Cookbook Awards, Best Cookbook, Americana Category
(2008) and SIBA (Southern Independent Booksellers Association)
Cookbook of the Year (2008)

Falling Off the Bone

From a Southern Oven

Mad for Muffins

Crisps, Cobblers, Custards & Creams

Jean Anderson's Preserving Guide

Kiln to Kitchen

Favorite Recipes from Beloved North Carolina Potters

Jean Anderson

PHOTOGRAPHS BY LISSA GOTWALS

The University of North Carolina Press   Chapel Hill

The University of North Carolina Press has been a member of the

Green Press Initiative since 2003.

Cover photograph courtesy of Lissa Gotwals

Maps created by Sally Scruggs

Library of Congress Cataloging-in-Publication Data
Names: Anderson, Jean, author. | Gotwals, Lissa, photographer.
Title: Kiln to kitchen: favorite recipes from beloved North Carolina potters /
Jean Anderson; photographs by Lissa Gotwals.
Description: Chapel Hill: The University of North Carolina Press, [2019] |
Includes index.
Identifiers: LCCN 2018059434| ISBN 9781469649450 (cloth: alk. paper) |
ISBN 9781469649467 (ebook)
Subjects: LCSH: Cooking, American—Southern style. | Potters—
North Carolina. | Cooking—North Carolina. | LCGFT: Cookbooks.
Classification: LCC TX715.2.S68 A529 2019 | DDC 641.5975—dc23
LC record available at https://lccn.loc.gov/2018059434

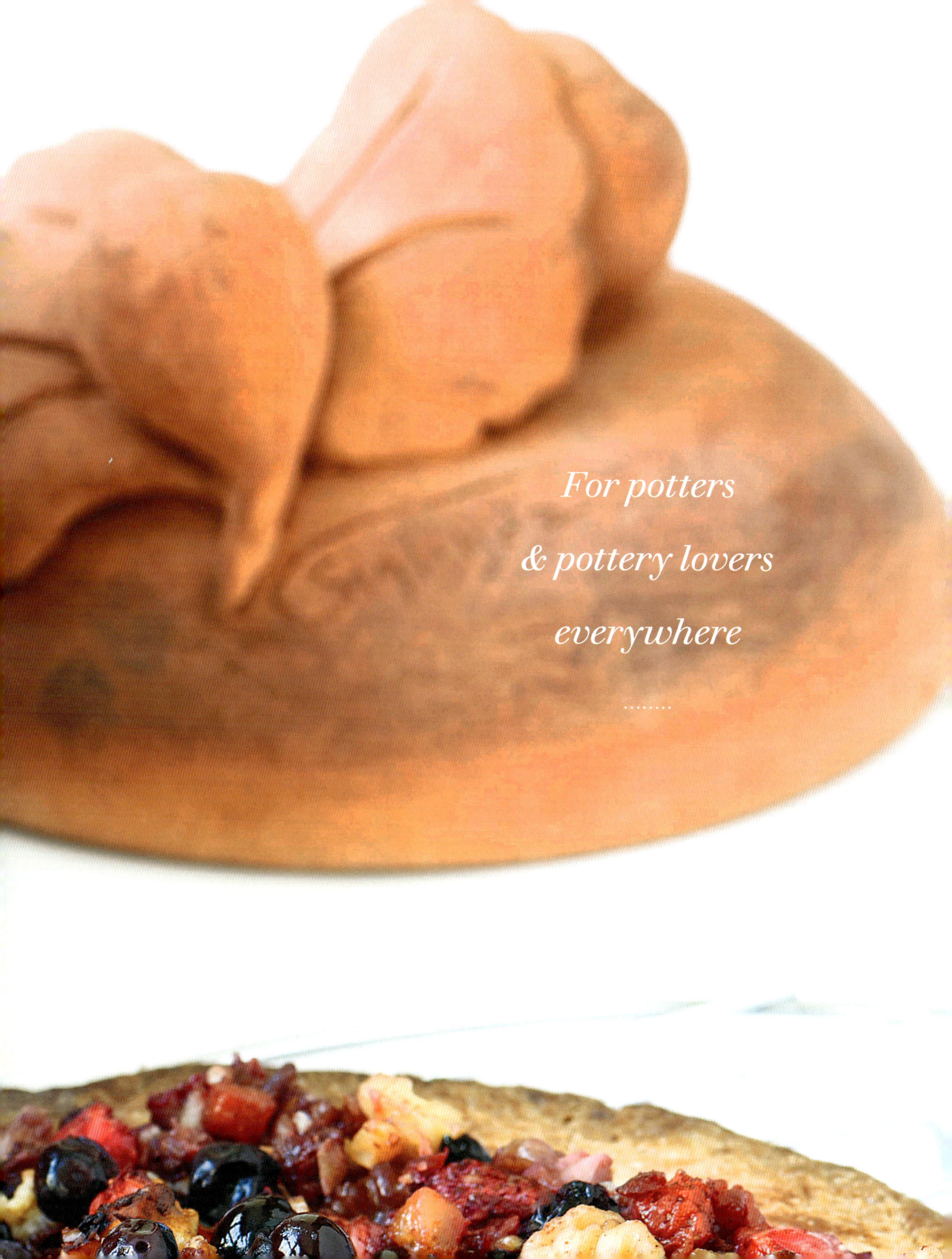
For potters
& pottery lovers
everywhere

CONTENTS

Maps

Acknowledgments

First, hats off to UNC Press for its support of North Carolina potters by publishing Nancy Sweezy's *Raised in Clay*; *The Potter's Eye: Art and Tradition in North Carolina Pottery* by Mark Hewitt and Nancy Sweezy; *Turners and Burners: The Folk Potters of North Carolina* by Charles G. Zug III; and now my own *Kiln to Kitchen*.

Special thanks to my editors, Elaine Maisner and Mary Carley Caviness; art director Kim Bryant; and the UNC Press team who shepherded this book into print with dedication and skill; and to photographer Lissa Gotwals for her wizardry with digital cameras, to Cecelia Murphy for area map ideas, and to styling assistant Julie Jones for her commitment, efficiency, and willingness to go the extra mile.

Sandy Gluck, Joanne Lamb Hayes, Maria Harrison Reuge, and Margaretta Yarborough: well done for taking such care when testing recipes.

Special thanks to Beth Gore of Cady Clay Works for being my Seagrove contact, and to Mark and Carol Hewitt for welcoming me into their home, introducing me to mountain potters I did not know, and the autographed copy of Mark's book, *The Potter's Eye*.

Thanks, too, to Linda Hilton Long for a signed copy of her *Hilton Homeplace Cookbook* as well as a lidded Hilton casserole to use for photography, and to Siglinda Scarpa for presenting several of her one-of-a-kind terra-cotta-colored unglazed stoneware pots to me and explaining why they must be cured before they are used. Likewise to Jon Ellenbogen of Barking Spider Pottery for online stoneware baking lessons.

I'm grateful, too, to *Our State Magazine* and UNC-TV for continuing to honor North Carolina potters both in print and on videos, among these a valuable discussion on the chemistry of clays with Ben Owen III on Frank Graff's *North Carolina Science Now* program. For the first time I understand what's required to make a proper stoneware pot.

I'd be remiss if I didn't recognize Jacques and Juliana Busbee, who established Jugtown some one hundred years ago, marketed Jugtown pots in New York, and are credited with rescuing North Carolina folk pottery from oblivion. So, too, Nancy Sweezy, who bought Jugtown after Mrs. Busbee's death, and introduced new designs and lead-free glazes while breathing new life into a pottery in distress.

A salute, too, to Nell Cole Graves, one of this state's first women potters, who sat at her wheel well into her eighties making the bowls, platters, pitchers, and vases that fill our home with color.

I'm indebted, too, to the North Carolina Pottery Center in Seagrove for its educational exhibits, demonstrations, research facilities, and unerring hospitality. Also to fellow pottery enthusiast Kathleen Ketterman, who introduced me to several potters I did not know; to Sara Moulton for her ongoing support; and to Bob Holmes, devout cook, longtime friend, and cookbook lover.

Unstinting thanks are due the booksellers who've hosted my demos and book signings over the years: McIntyre's at Fearrington Village, Flyleaf Books and A Southern Season in Chapel Hill, Quail Ridge Books in Raleigh, and my longtime home away from home, Nach Waxman's Kitchen Arts & Letters on the upper reaches of Lexington Avenue in New York.

Of course, there'd be no book without the cooperation of the potters featured in the pages that follow, artists who answered my call for recipes with a tantalizing mix despite their own crushing schedules. And particular thanks to you who so graciously gave or lent pottery to me to use in the photographs or gave me substantial discounts.

Finally, I'm blessed to have met Jugtown master potter Ben Owen, who charmed me with his "mud" magic long ago, and instilled in me a lifelong love affair with handcrafted pottery. I still use the Ben Owen "frogskin" mug I bought myself as a tenth birthday present—never mind that it blew my allowance. I'm pleased to say that after all these years, "It's as good as new. No chips, no cracks."

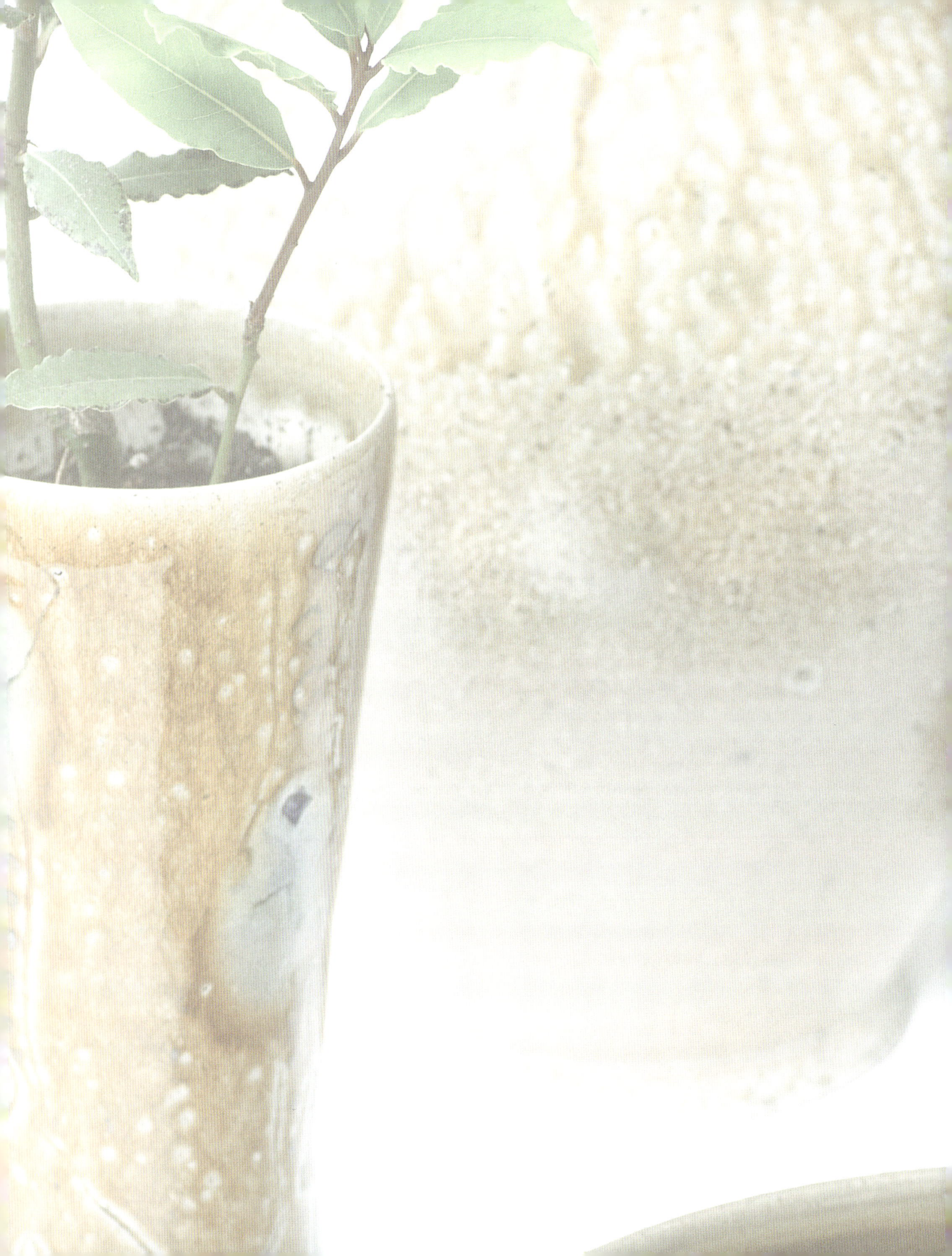

Kiln to Kitchen

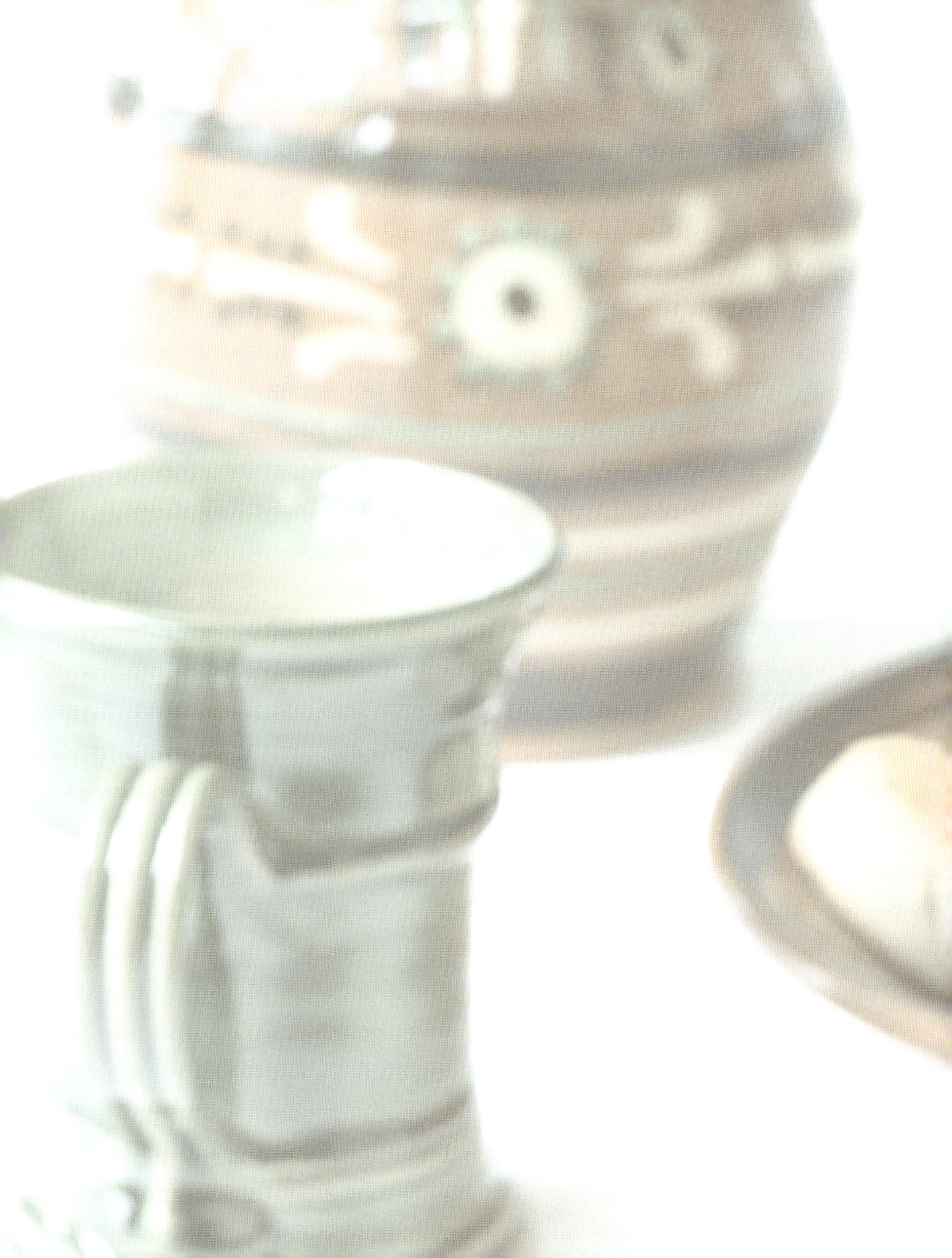

There are nearly a hundred potters clustered around the little town of Seagrove, deep in red clay country, so calling North Carolina "The World Capital of Pottery" is no idle boast.

My mother attributed her flaky piecrusts to the clay pie plates she'd bought at Jugtown, nine miles south of Seagrove. She filled her earthenware bean pot (in a Jugtown color called "tobacco spit") with her Illinois mother's pork and beans and bubbled them for hours in a slow oven. She even used that pot as a tureen for her midwestern corn chowder.

Mama was rare among yesterday's collectors, at least among those we knew, who considered handcrafted pottery decorative, something to exhibit on a living room shelf.

Today, thank goodness, more and more North Carolina potters are focusing on the functional—pottery in which food can be cooked and/or served.

Designs vary dramatically, and why not? Some of our potters are homegrown with ancestral roots reaching as far back as the 1700s; others grew up elsewhere—the Deep South, New York, and New England, like East Fork's Alex Matisse, whose statement, above, I excerpted from his gig on UNC-TV. There are expats here, too, Canadian, English, and Italian, all of them lured to this state by clay.

Many have introduced new glazes, new techniques, but just as many potters have remained true to the utilitarian pie plates, casseroles, jugs, platters, and pitchers that made North Carolina famous.

On recent pottery runs, I've discovered something else new: recipes tucked into everything from fluted angel food cake pans to no-nonsense casseroles. And once in a while there's even a nibble—a cube of pound cake, perhaps, or a bit of dip on a chip.

Introduction

North Carolina is a land made of clay.

It's everywhere.

—Our State *(PBS)*

With local potters beginning to share the recipes they prepare and/or serve in their own pots, why not a cookbook of potter family favorites? A colorful—make that irresistible—collection?

There would be southern recipes, to be sure, classics like Lucille Owen's Wild Persimmon Pudding, plus a few exotics: Mark Hewitt's mother's spicy South African beef Bobotie, Jon Ellenbogen's Puerto Rican shrimp and chorizo Asapao, and Siglinda Scarpa's Italian Crostata di Frutta. In other words, a "soup to nuts" potpourri of recipes to cook and/or serve in clay and other ovenproof ceramics.

Artists, I've discovered, are invariably good cooks, creative cooks, not to mention world travelers eager to check out the work of fellow potters. But there's an additional perk to these global jaunts: seductive new recipes to try (you'll find some of them in the pages that follow). Every recipe has been thoroughly tested, several times if necessary, and tweaked as needed so that it's foolproof for rookie home cooks as well as for old hands.

With hundreds of North Carolina potters firing kiln-loads of stoneware versatile enough for cooking and serving food, we are blessed. And to think that it all began at Jugtown some hundred years ago.

When I was a little girl, I looked forward to Saturday drives to Jugtown, a pottery owned by Raleigh acquaintances named Busbee. These outings were fun despite the geology lessons given en route because Daddy-the-science-professor always turned our car into a classroom.

Pausing at a road cut, he'd pull over, and ask me to stand beside him as he discussed the various strata, all of them created as volcanic ash weathered and morphed down the millennia. There'd be our stain-everything red mud, naturally. But also crumbly sandstone the color of country cream, schist, and, several tiers down, the putty-ish feldspar-rich clay that's essential for today's high-fired functional stoneware.

"Millions of years ago," Daddy would explain, "volcanic eruptions helped shape our state." So, too, the ocean, repeatedly rising and falling across beds of molten rock until tectonic plates collided heaving mountains into the sky. To a ten-year-old girl, surreal.

But the real magic for me was watching Jugtown master potter Ben Owen spin blobs of clay into jugs of perfect symmetry.

If I had had what potters call "the hands," I might have become a potter, myself. But having failed miserably at the potter's wheel, I became an aficionado. And I am not alone.

You've only to visit Jugtown, the studio of Owen's grandson Ben Owen III, or any of the other area potters to see binge-buyers loading their SUVs. Some own shops or galleries, but many, like me, are hard-core collectors of hand-crafted pottery, the decorative as well as the workaday.

Whenever New York friends fly down to visit, we spend a day pottery-hopping in and around Seagrove, and I'm always delighted—though not surprised—to see how blown away they are by the quality and variety of North Carolina pottery.

Our first potters—three thousand years back—were the Catawba and Cherokee Indians, but the shapes and patterns so familiar today were introduced some two and a half centuries ago by the English, who settled in the Piedmont and began transforming our red clay into storage jugs and crocks, churns and candlesticks.

Today there are potters all over the state, but for this book I focus on twenty-four, eight in each of three areas known for their functional

pottery: the Greater Triangle area (Raleigh–
Durham–Chapel Hill), the Seagrove–Asheboro
area ("pottery central"), and the Catawba Valley,
foothills, and mountains.

To simplify touring, I've worked out three
itineraries, one for each area, pinpointing the
location of its eight potteries on a map so that
you can drive from Pottery 1, to 2, to 3, and so
forth without backtracking. Or, equally easy,
from Pottery 8, to 7, to 6, and so on.

I, myself, am forever on the road ferreting
out new potteries, often with a fellow enthusiast
who's not only as passionate about pottery as I
but also an accomplished cook. We make a day
of it, lunching in some central spot midtour,
and usually end up "talking food," in particular
about what recipes the potters might cook or
serve in the pots they make.

Now, after two years of interviews, of recipe
tests and retests, there is a cookbook devoted
to North Carolina potters and their favorite
recipes—their apps and soups, their mains and
sides, and, yes, their breads and desserts.

You're holding that cookbook in your hands.

JEAN ANDERSON
Chapel Hill, North Carolina

Pottery Primer

Because pottery is handcrafted, the diameters and volumes of each piece vary slightly but rarely enough to affect a recipe. Here, then, a mini-guide to pottery:

BISQUE Pottery that's been fired but not glazed.

EARTHENWARE Porous, iron-rich pottery made from the local red clay. Early Quakers baked in it, even had "a fireproof frying pan." Today's may not be ovenproof. Always ask.

FOOD-SAFE Pottery that's not only free of toxic chemicals but also sturdy enough to withstand stacking and repeated trips to the oven and dishwasher—no chipping or cracking.

FUNCTIONAL POTTERY Utilitarian pottery made for preparing or serving food.

GREENWARE Pottery that's been shaped but not fired. Westmoore's Mary Farrell, however, calls her green-glazed pottery "greenware," a midrange stoneware.

OVENPROOF Pottery that can take oven heat, but make a note: both the pot and its ingredients must be at room temperature. Several factors determine oven-worthiness—the clay, the firing methods, and the glaze. My recipes all specify cold oven or preheated. *Note*: If you don't know whether a pottery pie pan, tube pan, or casserole is ovenproof, start in a cold oven. Ovenproof does not mean microwave-safe. The potter knows, so be sure to ask.

MORAVIAN AND QUAKER POTTERY Plain or decorative functional ware introduced by the Moravians and Quakers who settled in the Carolina Piedmont in the mid-1700s. Westmoore is noted for exquisite replicas of Moravian pottery, New Salem for Quaker slipware and redware.

REDWARE Iron-rust-red functional pottery plain or decorative, stoneware or earthenware.

STONEWARE Durable and nontoxic, stoneware is a mixture of clays, among them smooth, dense aluminum-and-silica-rich feldspar. Fired at 2,000°F-plus temperatures, it's ovenproof.

TERRA-COTTA Literally "baked earth." Glazed or unglazed, terra-cotta is used more often for bricks and roof tiles than for kitchen- or dinnerware.

Glazes

Glass fused onto the surface of pottery to make it waterproof as well as to add strength, design, and color. The subject of glazes is too complex to discuss here, but just know that to ensure the food safety of pottery, the federal government has set maximum allowable amounts of two toxic metals: lead and cadmium (often used for reds, oranges, and yellows).

According to Beth Gore of Cady Clay Works, "No responsible potter uses toxic glazes for functional ware." If in doubt, ask the potter directly. Also check the bottoms of pots to see if they've been stamped "Not for Food or Drink."

VINEGAR TEST FOR TOXICITY

Half fill a piece of glazed pottery with white vinegar and leave it on the counter for several days. Pour the vinegar out, wipe the pot dry, then compare the color and texture above and below the vinegar line. If there are significant differences, toxic chemicals will seep into any food or drink put into the pot. To avoid using this pot, write "TOXIC" on the bottom.

GLAZE TYPES

LEAD GLAZE Used by North Carolina's earliest potters ignorant of this metal's toxicity. By the mid-nineteenth century, however, they were fully aware and were substituting salt or wood ash (alkaline) glazes, both considered food-safe to this day.

SALT GLAZE Who knew that common salt, fired at temperatures beyond 2000°F, would fuse with the clay's silica and vitrify? Typically, salt-glazed pottery is mottled or streaked, usually in shades of gray and/or tans and browns.

UNGLAZED POTTERY Of the twenty-four potters featured in this book, Siglinda Scarpa is the only one whose stoneware pots are unglazed inside and out. And each must be properly seasoned or "cured" before it can be used. The process is too intricate to include here. Fortunately, Scarpa has printed the curing directions, which also include the care and keeping of unglazed pottery. Ask for these directions when buying.

Cooking in Clay Q & A

Q: Why do some recipes call for pottery baking dishes that can go into preheated ovens while others must be started in cold ovens?

A: Not all clays are created equal. Simple red clay (earthenware) dishes are so fragile they should be started in cold ovens. Ironstone, on the other hand, is sturdier and in most cases, can be started in a preheated oven. If in doubt, however, always start the dish in a cold oven. *Note: Each recipe in the book specifies a preheated or cold oven and suggests other containers that work equally well.*

Q: What about the various glazes? Does oven heat destroy them over time?

A: Rarely, although salt glazes are usually tougher than satiny ones, which may have been fired at lower kiln temperatures. Potter Mark Hewitt explains that the shock to a pot put into a preheated oven may occasionally crack or craze the glaze. If this should happen, use the pot as a serving piece.

Q: Why no microwave recipes for pottery?

A: Because the wattages of today's microwaves are so variable there's no way to give accurate cooking times.

Q: Is pottery dishwasher-safe?

A: The sturdier pieces, yes. But if doubt, always ask the potter.

Q: What's the best way to prepare clay casseroles, pie plates, and tube pans for baking? I've heard that things tend to stick—especially in tube pans.

A: Experienced cooks spritz pottery tube pans well with nonstick cooking spray just before adding the batter because if it's done earlier, the spray will merely puddle in the bottom of the pan and lose its effectiveness. Food pros find that greasing pottery tube and Bundt pans with vegetable shortening (Crisco) is even better. Then to make sure these cakes, breads, and other loaves unmold neatly, they line the bottom of the pan with a circle of baking parchment or nonstick aluminum foil and grease that, too.

BAKING POWDER Double-acting's the most reliable because it reacts first when moistened, second when heated.

BAKING SODA When this alkaline meets molasses or another acidic ingredient like lemon juice, the two release carbon dioxide gas, a powerful leavening.

BUTTER Old-fashioned stick butter, never margarine—salted unless unsalted is an option. *Note*: High-butterfat European-style butters (Plugrá, etc.) may be too rich for cakes.

CHOCOLATE AND COCOA Unsweetened, semisweet? My recipes leave no doubt. Cocoa means unsweetened cocoa powder, never a drink mix.

CORNMEAL Southerners fussy about cornmeal choose stone-ground. But supermarket granular meal is sometimes better. Each recipe IDs the one to use.

CORN SYRUP Glucose syrup made from the starch of yellow dent corn. It's used to increase volume and keep sugar from crystallizing. Light and dark corn syrup are both more caloric than granulated sugar (1 tablespoon = 48 calories).

- Dark corn syrup (1 tablespoon = 57 calories): This pecan pie favorite is a blend of light corn syrup, molasses, caramel coloring, and flavoring.
- Light corn syrup (1 tablespoon = 62 calories): Glucose syrup plus salt and vanilla.

CREAM From thin to thick. *Note*: The lower its butterfat content, the faster a cream will curdle when heated.

- Half-and-half: A 50–50 mix of whole milk and cream; 10 to 12 percent butterfat.

Ingredients Used in the Recipes

- Sour cream: Fermented with lactic acid bacteria; about 14 percent butterfat. Sour cream owes its creaminess to thickeners such as rennet, guar gum, and Irish moss.
- Light cream: About 20 percent butterfat.
- Whipping cream: Want billowing Alpine peaks? Then this 30- to 36-percent butterfat cream is the one to whip even though its peaks tend to deflate.
- Heavy cream: With 36 to 40 percent butterfat, heavy cream whips to sturdy peaks, especially if beaten with a little confectioners' (10x) sugar. *Note*: The ultra-pasteurized takes a bit longer to whip.

EGGS Large eggs only. All recipes containing egg must be cooked to an internal temperature of 160°F to avoid salmonella food poisoning. To test, insert an instant-read thermometer midway between the rim and the center of the baking dish. For meringues, insert horizontally into the middle. *Tip*: Even easier, use pasteurized eggs.

- For perfect hard-cooked eggs: Place eggs in a large, heavy pan, half-fill with cold water, then bring to a boil over high heat. Set off-heat, cover, and let stand for 15 minutes. Drain the eggs, then quick-chill in an ice bath. *Tip*: Eggs nearing their sell-by date shell more easily than fresh eggs.

EXTRACTS AND FLAVORINGS Pure extracts only, never the "faux," which can ruin a recipe.

FLOUR Always sift flour before you measure it, even if presifted, because flour compacts in storage. To measure: Spoon the sifted flour lightly into a dry cup measure (one of the "nested" Mary Ann cups), then level off the top with the edge of a small thin-blade spatula. Never shake the measuring cup to level the flour, and never rap it against the counter.

- All-purpose flour: Bleached unless unbleached is called for. And never self-rising unless self-rising is specified.
- Gluten-free flours: Three in this book—banana, potato, and rice (see Sources, page 164). *Note*: Spelt, a primitive wheat often said to be gluten-free, does contain gluten but in a more digestible form. Not for those with celiac disease.
- Self-rising flour: A time-saver with salt and baking powder added. Never substitute for all-purpose flour.
- Whole wheat flour: Few people associate this nutrient-dense flour with biscuits, but if mixed with an equal measure of sifted all-purpose flour, your biscuits will be light (see Lucille's Whole-Wheat Biscuits, page 94).

LARD AND VEGETABLE SHORTENING Never substitute one for the other. Lard is rendered hog fat, vegetable shortening is hydrogenated vegetable oil.

MILK Homogenized whole milk unless recipes call for something else.

- Buttermilk: Milk bacterially fermented to convert milk sugar into lactic acid. Low-fat (regular) and fat-free buttermilks are widely available. There are a few boutique "whole" buttermilks—expensive and pointless. Use soured milk instead; just buzz it till smooth in a food processor or electric blender.
- Evaporated milk: With 60 percent less water than fresh milk, this unsweetened canned milk has a faint caramel flavor that enriches any recipe to which it's added.

OLIVE OIL Find an extra-virgin olive oil that you like, and store it at room temperature; never refrigerate. Olive oil quickly goes rancid, so if you don't use it often, buy a small bottle.

PEPPER Freshly ground black pepper always.

RICE Recent FDA reports of arsenic in rice have raised red flags because organically grown rice may be as contaminated as inorganic. Soil and groundwater contain arsenic, and the greatest concentrations of it are in the South. Thus, where rice is grown matters more than how it's grown. The safest rice? California rice, also basmati, that popular slender-grained Indian rice whose Sanskrit name means "fragrant."

- Long-grain white rice: This country's most popular rice, if you don't count quick-cooking, and the one to use unless other options are given.
- Brown rice: With only the outer husk removed, brown rice is more nutritious and more flavorful than white rice. It also contains more arsenic.
- Wild rice: Not rice at all but the flowering head of an aquatic reed native to Minnesota and Wisconsin. It, too, contains arsenic, so use sparingly.

SALT Un-iodized table salt. Feel free to substitute coarse salt in soups, stews, and casseroles, but not in baked goods. It dissolves so poorly your cakes may be gritty.

SUGAR Whenever a recipe contains more than one kind of sugar, each type will be named. If there's one sugar only, that sugar is granulated.

- Brown sugar: Light or dark? Whichever recipes recommend. To measure, pack into a dry-cup measure, and level off with the flat side of a small thin-blade spatula.
- Confectioners' (10x) sugar: Sift or not, as recipes direct, then spoon lightly into a dry-cup measure, and level off with the edge of a small thin-blade spatula.
- Granulated sugar: To measure, spoon into a dry-cup measure, and level off with the edge of a small thin-blade spatula.
- Raw sugar: Also called demerara sugar, I think of this as granulated light brown sugar. Measure just as you would granulated sugar.

VEGETABLE OIL The lighter the better, and that goes for color, too.

Seasonings

FRESH GINGER Freshly grated always. The best grater? A fine-toothed Microplane.

HERBS With supermarkets selling fresh herbs, there's every reason to use them, and, oh, the difference in flavor. Rule of thumb: 1 tablespoon minced fresh herb = 1 teaspoon dried.

MATCHA Green tea powder (see Sources, page 164).

NUTMEG Grate your own using a fine-toothed Microplane.

ROSE WATER Popular throughout India and the Middle East, this liquid made by steeping rose petals contains no alcohol.

Sweeteners

HONEY Use a mellow golden one that won't overpower the other ingredients.

MAPLE SYRUP For cooking, only Grade B will do, because its deep flavor is strong enough to "shine through." Grade B is by no means inferior (see Sources, page 164).

MOLASSES Never blackstrap (too sludgy, too strong), preferably unsulfured. I keep a medium-brown unsulfured molasses in my pantry that serves me well.

Nuts: The Fresher the Better

ALMONDS California grows more almonds than anyone else. Buy them whole, skins on or off, slivered or sliced. To chop, pulse in your food processor.

> 1 cup slivered almonds = about ¾ cup moderately coarsely chopped

BLACK WALNUTS Cooks prize the faintly musky flavor of these nuts that grow wild across the eastern United States. Buy them recipe-ready (see Sources, page 164).

> 1 pound black walnuts = 3½ to 4 cups moderately coarsely chopped

HICKORY NUTS Called mockernuts by the British, hickories are New World nuts, first cousins to pecans, and thus interchangeable. They're the devil to shell, however, so order nut meats (see Sources, page 164).

> 1 pound hickory nuts = 3½ to 4 cups moderately coarsely chopped

PECANS The all-American nut, the most popular American nut, pecans are even better if lightly toasted: 6 to 8 minutes in a 350°F oven is all it takes.

> 1 pound pecans = 3½ to 4 cups moderately coarsely chopped

WALNUTS (ENGLISH) Next to pecans, these are the nuts we use most. They're Persian, not English, and 99 percent of ours come from California.

> 1 pound walnuts = 3½ to 4 cups moderately coarsely chopped

Seeds

The two used in this book are sold at health food stores and online (see Sources, page 164). Some attribute almost mystical powers to them.

- Black sesame: These oily seeds have a slightly nutty, slightly caramel flavor.
- Chia: They resemble poppy seeds but when wet are softly coated with something like gelatin.

Bread, Cracker, and Cookie Crumbs

BREAD CRUMBS Use firm-textured bread ("home-style"), and that goes for both white and whole wheat.

> 1 slice (with crust) = about ½ cup soft bread crumbs
>
> 1 slice crisp, dry toast (with crust) = ¼ to ⅓ cup moderately fine dry crumbs

GINGERSNAP CRUMBS Crush your own. It's easy. Arrange a layer of cookies between two sheets of plastic food wrap, then attack with your rolling pin.

> 16 (2-inch) round cookies = about 1 cup moderately fine crumbs

GRAHAM CRACKER CRUMBS Once again, crush your own. A 14.4-ounce box contains three sleeves of 2½-inch-square crackers.

> 1 sleeve graham crackers = about 1½ cups moderately fine crumbs.
>
> 13 to 14 (2½-inch square) crackers = about 1 cup medium-fine crumbs.

PANKO These super-crisp Japanese wheat bread crumbs are widely sold here. For crunchier main- or side-dish toppings, substitute panko for half of the other crumbs.

SODA CRACKER (SALTINE) CRUMBS To crush, place the crackers in a plastic zipper bag, and whack with a rolling pin or cutlet bat.

> 28 (2-inch square) soda crackers = about 1 cup moderately fine crumbs

Miscellaneous

CHEESE Cheddar, a sharp, hard or semi-hard cheese created in England, should be used wherever Cheddar is specified. By no means substitute softer processed American cheeses, usually sold in blocks. They can ruin a recipe if used in place of true Cheddar, whether imported or an American Cheddar like Vermont's or Wisconsin's). All cheeses will taste fresher if you grate them yourself. Parmesan means Parmigiano Reggiano. It's expensive, true, but cheaper by the chunk.

> ¼ pound cheese = 1 cup shredded or grated
>
> ½ pound = 2 cups shredded or grated
>
> 1 pound = 4 cups shredded or grated

CITRUS JUICE AND ZEST Fresh only. If a recipe calls for both juice and zest, grate first, then juice. *Note*: To zest on fast-forward, use a Microplane.

> 1 medium-size lemon = 2 tablespoons juice, 1 teaspoon grated zest
>
> 1 medium-size lime = 1½ to 2 tablespoons juice, 3/4 teaspoon grated zest
>
> 1 medium-size orange = ⅓ to ½ cup juice, 1 tablespoon grated zest

COCONUT The only time I'm willing to wrestle a whole coconut is for fresh coconut cake. Otherwise, commercial flaked or shredded coconut, sweetened or not, works well.

COCONUT MILK A blend of coconut liquid, guar gum (for creaminess), and water, coconut milk may be sweetened, unsweetened, full-fat, low-fat, or fat-free.

OATMEAL (ROLLED OATS) You'll get more crunch with old-fashioned rolled oats, and that's why they—not the quick-cooking—are best for toppings.

SESAME OIL Toasted Asian sesame oil only. The untoasted is tasteless.

TAHINI Sesame seed paste; Connie Matisse adds it to whipped cream (see page 142).

WILD PERSIMMONS Native to the South, "simmon" trees grow as far north as Indiana, and their Ping-Pong-size fruits drop after first frost. When soft, orange, and hazed with purple, wild persimmons are sweeter than a ripe peach. But woe to anyone who bites into a green one. Wild persimmon pulp shows up at farmers' markets and can be bought online (see Sources, page 164). If you're lucky and have your own source, here's a handy equivalent: 1 quart whole persimmons = about 2⅔ cups purée.

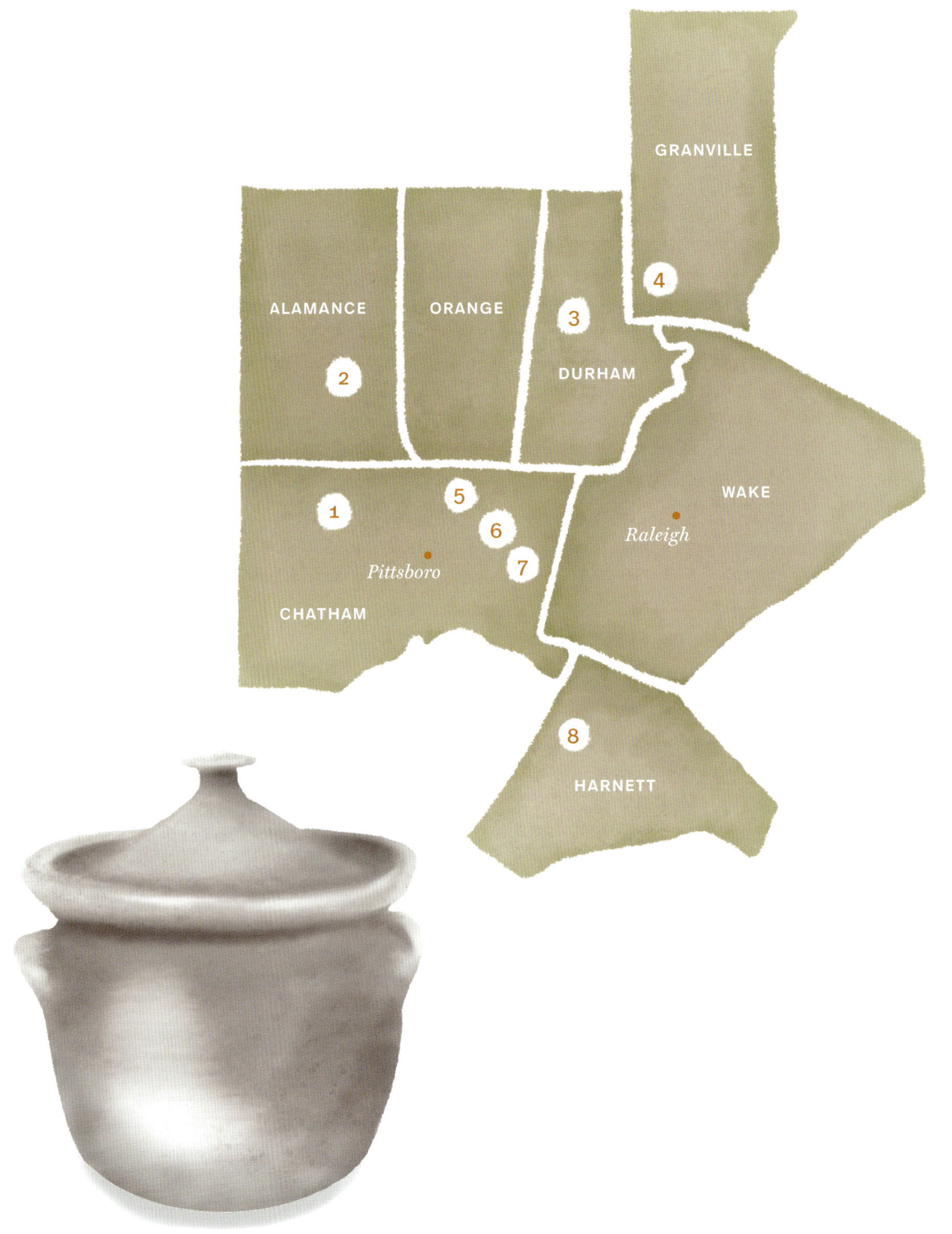

GRANVILLE
ALAMANCE
ORANGE
3
4
2
DURHAM
5
1
6
WAKE
7
Raleigh
Pittsboro
CHATHAM
8
HARNETT

Pottery numbers are keyed to the area map opposite.
For an easy-to-follow itinerary, begin at No. 1, or begin at
No. 8 and work your way back to No. 1.

Greater Triangle Area Potters

1 Goathouse Gallery (Siglinda Scarpa)

680 Alton Alston Road, Pittsboro

Contact: siglinda@earthlink.net

Goathouse Refuge open daily from noon to 4, but to meet
the potter and see her work, make an appointment.

2 Falcon Lane Pottery (Susan Kern)

108 Falcon Lane, Mebane

Contact: susanh.kern@gmail.com

Open by appointment only.

3 Julie Jones Pottery

119 West Seeman Street, Durham

Contact: juliejonespottery@gmail.com

Open by appointment only.

4 Brad Tucker Pottery

Cedar Creek Gallery

1150 Fleming Road, Creedmoor

Contact: bradtuckerpottery@gmail.com

5 Doug Dotson Pottery

326 Mockernut Road, Pittsboro

Contact: dougdotsonpottery@gmail.com

Open by appointment only.

6 Lyn Morrow Pottery

3449 U.S. 15-501, Pittsboro

Contact: lynmorrowpottery@gmail.com

7 Mark Hewitt Pottery

424 Johnny Burke Road, Pittsboro

Contact: carol@hewittpottery.com

Open by appointment only.

8 Cape Fear Pottery (Reuben and Ann York)

3309 U.S. 401 North, Lillington

Contact: info@ncpottery.org

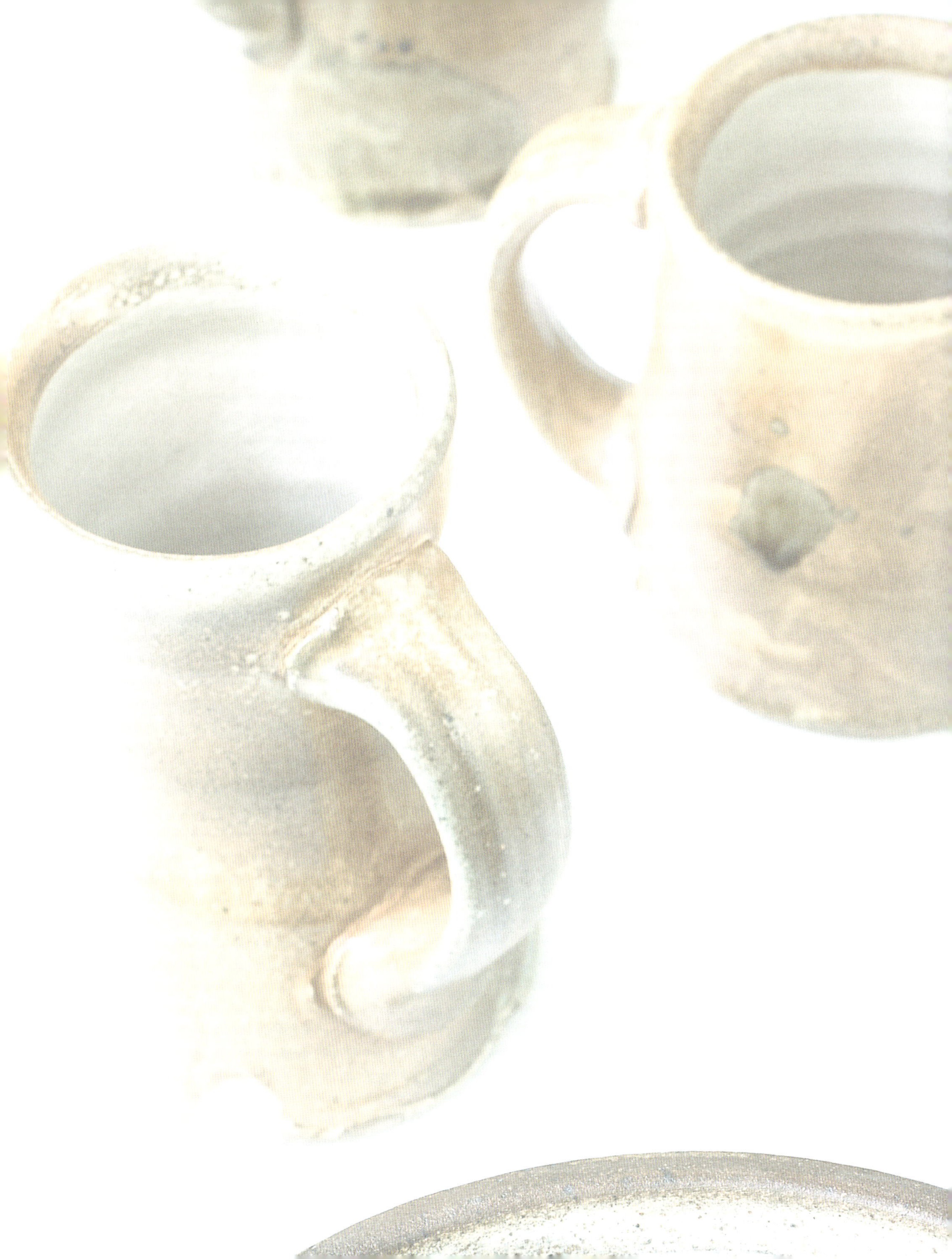

1

Goathouse Gallery:

Siglinda Scarpa

FOR MORE INFORMATION:

siglindascarpa.com

Born in Italy's Piemonte region during World War II, Siglinda Scarpa spent her childhood under the big kitchen table watching her great-grandmother cook. "We were so hungry we gathered any wild plants we could eat," she says. "And my mother turned potato peels into soups. So many potato skin soups!" As a teenager, Scarpa moved to Rome, studied clay sculpting with ceramicist Nino Caruso, and in time became a passionate clay artist of some renown. After a broken marriage and right-wing terrorists threatened both her studio and her life, Scarpa moved to New York City, then a few years later, accepted a job as Artist-in-Residence at the Garrison Art Center some 125 miles up the Hudson River valley.

Weary of New York's harsh winters, Scarpa was lured south by a friend at Duke, who offered to show her around. She came and bought a "little piece of heaven" near Pittsboro where she now gardens, keeps her pottery wheel spinning, and rescues orphaned cats—beware if you're allergic to cats. They're everywhere.

Scarpa's clay sculptures so ethereal they might be clouds have impressed potters across the country, and her unglazed, terra-cotta-colored stoneware pots like those her great grandmother used back in Italy are the cook's new must-haves. "They are like little ovens."

Scarpa's known for the bits of whimsy she adds to each pot: a little clay frog ready to jump off a casserole lid, a gecko snaking around the rim of a paella pan, a found metal object doubling as a handle.

Every Scarpa pot—whether casserole, fish poacher, or shallow baker—is unique, wholly functional, and sturdy enough to take stove-top heat if you follow Scarpa's lead.

Pollo Arrosto Ripieno (Roast Chicken Italian Style)

Makes 6 servings

One friend's immediate reaction to this recipe? "What a wonderful chicken-in-a-pot! I will definitely be making this recipe."

Notes: The chickens Siglinda prefers are hormone- and antibiotic-free. Remove the giblets from the chicken and from their packet. Slip into a small plastic zipper bag, press out all the air, then label and date and store in the freezer. Use within three months when making stock, soup, or gravy. The best potatoes? Ping-Pong-ball-size redskins, if possible (you'll get about ten of them in two pounds and half as many medium-size, which should be pared into "Ping-Pongs") plus vivid orange Jewel or Beauregard sweet potatoes.

Tip: Always start with a cold oven when baking in one of Siglinda's pots.

2 pounds small redskin potatoes, peeled but left whole (see headnote)

2 pounds medium-size sweet potatoes, peeled and cut into pieces about the same size as the redskins (see headnote)

1 pound medium-size Granny Smith apples, peeled, cored, and sliced ¼ inch thick

¾ cup dried cranberries

6 large garlic cloves, coarsely chopped

1 tablespoon coarsely chopped fresh rosemary

1 tablespoon coarsely chopped fresh sage

1 tablespoon sea salt

1 teaspoon crushed black peppercorns

1 (4¾- to 5-pound) oven-ready chicken (see *Notes* above)

¾ cup brandy

4 (4- to 5-inch) sprigs fresh rosemary (garnish)

1. Lay half of the redskins and sweet potatoes in the bottom of a lidded 6- to 7-quart ovenproof stoneware, other pottery, or heavy-duty ceramic roasting pot or casserole.

2. Combine the next 7 ingredients (apples through black peppercorns) in a bowl, then rub half of the mixture inside the chicken, and sew the cavity shut.

3. Lay the chicken breast-side up on top of the potatoes in the casserole, then arrange the remaining redskins and sweet potatoes around the bird. Sprinkle with the remaining apple-cranberry mixture, and pour the brandy evenly over all.

4. Set the lid on the pot, slide onto the middle shelf of a cold oven, set the thermostat at 450°F, and roast for 1½ to 2 hours or until the bird is golden brown and an instant-read thermometer, inserted in the meatiest part of a thigh not touching bone, registers 165°F.

5. Turn the oven off and let the casserole rest about 20 minutes before removing from the oven. To garnish, crisscross the rosemary sprigs on top of the chicken.

6. Serve the chicken at table, first separating the thighs, drumsticks, and wings from the body, then cutting the breast into thin slices. Make sure everyone gets the meat of their choice (light or dark) along with plenty of redskins and sweet potatoes.

7. Accompaniments? How about a simple vinaigrette-dressed salad of bitter greens and some good country bread to sop up the casserole juices?

Tagliatelle alla Novarese with Portabella Mushrooms

Makes 8 servings

"Alla Novarese" means "in the style of Novara," the northern Italian town where Siglinda was born. It's essential to use a good ricotta for this pasta classic, and the best she's found here is Calabro fresh whole-milk ricotta. As for the tagliatelle (fettuccine-like flat ribbon pasta), use a good commercial brand (Siglinda likes De Cecco). "But," she urges, "Please do not add oil to the drained pasta." Do, however, save ¼ cup of the pasta cooking water to loosen the sauce, which should be poured on the drained the pasta pronto!

Note: "Portabella" (the mushroom we spell "portobello") means "beautiful door." The gills on the underside of the caps tend to be bitter, so scrape them out with a spoon before slicing.

Tip: You'll find the rich European-style butters at high-end supermarkets. Brands: Cabot, Kerrygold, Plugrá.

¾ cup dried Italian porcini mushrooms
    (see Sources, page 164)
1 cup lukewarm water
6 tablespoons (½ stick plus 2 tablespoons)
    unsalted European-style butter (see *Tip* above)
3 large garlic cloves, finely chopped
2 tablespoons moderately coarsely chopped fresh
    sage leaves
6 portobello mushrooms roughly the size of your
    hand (about 2 pounds), stemmed, wiped clean,
    and thinly sliced (see *Note* above)
1 cup ricotta cheese (see headnote)
½ cup coarsely chopped fresh Italian parsley
    plus 1 tablespoon for garnish
¾ teaspoon salt, or to taste
½ teaspoon freshly ground black pepper, or to taste
1 pound tagliatelle, cooked and drained by package
    directions (see headnote)
¼ cup reserved pasta cooking water
½ cup freshly grated Parmigiano-Reggiano cheese

1. Soak the porcini in the warm water while you proceed with the recipe.

2. Melt the butter in a large, heavy skillet over moderate heat with the garlic and sage. Add the portobellos and sauté, stirring occasionally, for 5 to 8 minutes or until the mushrooms give up their juices and these evaporate.

3. Drain the porcini, reserving their soaking liquid, and add the porcini to the skillet. Quickly strain the porcini soaking liquid through a coffee-filter-lined small sieve directly into the skillet.

4. Reduce the heat to low, and continue cooking the mushroom mixture uncovered, stirring occasionally, for 8 to 10 minutes or until the portobellos are tender and the flavors have married.

5. Add the ricotta, the ½ cup parsley, and the salt and pepper, and stir for 1 to 2 minutes or just until warm.

6. Mound the tagliatelle in a large, shallow pottery serving bowl, pour on the ricotta-mushroom sauce along with the reserved pasta cooking water, and toss to mix. Add ¼ cup of the Parmigiano-Reggiano and toss well again.

7. Sprinkle the remaining Parmigiano-Reggiano and the chopped parsley garnish on top of the pasta, carry to the dinner table, and serve. Accompany with a tartly dressed salad of bitter lettuces such as arugula, radicchio, and endives.

Crostata di Frutta (Fresh Fruit Tart)

Makes one 10-inch tart (8 to 10 servings)

Siglinda says that this beloved Italian dessert works well with any fruits in season—berries, cored and sliced peaches, pears, apples, or a mixture. Our preference: equal parts fresh blueberries and strawberries. Siglinda doesn't sugar the fruit because it becomes too sweet. "The crust that gives the name to this tart brings just enough sweetness," she explains. "The dough comes together slowly as the butter melts in the warmth of your hands. Never add liquid of any kind because you will ruin the pastry."

Note: European-style butter? It's richer than everyday butters because it's pure butterfat. Cabot, Kerrygold, and Plugrá all qualify and can be found at many supermarkets. American butters containing milk solids can be substituted, but the pastry will be firmer.

PASTRY

2 cups unsifted unbleached all-purpose flour

1 cup sugar

½ teaspoon salt

½ cup (1 stick) plus 2 tablespoons cold unsalted European-style butter, cut into small dice (see *Note* above)

4 large egg yolks

¼ cup apricot jam

FRUIT FILLING

1 cup mixed dried fruits (cranberries, raisins, and diced apricots) soaked in ½ cup brandy, then drained and 2 teaspoons soaking brandy reserved

2 teaspoons reserved soaking brandy mixed with ⅛ teaspoon cayenne pepper

4 cups fresh berries, stemmed, washed, drained, and sliced, if needed (see headnote)

1 cup coarsely chopped walnuts

½ teaspoon ground cinnamon

1. *For the pastry*: Combine the flour, sugar, and salt in a medium-size mixing bowl and make a well in the center. Work the butter in with your hands, kneading until it melts and combines with the flour—have patience; this may take a while.

2. Mix the eggs in one by one, then continue kneading the dough until you can shape it into a smooth, firm ball—no crumbs or stray bits of pastry. Flatten the dough, wrap in damp toweling, and set aside while you prepare the filling.

3. *For the fruit filling:* Place all ingredients in a large nonreactive mixing bowl, then toss well to mix.

4. To finish the crostata: Press the pastry dough over the bottom and up the sides of an ungreased 10-inch ovenproof stoneware, other pottery, ceramic, or heat-resistant glass pie pan, leaving a 1- to 1½-inch overhang all around.

5. Spread the jam over the bottom of the pie shell, then add the fruit filling. Bring the pastry

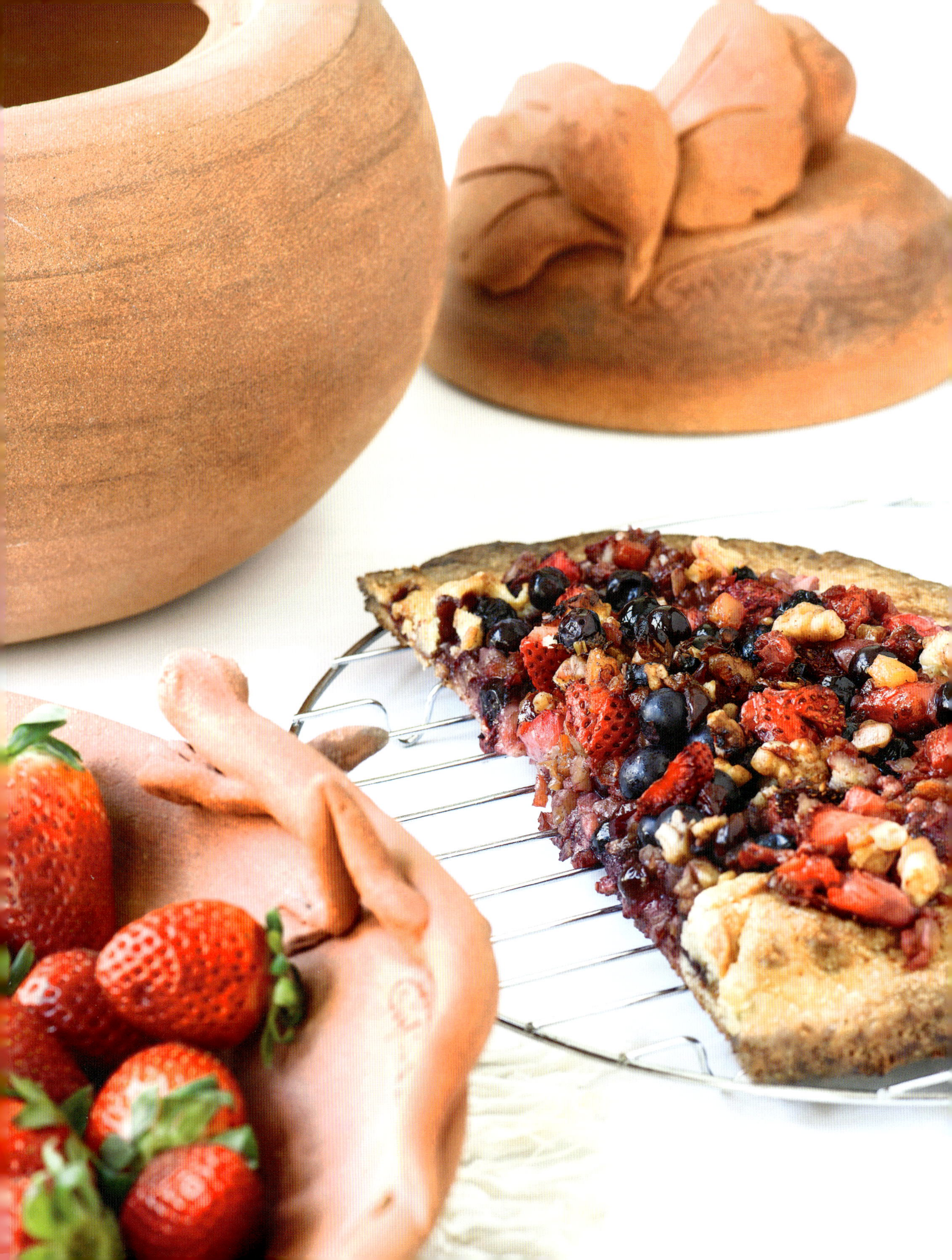

overhang up over the filling, trimming and
crimping into a free-form edge.

6. Slide the crostata onto the middle shelf
of a cold oven, set the thermostat at 350°F and
bake for 45 minutes to 1 hour or until the filling
is bubbly and the pastry is golden brown.

7. Transfer the pan of crostata to a wire rack
and cool to room temperature.

8. To serve, cut the crostata into wedges.
Nothing more is needed, though Americans—
shhhhh!—would be tempted to add a scoop
of gelato to each portion or a trickle of heavy
cream. Bliss.

2

Falcon Lane Pottery:

Susan Kern

FOR MORE INFORMATION:

falconlanepottery.com

"When someone uses one of my pots," Susan says, "I hope they experience a moment of slow time in a fast world."

For throwing pots on a wheel, firing, glazing, then firing again is slow work, even for artists as skilled as Susan Kern.

She describes her work as "functional stoneware that adds grace to the ordinary rituals of home and office. I'm drawn to texture that invites touch," she adds, "colors that engage the eyes, and substantial forms that offer both balance and movement."

Though southern New Jersey was home during Susan's growing-up years, the two events that would change her life took place in England during her semester abroad: meeting the fellow Jersey-ite she would marry at twenty-one and buying her first handcrafted pot.

But Susan clearly inherited "the artistic gene" from her mother, a painter and pottery collector. Settling into married life in Durham, Susan discovered a world of potters orbiting around what might be described as "the solar energy" of Seagrove, and caught the bug.

She took her first pottery lesson in Chapel Hill, where she'd earned a master's degree in library science at UNC, then put potting on hold for twenty years not only to raise her own children but also to teach three-year-olds at preschool.

Finally back at her wheel, Susan took classes with Marie Summers at the Cane Creek Gallery in Creedmoor, and before long she was selling her own pots while honing her skills at the Arrowmont School of Arts and Crafts in Gatlinburg, Tennessee.

And today? Susan continues to create wheel-thrown and hand-built pottery so stylish it's "at home" in private collections all across this country as well as the United Kingdom.

Summer Squash and Roasted Tomato Pie

Makes one 9-inch pie (6 servings)

"Many years ago I was invited to lunch at the home of my first pottery teacher, Marie Summers, who operated Cane Creek Pottery," Susan says. "She served a tomato pie so delicious it began my interest in savory pies. This one has many variations, but the centerpiece remains fresh tomatoes."

Note: The cheese Susan prefers is an Ashe County yellow Cheddar, but any Cheddar—sharp or mild—will do.

Tip: By all means make your own pie shell, but it's OK, too, to use a refrigerated piecrust sheet that you can shape, fill, and bake.

3 firm-ripe tomatoes about the size of tennis balls, sliced ½ inch thick but not peeled

2 large garlic cloves, finely minced

1 tablespoon extra-virgin olive oil

1 large yellow squash, trimmed and sliced about ¼ inch thick

1 cup coarsely shredded Cheddar cheese (see *Note* above)

½ cup coarsely shredded Asiago or Parmigiano-Reggiano cheese

1 (9-inch) pie shell fitted into a 9-inch ovenproof stoneware, other pottery, ceramic, or heat-resistant glass pie pan, then crimped with a high fluted edge (see *Tip* above)

3 medium-size eggs

¾ cup milk blended with 1 tablespoon all-purpose flour

¾ teaspoon salt

¼ teaspoon freshly ground black pepper

1 teaspoon coarsely chopped fresh thyme or ¼ rounded teaspoon crumbled dried leaf thyme

1. Preheat the oven to 425°F. Lightly grease a rimmed baking sheet with olive oil, then arrange the sliced tomatoes, not touching, on top. Sprinkle evenly with the garlic.

2. Slide the baking sheet onto the middle shelf of the preheated oven and roast the tomatoes uncovered for 8 to 10 minutes or just until they begin to bubble—watch carefully lest they burn.

3. Remove the pan of tomatoes from the oven, ease the slices into a large colander set in the sink, arranging them in a single layer over the bottom and up the sides, then set aside. Also turn the oven off.

4. Heat the olive oil in a heavy, medium-size skillet over moderately high heat for about 1½ minutes or until ripples appear on the pan bottom. Add the sliced squash and cook, stirring

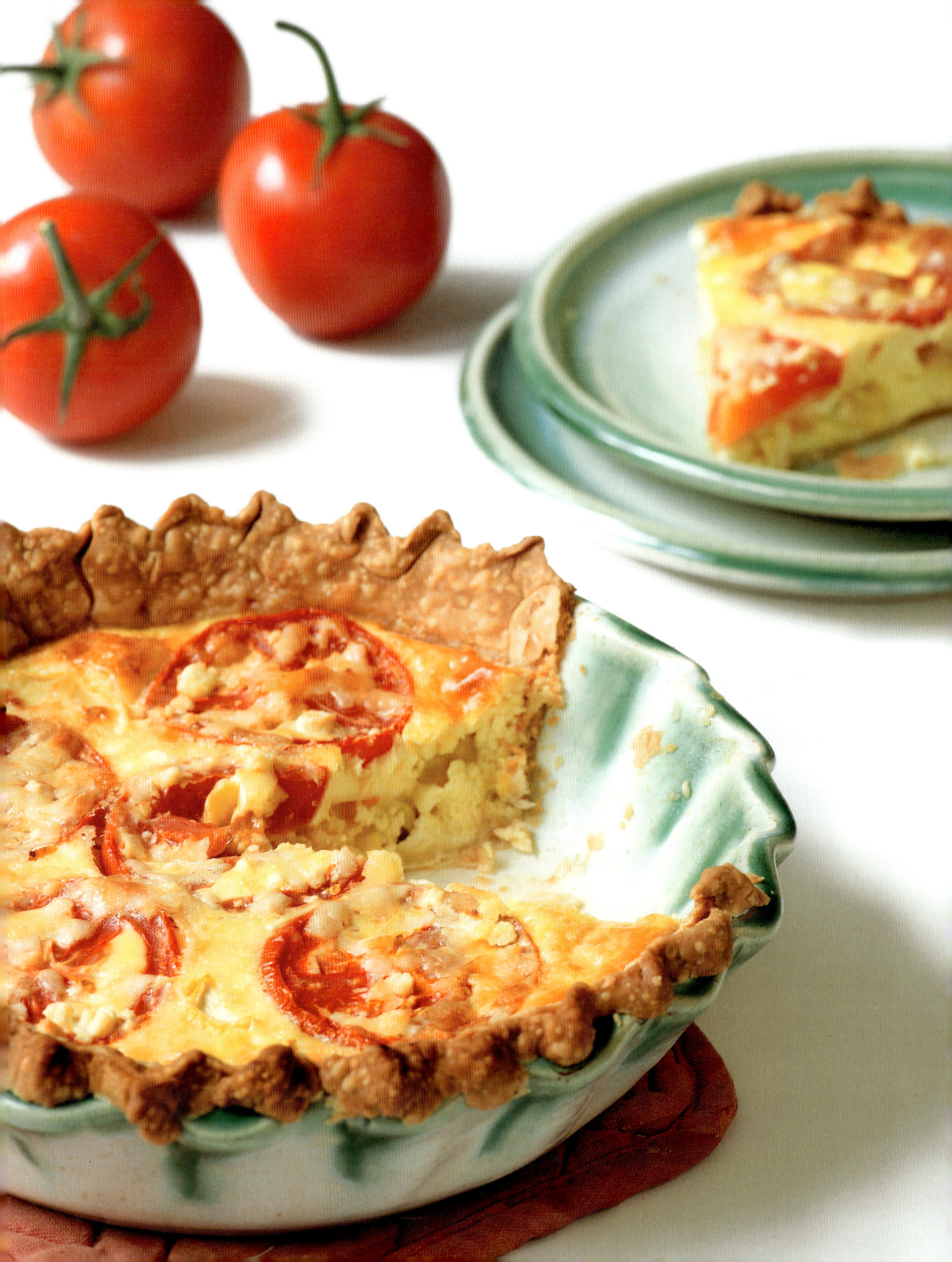

occasionally, for 5 to 6 minutes or until beginning to soften.

5. Scatter ⅓ of each cheese (the Cheddar and
Asiago) evenly over the bottom of the pie shell,
top with the cooked squash slices, another ⅓
of each cheese, and then the roasted tomatoes,
distributing as evenly as possible. Finally, scatter the remaining Cheddar and Asiago on top.
Set the partially filled pie on a rimmed baking
sheet.

6. Whisk the eggs, the milk mixture, salt, and
pepper until smooth, and pour into the pie—
carefully, so that you don't drown the tomatoes—
and scatter the thyme on top.

7. Slide the baking sheet onto the middle
shelf of a cold oven, set the thermostat at 350°F,
and bake the pie uncovered for about 1 hour
or until a cake tester inserted midway between
the rim and the center comes out clean. *Note*:
If at any point the crimped edge of the crust is
in danger of overbrowning, cover with strips
of foil.

8. Remove the pie from the oven and from
the baking sheet, then cool on a wire rack for
20 to 25 minutes.

9. Serve as the main course of a brunch,
light lunch, or supper accompanied by a simply
cooked and seasoned green vegetable. Asparagus or broccoli would be perfect.

My Father's Baked Beans

Makes 8 to 10 servings

"My father's mother was famous for the beans she baked all night in a very slow oven," Susan says. "When my father took up cooking, post retirement, he made those beans in a less labor-intensive way." Susan follows his lead but bakes the beans in one of her own stoneware baking dishes.

1 pound dried great northern beans, washed, sorted, soaked overnight in enough cold water to cover, then drained very well

4 to 6 slices (¼ to ⅓ pound) bacon, cut into 1-inch pieces

1 medium-small yellow onion, coarsely diced

¼ cup plus 1 tablespoon medium-brown unsulfured molasses

½ teaspoon powdered mustard

2 teaspoons salt, or to taste

½ teaspoon freshly ground black pepper, or to taste

¼ cup firmly packed light brown sugar

1. Place the drained beans in a large, deep saucepan, add enough cold water to cover, then set over moderately high heat, and bring to a boil.

2. Reduce the heat so the water ripples gently, cover, and cook the beans, stirring now and then, for about 40 minutes or until firm-tender. Remove the beans from the heat and drain, reserving the cooking water.

3. Using a slotted spoon, scoop ¼ of the beans into an ungreased, fairly deep 2½- to 3-quart ovenproof stoneware, other pottery, ceramic, or heat-resistant glass baking dish, and layer the ingredients in this way: ¼ of the bacon, ¼ of the onion, 1 tablespoon molasses, then sprinklings of powdered mustard, salt, and black pepper.

4. Repeat 3 times, beginning each time with the beans. Drizzle the fifth tablespoon of molasses evenly over all, and sprinkle with the brown sugar. Finally, ladle enough of the reserved cooking water into the baking dish to be visible just below the beans but not enough to cover them. Do not stir; also reserve the remaining cooking water.

5. Set the baking dish lid in place, or if it has no lid, cover with aluminum foil. Slide the beans onto the middle shelf of a cold oven, and set the thermostat at 300°F.

6. Bake the beans for 2 to 2½ hours or until bubbling, brown, and tender, stirring every 45 minutes. *Note*: If at any point the beans seem to be drying out, add another ½ to 1 cup of the reserved cooking water.

7. To serve, carry the baked beans from oven to table and accompany with coleslaw or a tartly dressed green salad.

Apple-Pecan Crisp

Makes 6 to 8 servings

"I use an old-fashioned apple peeler with a spit
and turning handle, which makes this super-
fast," Susan says. "It was a gift from my father."
As for apples, Susan likes Stayman, Rome,
"or similar apple with some tartness." You might
use a mix of tart apples (Granny Smiths, for
example) and sweeter ones like Gala and/or
Golden Delicious, which hold their shape when
baked.

Note: Susan bakes this crisp in her 10-inch
stoneware baker and starts it in a cold oven to
prevent cracking.

6 large apples (2 Grannies, 2 Galas, 2 Golden
    Delicious), peeled, cored, halved, and each
    half sliced about ¼ inch thick
¼ cup apple cider blended with 1 tablespoon
    all-purpose flour

TOPPING

1 cup firmly packed light brown sugar
½ cup old-fashioned rolled oats (oatmeal)
½ cup sifted all-purpose flour
½ cup (1 stick) butter, cut into pats and at
    room temperature
¼ teaspoon ground cinnamon
1 cup coarsely chopped pecans or walnuts

1. Lightly butter one of Susan's 10-inch
stoneware bakers or a 10-inch ovenproof stoneware, other pottery, ceramic, or heat-resistant
glass pie pan. Add the apples, spread to the
edge, then drizzle the apple cider mixture
evenly over all, and reserve.

2. *For the topping*: Pulse the first 5 ingredients (brown sugar through cinnamon) 7 to 8
times in a food processor fitted with the metal
chopping blade or just long enough to reduce
the butter to pieces the size of lentils. Add the
pecans and pulse 2 to 3 times. Spread the topping over the apples, and press down lightly,

3. Slide the crisp onto the middle shelf of
a cold oven, set the thermostat at 350°F, and
bake for 1 hour to 1 hour and 10 minutes or
until bubbling and lightly browned.

4. Serve the crisp hot with or without dollops
of whipped cream or scoops of ice cream—
vanilla or dulce de leche would be my choice.

3

Julie Jones Pottery

FOR MORE INFORMATION:

juliejonespottery.com

A pharmacist turned potter? If that pharmacist is Julie Jones of Durham, yes.

She and husband Steven, who met in high school, majored in pharmacy at the University of Mississippi, then landed jobs in Durham in 2003.

"We had visited friends in the Triangle Area and loved how much there was to do music- and art-wise," Julie says. "Steven plays guitar and bass, and joined a few bands once we moved here. We'd go to live shows several times a week and found a great community of musicians and artists."

But Julie's interest in pottery actually began a few years earlier. "My mother-in-law bought a potter's wheel for my sister-in-law and me to share. She thought I'd like it because I did a lot of painting and was into arts and crafts."

Once Julie was at that pottery wheel, she was "hooked" and wanted "to learn everything." As luck would have it, her next-door neighbor owned Clay-makers in downtown Durham.

"I took classes," Julie says, "and met other potters."

Then when her pharmacy closed, Julie studied wood kiln firing with Michael Kline at the Penland School of Crafts some fifty miles northeast of Asheville. Other classes followed, two apprenticeships, and by 2011 Julie had turned her basement into a pottery studio.

Her daughter's birth a year later meant a break in pottery making, but Julie's back at it now, concentrating on functional pottery "so that I can fill my home with my own pottery."

She and Steven both cook, often in tandem, using Julie's pottery for pickling, for baking, and not least, for serving whatever they've made to family and friends.

Kimchi

Makes 3 quarts

Because her husband "loves all things pickled and fermented," he and Julie make their own kimchi, the mix of peppery pickled vegetables that's the national dish of Korea, and ferment it in the deep stoneware crocks she makes. Because they eat kimchi so fast, Julie refrigerates jars of it instead of going the water-bath route.

Note: Gochugaru may not be as exotic you think—I found it on the McCormick rack. For Korean gochugaru, see Sources (page 164).

Tip: For a vegan version, use 1 tablespoon each red miso paste and soy sauce.

2 medium-size heads napa cabbage (about
    5 pounds), trimmed, cored, quartered, and
    each quarter cut into 2-inch chunks

3 medium-size carrots, peeled and cut into
    matchstick strips

1 small Korean or daikon radish, cut into
    matchstick strips but not peeled

8 to 10 medium-size scallions, trimmed and
    thinly sliced (include green tops)

2 tablespoons kosher salt

8 medium-size garlic cloves, finely chopped

1 (2-inch) knob fresh ginger, peeled and finely
    chopped

½ cup gochugaru (Korean red pepper flakes,
    see *Note* above)

2 tablespoons Asian fish sauce (see *Tip* above)

2 tablespoons unbleached organic sugar or
    raw sugar

1 teaspoon Asian toasted sesame oil

1. Place the cabbage, carrots, radishes, and scallions in a very large nonreactive bowl. Add the salt and mix gently. Cover with cheesecloth and let stand at room temperature for 1½ to 2 hours. Pour off the accumulated brine and reserve.

2. Combine the next 6 ingredients (garlic through sesame oil) in a small nonreactive bowl, then add 2 to 3 tablespoons of the reserved brine or enough to make a paste about as thick as peanut butter.

3. Wearing disposable gloves, mix this paste into the cabbage mixture, massaging as you go, until fully incorporated.

4. Pack the kimchi into a pristine 3-quart, deep stoneware crock, and if needed, add enough of the remaining reserved brine to cover the kimchi.

5. Place an impeccably clean large, heavy nonreactive stockpot lid on top of the kimchi, then weight with a heavy pan. Cover the crock loosely with cheesecloth, then set the crock lid in place or cover snugly with aluminum foil.

6. Transfer the covered crock to a cool (60° to 72°F) spot, and allow to ferment for 48 to 72 hours.

7. Spoon the kimchi into 3 sterilized 1-quart preserving jars, wipe the rims with a damp cloth, then screw the lids down tight. Label, date, and refrigerate.

8. Use within 2 weeks.

Kimchi Deviled Eggs

Makes 6 servings

"My husband, Steven, has an adventurous palate," Julie says, "and started making kimchi deviled eggs whenever we needed to take an appetizer to share at gatherings. They disappear rapidly because they're both exotic and delicious."

Note: Gochujang is a pungent fermented hot red pepper paste or sauce. Look for it at Asian or specialty groceries or order it online (see Sources, page 164). In a pinch, substitute sriracha sauce. My New York friend Maria Harrison Reuge tried this recipe and raved, "Loved, loved, loved these deviled eggs. And what an original recipe!"

Tip: For a foolproof way to hard-cook eggs, see page 8. Also, for a creamier filling, add 1 more teaspoon mayonnaise.

EGGS

1 dozen large hard-cooked eggs, shelled (see *Tip* above)

¼ cup finely chopped kimchi (recipe precedes) or substitute store-bought

3 tablespoons mayonnaise (see *Tip* above)

½ tablespoon kimchi liquid

1 tablespoon gochujang (Korean red pepper paste; see *Note* above)

½ teaspoon Asian toasted sesame oil

½ teaspoon rice vinegar

¼ teaspoon salt, or to taste

¼ teaspoon freshly ground black pepper, or to taste

GARNISH

1 medium-size scallion, trimmed and thinly sliced (include green tops), and if you like, cut a second medium-size scallion into thin sticks to cluster on the deviled egg platter

¼ teaspoon black sesame seeds (see Sources, page 164)

1. Halve the hard-cooked eggs lengthwise, pop the yolks into a medium-size nonreactive bowl, and mash well with a fork. Arrange the whites on a large rimmed baking sheet lined with several thicknesses of damp paper toweling and set aside.

2. Add all the remaining ingredients (kimchi through black pepper) to the mashed yolks and mix thoroughly.

3. Spoon the yolk mixture into the egg whites, dividing as evenly as possible. Or if you want to get fancy, pipe the yolk mixture through a pastry bag fitted with a plain or fluted No. 10 nozzle, swirling it into a decorative pattern.

4. Cover the pan of deviled eggs and refrigerate overnight or until ready to serve the next day.

5. Just before serving, garnish the deviled eggs with sprinklings of thinly sliced scallion and a light scattering of black sesame seeds. Arrange on a large pottery platter (Julie uses one of her own), then if you like, cluster thin scallion sticks in the center of the platter.

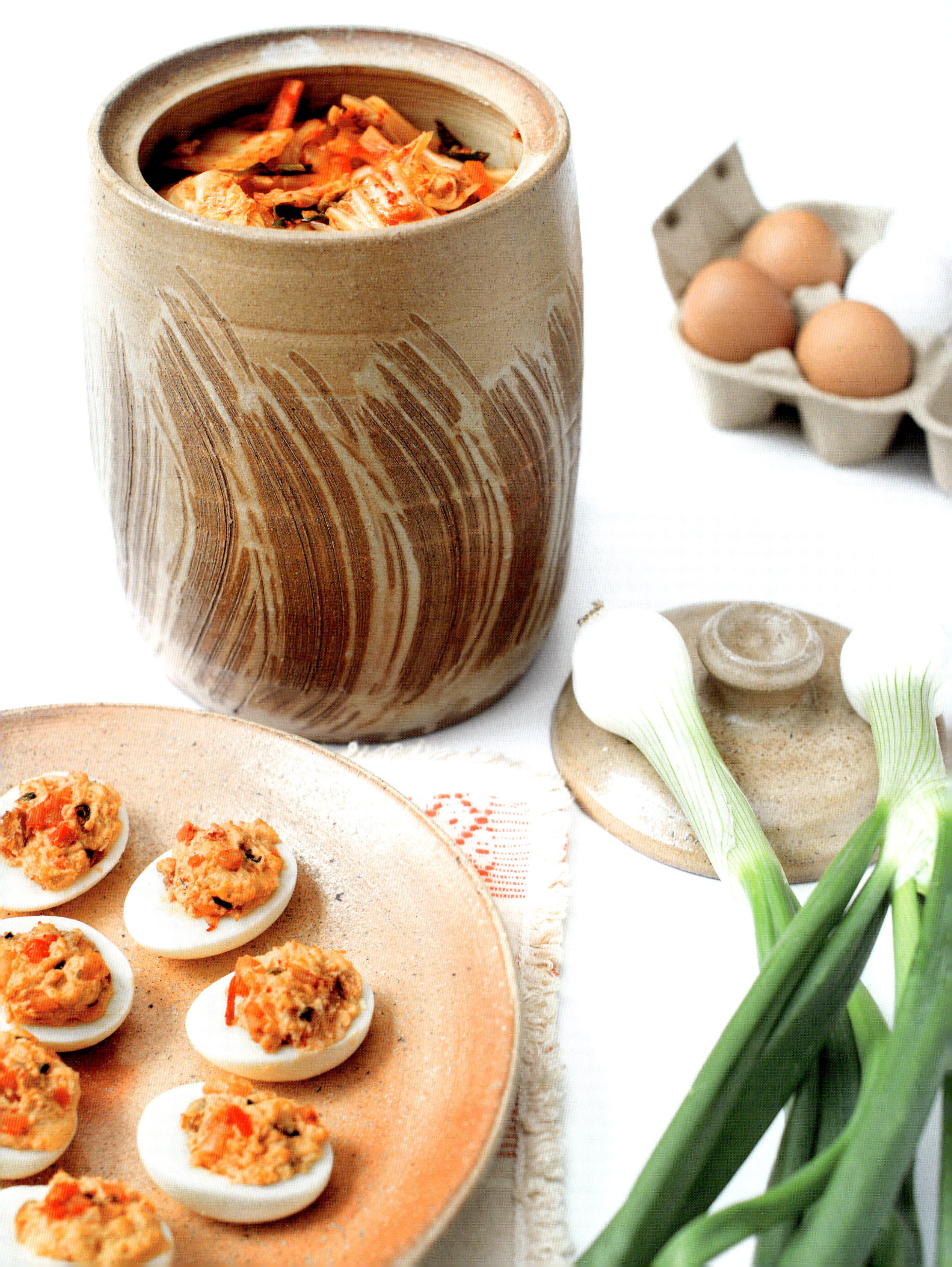

Sweet Potato Bread with Walnuts and Dried Cranberries

Makes an 8½-inch tube loaf (about 8 servings)

Julie's father used to grow sweet potatoes, so is any quick bread more appropriate than this one? Julie bakes it in her shallow stoneware tube pan—our choice here.

Note: This bread may crack a bit on top as it bakes but no prob. It'll be upside down when cut into wedges, so only you will know.

Tip: For 1 cup mashed sweet potatoes, you'll need to cook ¾ to 1 pound of sweet potatoes.

2 cups sifted all-purpose flour

1 teaspoon baking soda

½ teaspoon baking powder

½ teaspoon salt

1 cup raw sugar

¾ cup coarsely chopped walnuts or black walnuts (see Sources, page 164)

½ cup coarsely chopped dried cranberries

1 cup firmly packed unseasoned mashed sweet potatoes (see *Tip* above)

⅓ cup buttermilk (or more as needed)

⅓ cup melted butter

2 large eggs

1 tablespoon fresh orange juice

1. Stand an 8½-inch, 6- to 7-cup ovenproof stoneware, other pottery, ceramic, or heat-resistant glass tube pan or ring mold on a piece of aluminum foil. Trace around the bottom of the pan and cut around the traced lines. Fold the foil circle in half, then in half again, and snip off the point to accommodate the pan's central tube. Place the foil liner shiny side down in the bottom of the ring mold or tube pan and set aside.

2. Whisk the flour, baking soda, baking powder, and salt together in a large bowl, add the sugar, and whisk well to combine. Mix in the walnuts and dried cranberries, then make a well in the middle of the dry ingredients, and set aside.

3. Using a hand electric mixer at high speed, beat the remaining ingredients (mashed sweet potatoes through orange juice) for 1 to 2 minutes in a medium-size bowl until smooth, or alternately churn and pulse 4 to 5 times in a food processor.

4. Pour the liquid ingredients into the well in the dry ingredients and fold in—gently. No matter if a few floury specks show. *Note*: If the batter is too stiff to pour, mix in another 2 to 3 tablespoons buttermilk.

5. Spritz the tube pan well with nonstick cooking spray, paying particular attention to the central tube and pan sides. Scoop the batter into the prepared pan, smoothing and spreading to the edge.

6. Slide the pan onto the middle shelf of a cold oven, set the thermostat at 350°F, and bake for 1 to 1¼ hours or until the bread begins to pull from the sides of the pan, is springy to the touch, and a cake tester inserted midway between the edge and central tube comes out clean.

7. Cool the bread in the pan right-side up on a wire rack for 20 minutes.

8. Carefully run a small thin-blade spatula around the edge of the pan and central tube to loosen the bread, invert on the rack, and peel off the foil liner. Cool the bread to room temperature, then ease the upside-down loaf onto a round platter.

9. To serve, cut the sweet potato bread into wedges using your sharpest serrated knife. Delicious as is, even better with whipped cream cheese and/or marmalade.

Danish Pudding Cake

Makes one 7-inch tube cake (8 servings)

When Julie sent me a banana bread recipe, I told her I already had a good one and wanted something quite different. "I'm searching for recipes with my cousin," Julie replied, "and I'm going to try a Danish pudding cake that I've had but not cooked myself." Laden with chopped dates and pecans and finished with an orange sauce, we found it memorable and party-perfect.

10 tablespoons (1 and ¼ sticks) butter,
    at room temperature
⅔ cup granulated sugar
3 tablespoons firmly packed light brown sugar
1 tablespoon orange marmalade blended with
    1 tablespoon finely grated fresh ginger
2 large eggs
2 cups sifted all-purpose self-rising flour
⅔ cup milk
1 (7¼-ounce) package pitted dates,
    moderately coarsely chopped
⅔ cup moderately coarsely chopped pecans

SAUCE

⅔ cup firmly packed orange marmalade
¼ cup fresh orange juice
2 teaspoons fresh lemon juice

1. Cream the butter, both sugars, and the marmalade mixture at high speed in a large electric mixer bowl for about 2 minutes or until light. Beat in the eggs one by one.

2. With the mixer at low speed, add the flour alternately with the milk, beginning and ending with the flour, and beating after each addition only enough to combine. Using a large rubber spatula, fold in the dates and nuts.

3. Line the bottom of a 7-inch, 6½-cup ovenproof stoneware, other pottery, ceramic, or heat-resistant glass tube pan with a circle of baking parchment or nonstick aluminum foil, then spritz well with nonstick cooking spray, paying particular attention to the central tube and sides of the pan.

4. Scoop the batter into the prepared tube pan, smoothing the top and spreading to the edge.

5. Slide the pudding cake onto the middle shelf of a cold oven, set the thermostat at 325°F, and bake for 50 to 60 minutes or until springy to the touch and a cake tester, inserted midway between the rim and the central tube, comes out clean.

6. When the pudding cake is done, transfer to a wire rack, and cool right-side up in the pan for 10 minutes.

7. *Meanwhile, prepare the sauce*: Combine the orange marmalade, orange juice, and lemon juice in a small nonreactive saucepan, set over low heat, and heat, stirring occasionally, for about 3 minutes or just until the marmalade melts. Set off the heat.

8. Using a small thin-blade spatula, carefully loosen the pudding cake around the edge and the central tube, and invert on a large, rimmed cake plate. Spoon the hot sauce slowly and evenly on top of the pudding cake so that it soaks in, then cool to room temperature.

9. To serve, cut the pudding cake into slim wedges, arrange on decorative dessert plates, and don't be surprised if guests beg for the recipe.

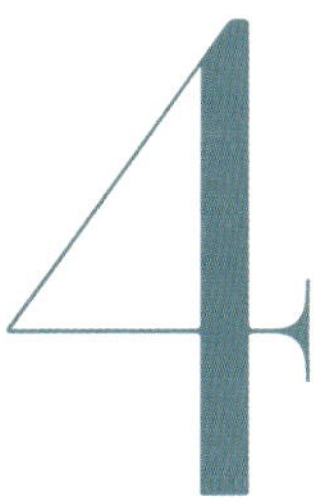

Brad Tucker Pottery

Red clay country, children quickly learn, is both playground and classroom. First there's the ecstasy of splashing through rust-red mud puddles, then the thrill of squashing mud into patty cakes, then a little later, the pride of shaping red clay into crude jugs and bowls.

Tucker came to red clay country at the age of nine when his family relocated from the Bronx to Raleigh. "That's where I grew up," he says, mentioning neither red clay nor pottery.

He credits his girlfriend, a hobby potter (and now wife of thirty-four years) for introducing him to the world of North Carolina pottery. "She took me to Cole's and to Jugtown."

"From the start I was attracted to the challenge of making functional pots that create a bond between the user and the maker . . . and in particular the great visual pleasure and constant inspiration of teapots" (Tucker's hosted the National Teapot Show for twenty-six years).

But before teapots, before pottery, Tucker majored in English at Atlantic Christian College in Wilson, North Carolina. Next came an A.B. in pottery production at Montgomery Tech almost within hollering distance of Jugtown, then a two-year apprenticeship at Creedmoor's Cedar Creek Pottery followed by a summer at the Penland School of Crafts in the Blue Ridge.

Returning to Cedar Creek, Tucker rented a studio, fired his first kiln load, and disaster!

"By some cruel twist of fate, a video crew was on hand to record my failure," he says. But Tucker pressed on, perfected his skills, and by 1982 had opened his own pottery.

For decades now, Tucker has been turning out "the traditional wares of North Carolina—sturdy, simple forms designed to bring many years of useful and visual enjoyment." And en route he has won the approval of the state's pottery establishment, not to mention cheers from dozens of stoneware collectors.

Grilled Corn Grits

Makes 8 servings

"My wife and I love going to the Raleigh Farmers Market in spring and summer," Brad says. "We always look forward to the weekends when corn is in abundance, and when the price drops, we end up with far more corn than we can use right away. When this happens, I grill the corn, cut it from the cob, and use it in this recipe." Grilling corn over charcoal and wood chips gives the grits a smoky sweetness that pairs perfectly with Brad's Grilled Pork Steaks (recipe follows).

Note: Brad uses his own stoneware baking dish—"the 9-inch, 1½-quart round one with handles is perfect," he says.

Tip: To grate the Parmigiano-Reggiano, use the second coarsest side of a box grater.

5 medium-size ears sweet corn, shucked ("butter-and-sugar" corn if you can find it)

2 cups milk

2 cups chicken stock or broth

1 cup stone-ground white grits

3 tablespoons butter

1 cup coarsely shredded sharp Cheddar cheese

1 cup coarsely grated Parmigiano-Reggiano cheese (see *Tip* above)

1 teaspoon salt, or to taste

½ teaspoon freshly ground black pepper, or to taste

1. Mound charcoal briquettes and a few hickory chips in the middle of your grill, light, and burn for about 15 minutes or until the coals are covered with gray ash. Set the grilling rack in place.

2. Arrange the ears of corn side by side—not touching—on the rack and grill for 10 to 15 minutes, turning as needed for an even char. The younger the corn, the faster it grills.

3. Remove the corn from the grill, cool until easy to handle, then cut the kernels from the cob. Measure out and reserve 2 cups of the grilled corn kernels; freeze the rest, if any, to use later in soup or salad.

4. Bring the milk and chicken stock to a simmer in a large, heavy saucepan over moderate heat, then stirring vigorously, add the grits slowly and bring to a gentle simmer.

5. Reduce the heat to low, cover the grits, and cook for 55 to 60 minutes or until creamy with a tiny bit of bite. Mix in the 2 cups reserved grilled corn kernels and cook, stirring now and then, for about 5 minutes.

6. Finally, set off the heat, and mix in the butter, half of the Cheddar, and half of the Parmigiano-Reggiano along with salt and pepper to taste.

7. Position the broiler rack 8 inches below the heating element and preheat the broiler. Also spritz a 9-inch, 1½-quart ovenproof stoneware, other pottery, ceramic, or heat-resistant glass casserole with nonstick cooking spray.

8. Scoop the grits mixture into the casserole, smoothing the top and spreading to the edge, then scatter the remaining Cheddar and Parmigiano-Reggiano on top.

9. Slide into the preheated broiler, and broil for 5 to 7 minutes or until the cheese bubbles and is tipped with brown.

10. Remove the corn grits from the broiler, cool for about 5 minutes or until the grits firm up a bit, then cut into wedges and serve.

Grilled Pork Steaks

Makes 4 servings

This is one of Brad's all-time favorites, grilled with skill, then sliced and served on one of his prettiest stoneware platters accompanied by Grilled Corn Grits (recipe precedes). Brad sets up his charcoal grill with a hot zone and a cool zone. "You'll need to move the steaks around to get an even sear and tender meat," he says.

Note: There are two shoulder cuts on a hog: Boston butt behind the ears and picnic in front of the loin. Blade steaks come from the butt, arm steaks from the picnic. Both are tender enough to grill because hogs, unlike beef cattle, get little exercise.

Tip: To be safe to eat, pork must be cooked to an internal temperature of 140°F. Many people prefer 150° to 155°F—juicy and succulent with a tinge of pink.

4 (½-inch) bone-in pork blade or arm steaks (about 2½ pounds; see *Note* above)

1 tablespoon plus 1 teaspoon light brown sugar

1 teaspoon salt

1¼ teaspoons fennel seeds

1 large garlic clove, finely minced

1½ tablespoons finely chopped yellow onion

1¼ teaspoons chili powder

¾ teaspoon ground ginger

¾ teaspoon ground cumin

¾ teaspoon freshly ground black pepper

1. Wipe the pork steaks, then trim off and discard any excess fat. Set the steaks aside while you prepare the rub.

2. For the spicy rub: Buzz all the remaining ingredients for about a minute in a small electric spice grinder, or mash until smooth in a mortar and pestle, grinding the fennel seeds first, then adding the remaining ingredients. Alternately, grind and pound for about 3 minutes until you have a fairly smooth paste.

3. Massage the spicy rub into both sides of each steak, sleeve the steaks in a large plastic zipper bag, and refrigerate overnight.

4. When ready to proceed, remove the steaks from the refrigerator and let stand at room temperature while you prepare the grill.

5. Mound charcoal briquettes and a few hickory chips in the middle of your grill, light, and burn for about 15 minutes or until the coals are covered with gray ash. Set the grilling rack in place.

6. Arrange the steaks—not touching—in the middle of the grill rack and grill for 4 to 5 minutes on each side. *Note*: Watch for flare-ups; pork steaks are fairly fatty and may burn if not monitored carefully.

7. Once the steaks are nicely seared, move to the cooler or indirect heat zone of the grill, and allow them to continue cooking for about 5 minutes or until an instant-read thermometer, inserted in the middle of a steak not touching bone, registers 150°F.

8. Remove the steaks from the grill, bone each one, then slice and arrange on a colorful stoneware platter that will showcase the fanned-out slices.

Butternut Squash Parmesan

Makes 6 to 8 servings

To save time, Brad uses supermarket precut butternut squash cubes, then recuts, if needed, into ¾-inch cubes. He's fussy about the Parmesan cheese and uses only "the good stuff, never stuff out of a can or jar." That means freshly grated Parmigiano-Reggiano. To grate this hard Italian cheese zip-quick, wedge into smallish chunks, drop into a food processor fitted with the metal chopping blade, then alternately churn and pulse for 10 to 15 seconds or until about the texture of kosher salt.

2 pounds ¾-inch butternut squash cubes

1 cup heavy cream blended with 2 tablespoons
    all-purpose flour

1 tablespoon cold unsalted butter, cut into
    ¼-inch dice

1½ teaspoons salt

¾ teaspoon freshly ground black pepper

¾ cup freshly grated Parmigiano-Reggiano cheese
    (see headnote)

1. Preheat the oven to 350°F. Meanwhile, temper a lidded 2-quart ovenproof stoneware, other pottery, ceramic, or heat-resistant glass casserole that can go into a preheated oven under the hot water tap for about 3 minutes. Drain the casserole and wipe dry (don't forget the lid), then spritz with nonstick cooking spray.

2. Drop the squash cubes into the prepared casserole, pour the cream mixture over all, dot with the butter, sprinkle with the salt and pepper, then stir in half of the cheese.

3. Cover the casserole, slide onto the middle shelf of the preheated oven, and bake for about 40 minutes or until the squash is fork-tender.

4. Remove the casserole lid, sprinkle the remaining cheese evenly over the squash, and bake uncovered for about 20 minutes or until the cheese has melted and the squash is light golden brown.

5. Remove the casserole from the oven and let stand uncovered for about 15 minutes or until the sauce thickens a bit. It should be about the consistency of a medium white sauce.

6. Serve hot with roast chicken, turkey, or pork. Add a green vegetable—broccoli, perhaps, or even better, stemmed broccoli rabe that's been quickly blanched and softened in salt water. Its bitterness perfectly counters the richness of the creamed butternut squash.

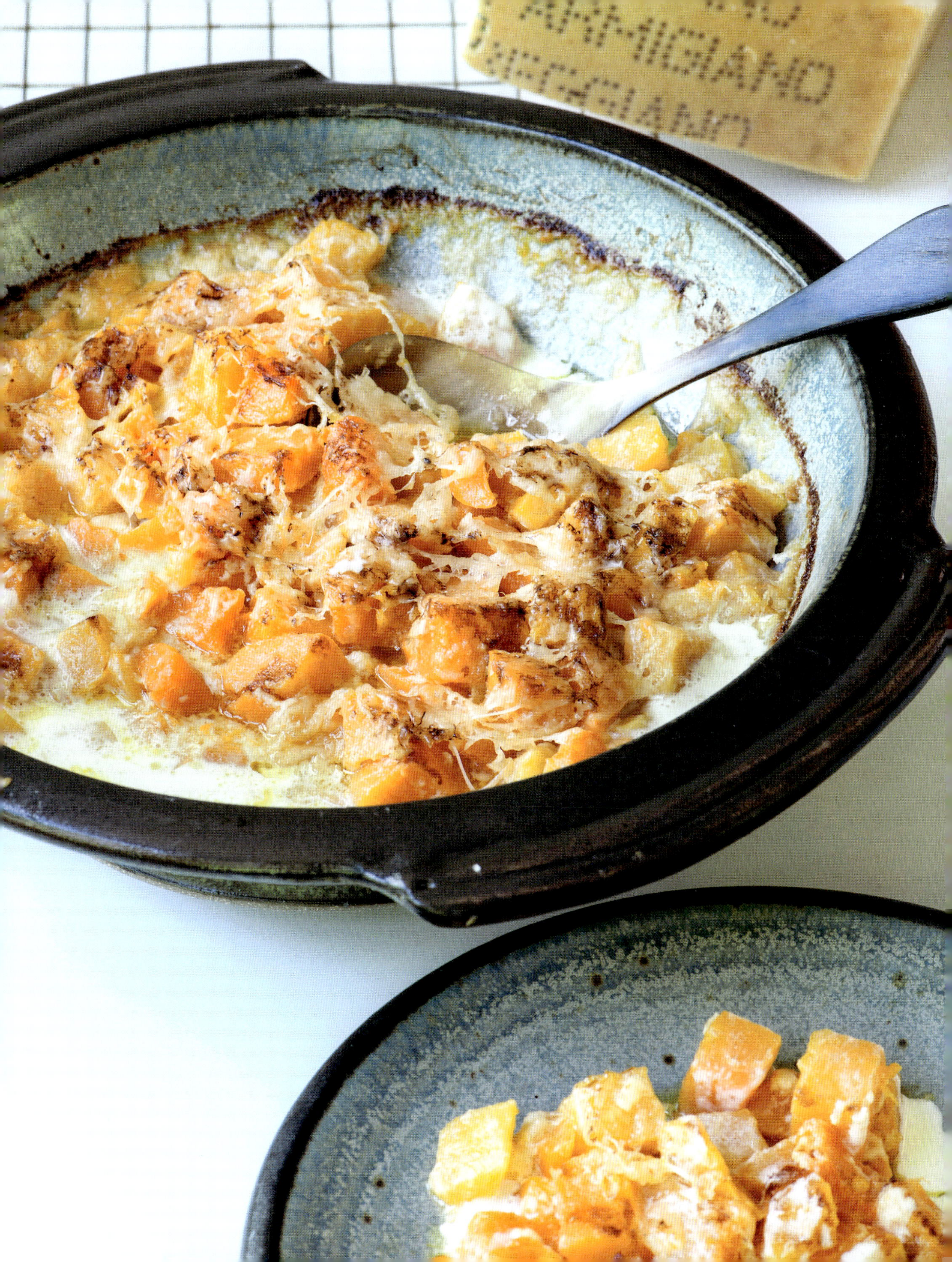
PARMIGIANO
REGGIANO

5

Doug Dotson Pottery

FOR MORE INFORMATION:

dougdotsonpottery.com

When an eighth-grade art class in Virginia Beach introduced Dotson to the potter's wheel, it was love at first spin. But his passion didn't catch fire until he'd settled in the Triangle years later.

As the son of a navy captain, Dotson spent his childhood bouncing about the South and South Pacific, then after earning an engineering degree at the University of Florida, he became a computer programmer at SAS, one of the Triangle's white-hot tech companies.

To chill out and meet people, Dotson took a pottery class at the Duke Art Center and "was immediately obsessed."

"I don't have potters in my family," he says, "but there are artists and craftsmen"—a mother who's a skilled painter, an uncle and a brother who make furniture.

After a brief leave of absence to study pottery at the Penland School of Crafts, "I was on fire," Dotson says. "A whole new world had opened up for me."

Still working at SAS, Dotson eased into this new world by renting a studio in Durham and selling his pots at street fairs. People liked their looks and functionality.

Determined to spend more time at his pottery wheel, Dotson built a post-and-beam studio on the Chatham County acreage he and his brother had bought, tumbling densely forested land strewn with boulders. Then thanks to an Emerging Artists Grant from the Durham Arts Council, Dotson added a kiln for soda firing.

Keeping his day job at SAS, Dotson says, "My obsession with clay happily continues in the forest where I live with my wife and two sons." So, too, his experiments with the local red clay and granite, not to mention soda firing—today a Dotson hallmark.

"I like connecting nature with my work," Dotson explains, adding that whenever he sees food being served in his pottery, "I feel that a circle has been completed."

Seven Vegetable Casserole

Makes 4 main-dish or 8 side-dish servings

"This recipe came from a housemate when I was a vegetarian," Doug says, "and has been tucked lovingly in my old *Moosewood Cookbook*. It's a cool weather dish, good with thinly sliced pan fried flank steak."

Notes: Doug likes to cut the celery, carrots, and parsnips into 2-inch sticks because "they're fun to eat." But if he's in a hurry, he cross-cuts them. A friend who tasted this dish said, "It's one of the best vegetarian dishes I've ever had." Then added that to turn it into a vegan dish that's as delicious as it is nutritious, you've only to substitute olive or vegetable oil for butter and a vegan cheese for Cheddar. Hardly scant praise.

2 tablespoons unsalted butter

4 medium-size leeks, carefully trimmed and washed, then the white part of each leek cut crosswise into 1-inch chunks

2 medium-size celery ribs, trimmed and cut into 2 × ½-inch sticks

2 large Yukon Gold potatoes, peeled and cut into 1-inch cubes

2 medium-size carrots, peeled and cut into 2 × ½-inch sticks

2 medium-size parsnips, peeled and cut into 2 × ½-inch sticks

½ medium-size cauliflower, trimmed and divided into florets

1 (16-ounce) can chickpeas, well drained

1¼ cups apple cider blended with 2 tablespoons tomato paste

1 teaspoon salt, or to taste

½ teaspoon freshly ground black pepper, or to taste

1½ cups coarsely shredded sharp Cheddar cheese

½ cup soft white bread crumbs

1. Melt the butter in a large, heavy skillet over moderately high heat, reduce the heat to low, then add the leeks and celery, and cook, stirring often, about 5 minutes until golden and beginning to soften.

2. Add all but the last 2 ingredients (cheese and bread crumbs), then cook, stirring often, for about 15 minutes or just until the mixture steams.

3. Transfer all to an ungreased deep 2½-quart ovenproof stoneware, other pottery, ceramic, or heat-resistant glass casserole, and cover.

4. Slide a rimmed baking sheet onto the middle shelf of a cold oven, center the covered casserole on top, then set the oven thermostat at 400°F, and bake the vegetables for 45 minutes

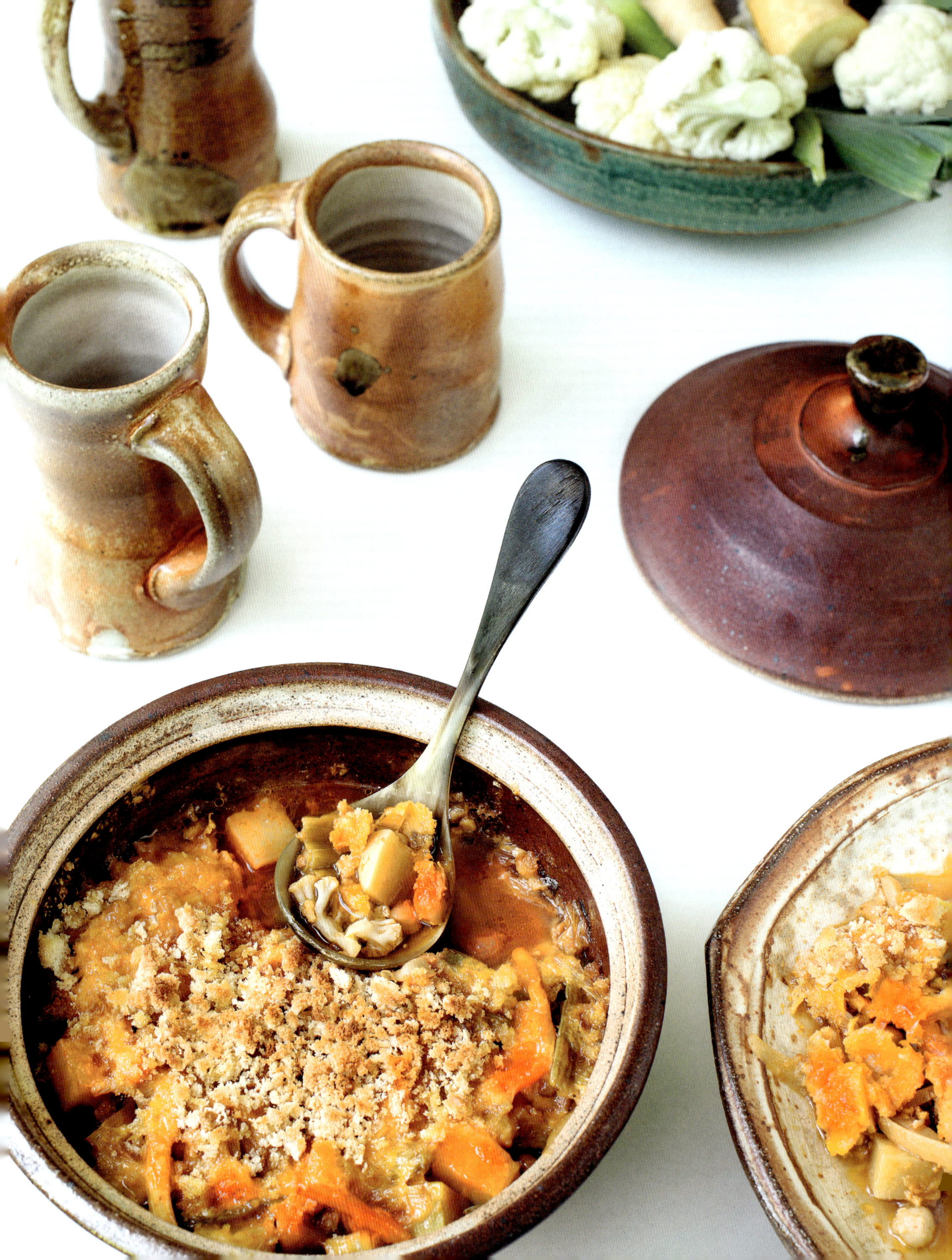

to 1 hour or until they are fork-tender and their flavors nicely married.

5. Uncover the casserole, scatter the shredded cheese evenly over all, then sprinkle the bread crumbs on top. Return the casserole to the oven and bake uncovered for 15 to 20 minutes or until the cheese melts and the crumbs brown lightly.

6. Serve the casserole at table as the main course of a light supper, adding an accompaniment of your choice—maybe just a crusty-chewy country or sourdough bread. Or serve as a side dish with beef, lamb, or fish.

Faux-but-Fabulous Chicken Pot Pie

Makes 6 servings

"This is one of those recipes that I just start cooking without following a recipe very closely," Doug says, adding that the yeast gravy flavors are "very forgiving." He bakes this cool-weather favorite in one of his lidded casseroles and accompanies the dish with cornbread because "it kind of takes place of the crust in a real chicken pot pie." Make the gravy first so it's ready the minute you need it.

Note: Because of the saltiness of the tamari sauce, this recipe needs no salt.

Tip: Health food stores sell nutritional yeast, as do many supermarkets.

YEAST GRAVY

2 tablespoons canola or other vegetable oil

¼ cup unsifted all-purpose flour

1½ cups water, chicken broth, or stock
   (low-sodium, if you like)

¼ cup nutritional yeast (see *Tip* above)

2 tablespoons tamari sauce, or to taste
   (see *Note* above)

CHICKEN

2 tablespoons canola or other vegetable oil

1½ pounds skinless, boneless chicken thighs
   and/or breasts, cut into ½-inch cubes

1 small Vidalia or Bermuda onion, cut into
   ½-inch cubes

2 medium-size Yukon Gold potatoes, peeled and
   cut into ½-inch cubes

2 medium-size celery ribs, trimmed and cut into
   ½-inch chunks

1 cup fresh or solidly frozen green peas

½ teaspoon freshly ground black pepper,
   or to taste

1. *For the yeast gravy*: Heat the canola oil in a small, heavy saucepan over moderate heat for about 1½ minutes or until ripples appear on the pan bottom.

2. Blend in the flour, cook and stir for 3 minutes, then add the water and cook, stirring constantly, for 3 to 4 minutes or until thickened and smooth.

3. Set off the heat, blend in the nutritional yeast and tamari sauce, and set aside. Stir the gravy occasionally to keep it from skinning over.

4. *For the chicken*: Heat the canola oil in a large, heavy skillet over moderately high heat for 1½ to 2 minutes or until ripples appear on the pan bottom.

5. Add the chicken and onion and cook, stirring often, for 2 to 3 minutes or until the onion is translucent and the chicken is barely cooked through.

6. Mix in the reserved yeast gravy along with the potatoes, celery, green peas, and black pepper.

7. Transfer to a lightly greased deep 1½-quart ovenproof stoneware, other pottery, ceramic, or heat-resistant glass casserole, and set the lid in place.

8. Slide a rimmed baking sheet onto the middle shelf of a cold oven, center the covered casserole on top, then set the oven thermostat at 350°F, and bake for about 1 hour and 20 minutes or until the potatoes are fork-tender and the flavors have melded.

9. Carry the casserole to the table and serve as the main course of a hearty family supper, accompanying, if you like, with cornbread. It's Doug's choice. But rice and quinoa are equally delicious.

Mockernut Pumpkin Pie

*Makes one 11 to 11½-inch pie
(8 to 10 servings)*

Mockernut? Just another name for the hickory nut, a wild pecan indigenous to North America. Doug Dotson's pottery is hidden in a forest of hickory trees, and in fall, mockernuts rain down by the millions, hitting metal roofs and cars with the crack of a rifle.

I bake this pie in Doug's deep, straight-sided 11½-inch round stoneware platter. It looks like a ceramic quiche pan.

Note: Because pastry crusts, cradling a soupy filling, started in a cold oven, and baked long and slow, emerge as soggy as swamp mud, I've substituted a crumb crust—two parts graham cracker crumbs, one part gingersnap.

Tip: Because graham crackers come in many different-size packages and because the crackers themselves vary in size, check out the section on crumbs on page 10 for a list of equivalents that includes gingersnaps.

CRUMB CRUST (SEE NOTE AND TIP ABOVE)

2 cups graham cracker crumbs

1 cup gingersnap crumbs

¼ cup granulated sugar

¼ teaspoon freshly grated nutmeg

½ cup (1 stick) plus 2 tablespoons melted unsalted
  butter (or, if needed, 1 to 2 tablespoons more)

PUMPKIN LAYER

1 cup firmly packed canned solid-pack pumpkin
  (not pumpkin pie mix)

¼ cup granulated sugar

1 large egg

1 tablespoon heavy cream

½ teaspoon ground cinnamon

¼ teaspoon ground ginger

¼ teaspoon freshly grated nutmeg

MOCKERNUT LAYER

⅔ cup light corn syrup

2 large eggs

⅓ cup raw sugar

3 tablespoons melted unsalted butter

½ teaspoon vanilla extract

⅛ teaspoon salt

1 cup coarsely chopped hickory nuts (see Sources,
  page 164) or pecans

1. *For the crumb crust*: Combine all the ingredients (the crumbs should hold together when you pinch them), and press over the bottom of an 11- to 11½-inch ovenproof stoneware, other pottery, ceramic, or heat-resistant glass pie or quiche pan that has been liberally spritzed with nonstick cooking spray—sides as well as bottom. Do not push the crumb mixture up the sides of the pan. Set aside.

2. *For the pumpkin layer*: Whisk all the ingredients together in a medium-size bowl until smooth, or if you prefer, alternately churn and pulse in a food processor just long enough to

combine. Spread over the bottom of the crumb crust and set aside.

3. *For the mockernut layer*: Whisk all but the final ingredient (hickory nuts) together (or pulse briskly in a food processor to combine), then stir in the hickory nuts, and pour slowly over the pumpkin layer—carefully, so that it floats on top—and spread until it touches the crust all around.

4. Slide the pie onto the middle shelf of a cold oven, set the thermostat at 350°F, and bake for 50 to 60 minutes or until the filling is set and a cake tester inserted midway between the rim and the center comes out clean.

5. Transfer the pie to a wire rack and cool to room temperature, then refrigerate 1½ to 2 hours before serving. *Tip*: I lay a baking sheet on the shelf directly above the pie so that it's protected from spills.

6. Cut the pie into slim wedges and serve at the end of a festive meal. Thanksgiving is perfect.

6

Lyn Morrow Pottery

FOR MORE INFORMATION:

lynmorrowpottery.com

There's a little town in eastern North Carolina few people know. Founded in 1776, it was the first American town named for our first president. But most people call it "Little Washington" to distinguish it from the one in D.C.

Acclaimed movie director Cecil B. DeMille grew up in Little Washington, and so, too, potter Lyn Morrow. Among her cherished memories are visiting her Grandmother Mallison, who had a house on the Pamlico River and charmed her nine grandchildren with arts projects. Morrow's arts project? "Digging clay from the river bank and making ashtrays. We baked them in the oven, then painted them." But by end of a humid southern summer, those little art projects had softened back into clay.

"I never thought about clay again," Morrow continues, "until I went to Stratford (a junior college in Danville, Virginia), saw a potter's wheel, and was hooked." She majored in ceramics and sculpture at Atlantic Christian College in Wilson, North Carolina, studied sculpture, fresco, and art history at Accademia di Bella Arti "Pietro Vannucci" in Perugia, then came home to earn a master of fine arts at UNC Greensboro.

After teaching in a few colleges and universities, Morrow realized that what she wanted more than anything was to work in her studio.

"I'm not happy unless I'm working," she admits. "I travel quite a bit, too—China, Egypt, South America, Europe, all over." Eager always to learn something new, she tries to spend time with the local potters wherever she goes.

Her advice to young potters? "Learn the basics, then learn to be an artist."

Lyn's Couldn't Be Easier Tomato Pie

Makes one 9-inch pie (6 to 8 servings)

Delicious warm or at room temperature, perfect for a light lunch or supper. Fresh, firm-ripe homegrown tomatoes are a must, ditto grating the cheeses yourself instead of settling for packages of pre-grated. Use genuine Parmigiano-Reggiano, not some domestic imitation that lacks its unique nutty flavor.

Note: Southerners insist upon Duke's mayonnaise, but Hellmann's is certainly an acceptable substitute.

1 (8-ounce) refrigerated tube crescent rolls

1½ cups coarsely shredded mozzarella cheese

2 medium-size firm-ripe tomatoes (about 10 ounces), sliced ¼ inch thick but not peeled

½ cup moderately coarsely chopped fresh basil leaves

⅓ cup firmly packed mayonnaise (see *Note* above)

¼ cup freshly grated Parmigiano-Reggiano cheese

2 medium-size garlic cloves, moderately finely chopped

2 tablespoons panko crumbs

1. Preheat the oven to 400°F.

2. Separate the crescent dough triangles or rounds and shape into a pie shell in an ungreased 9-inch metal or heat-resistant glass pie pan, pressing all seams to seal, pushing the edges up onto the rim, and crimping with the tines of a table fork.

3. Slide the pie shell onto the middle shelf of the preheated oven and bake for 5 to 7 minutes or until lightly browned. Remove the pie shell from the oven and reduce the temperature to 375°F.

4. Scatter the mozzarella over the warm pie shell, then spread out to the edge.

5. Arrange the tomato slices in concentric rings on top of the mozzarella and set aside.

6. Quickly combine the chopped basil, mayonnaise, Parmigiano-Reggiano, and garlic in a small bowl, then spread the mixture on top of the tomatoes. Finally, sprinkle the panko crumbs evenly over all.

7. Slide the pie pan onto the middle shelf of the 375° oven and bake for 25 to 30 minutes or until bubbling and touched with brown.

8. Remove the tomato pie from the oven and cool on a wire rack for 15 to 20 minutes.

9. To serve, cut into wedges, place on colorful pottery plates, and accompany, if you like, with a tartly dressed salad of crisp greens. Good, too, with sautéed broccoli or green beans.

Plantation Coconut Meringue Pie

Makes one 9-inch pie (8 servings)

Lyn says she scribbled this recipe down more than forty years ago, adding that it comes from the Bellamy Plantation in Wilmington. "My mother's family came from Wilmington," she says, "and back then, coconut was exotic." The original recipe calls for one coconut, but with Lyn's OK, I've substituted Angel Flake. She thinks the pie's better if you make it one day and serve it the next because the sherry "tastes less strong."

Note: Before you bake the pie shell, thaw it, recrimp into a high fluted edge, then set the pie shell, still in its foil pan, in a 9-inch metal or heat-resistant glass pie pan.

Tip: Your meringue will less likely to weep if you make it with a 50–50 mix of granulated and confectioners' (10X) sugar.

FILLING

½ cup granulated sugar

6 tablespoons (¾ stick) butter, at room temperature

5 large egg yolks

¼ cup medium-dry amontillado sherry or, if you
   prefer, malmsey (sweet Madeira)

2 cups sweetened shredded coconut (see headnote)

½ cup meringue (spoon lightly into the cup measure)

MERINGUE

4 large egg whites

½ cup plus 2 tablespoons granulated sugar or
   5 tablespoons each granulated sugar and
   confectioners' (10X) sugar (see *Tip* above)

PIECRUST

1 (9-inch) frozen deep-dish pie shell, baked by
   package directions (see *Note* above)

1. *For the filling*: Using a hand electric mixer at moderate speed, beat the sugar, butter, egg yolks, and sherry in the top of a medium-size double boiler for about 3 minutes or until smooth.

2. Set over simmering—never boiling—water and cook, stirring constantly, for about 7 minutes or until thickened and the custard coats a metal spoon. Remove the double boiler top from the bottom, and set on a heatproof counter. Smooth a sheet of plastic food wrap flat on the top of the custard to keep it from skinning over, and cool to room temperature.

3. *Meanwhile, prepare the meringue:* Preheat the oven to 350°F. With pristine beaters and bowl, beat the egg whites at moderate speed until silvery, then add the sugar 1 tablespoon at a time, beating all the while, and continue beating for about 4 minutes or until soft peaks form. *Note*: Resist the temptation to beat the meringue to stiff peaks because it may break down and weep onto the filling as it bakes.

4. Fold the coconut into the cooled custard, then scoop up ½ cup of the meringue and fold it gently into the filling. Pour the filling into the baked pie shell, smoothing the top and spreading to the edge. Finally, swirl the meringue on top, making sure that it touches the crust all around.

5. Slide the pie onto the middle shelf of the preheated oven and bake for about 12 to 15 minutes or until tipped with brown.

6. Set the pie on a cake rack and cool to room temperature. Cover with a large cake keeper or upside-down metal bowl, and refrigerate overnight.

7. Slip the cooled pie (still in its metal pan) into a slightly larger stoneware pie pan if you have one, cut the pie into wedges, arrange on bright pottery plates, and expect raves.

OMG Pecan Pie

This recipe—or rather its ingredients—were jotted on the flyleaf of Lyn's *Joy of Cooking* but this is not a *Joy* recipe. It's a southern brown sugar pie with toasted pecans baked in.

Note: To toast the pecans, spread on an ungreased baking sheet, slide onto the middle shelf of a preheated 350°F oven, and toast for 6 to 8 minutes or until the aroma's irresistible. Cool the nuts before adding to the pie.

Tips: Follow Lyn's lead and use pure Madagascar vanilla extract. No time to make the pie shell? No problem. Simply use a deep-dish frozen pie shell or one of the refrigerated unfurl-and-shape pie dough circles that supermarkets sell (you get two in each 14.1-ounce package).

**1 (9-inch) thawed frozen deep-dish pie shell
(see *Tips* above)**

**1 cup toasted pecan halves, coarsely chopped
(see *Note* above)**

1 cup firmly packed dark brown sugar

½ cup (1 stick) butter, melted

3 large eggs

1½ teaspoons vanilla extract (see *Tips* above)

¼ teaspoon salt

1. Preheat the oven to 350°F. Set the thawed pie shell, still in its flimsy aluminum tin, inside a standard 9-inch metal or heat-resistant glass pie pan, then recrimp the edge into a high fluted zigzag to minimize the risk of spillovers. Scatter the pecans evenly over the bottom of the pie shell, and set the pie aside.

2. Using a hand electric mixer at moderate speed or a whisk, beat the remaining ingredients (brown sugar through salt) for about 1 minute or until smooth.

3. Pour the filling into the pie shell, and gently spread to the edge, disturbing the pecans as little as possible.

4. Slide the pie onto the middle shelf of the preheated oven and bake for 30 to 35 minutes or until the filling jiggles slightly when the pie is nudged.

5. Remove the pie from the oven, and cool to room temperature on a wire cake rack. *Note*: The filling will fall somewhat as the pie cools, but this is the nature of all southern pecan and chess pies.

6. Slip the cooled pie (still in its metal pan) into a slightly larger stoneware pie pan (if you have one), cut the pie into slim wedges, and arrange on colorful pottery plates. Resist the temptation to "cut the richness," as southerners say, by adding a scoop of vanilla ice cream or dollop of whipped cream. Nothing more needed.

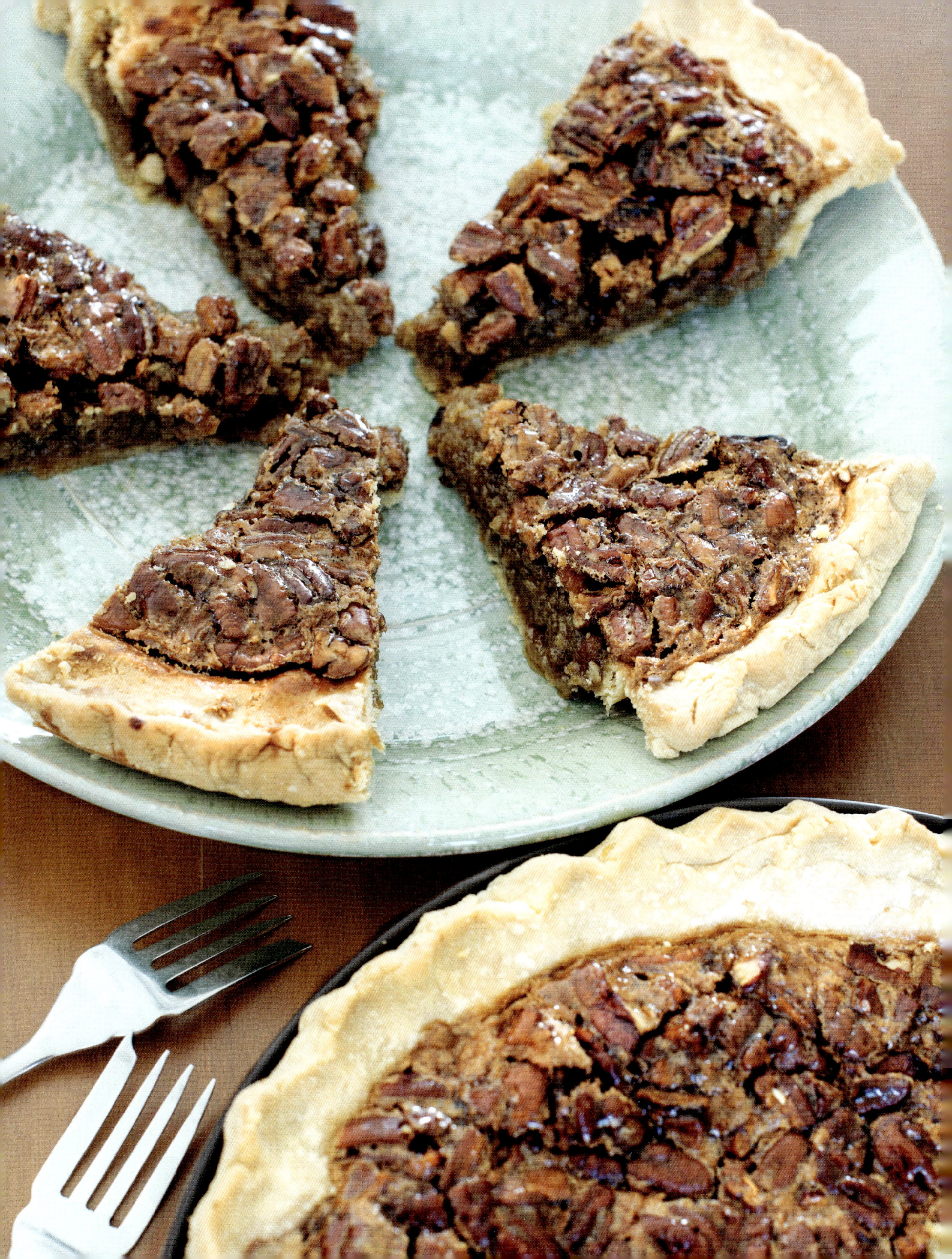

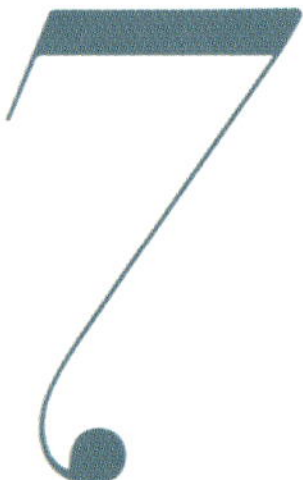

Mark Hewitt Pottery

FOR MORE INFORMATION:

hewittpottery.com

. . . .

"In the 1700s a group of potters from Staffordshire, England, settled in the Sandhills section, and their descendants still fashion churns, crocks, bowls, jugs, plates, pitchers, cups and saucers in beautiful forms and colors" (*The North Carolina Guide*).

Fast-forward two hundred years and meet another Staffordshire potter who settled in red clay country. Born in Stoke-on-Trent, where both his father and grandfather had been directors at Spode (fine china), Hewitt experienced an "aha" moment at Bristol University while reading Bernard Leach's *A Potter's Book*. Shaping clay is what he wanted, not the executive suite.

So he apprenticed for three years with Michael Cardew, who's credited with reviving England's handcrafted pottery quashed by big industry, then worked with Connecticut woodfire potter Todd Piker at Cornwall Bridge, where he met his future wife, Carol Peppe, on a blind date.

"We each thought we were being fixed up with someone else," Carol says. But they hit it off so well that shortly after returning to England, Hewitt U-turned "for another year at Todd's," then took off on a four-month pottery tour of Southeast Asia. Carol caught up with him in England, met his family, met his mentor, Michael Cardew, and married Hewitt in 1983.

After scouring the East Coast for a place to live, Carol says, "we were enormously fortunate to find our place near Pittsboro. It was in terrible shape, which meant that we could afford it . . . and we're grateful every day."

Before long Hewitt began making his mark apprenticing rookies . . . coauthoring *The Potter's Eye* with Nancy Sweezy . . . lecturing . . . presiding over the North Carolina Pottery Center's board . . . winning a kiln-load of awards . . . landing in museums from London to California to Tokyo . . . and, not least, turning and burning the majestic jugs, urns, vases, and utilitarian pots that have established him as a great American master.

Bobotie

Makes 6 to 8 servings

"This South African casserole," Carol Hewitt says, "is one Mark's mother, Sybil Fraser Hewitt, learned to make in Newcastle, South Africa, where she was born and raised. There are many Bobotie variations, but this is the way Sybil made hers. So I dove in and did my best to channel Sybil (who is now in heaven's kitchen), and started dicing onions." The last step in the recipe, Carol adds, "is what takes Bobotie from an unusual meatloaf to a very classy, deeply flavorful dish. With that little egg custard on top, it comes out so pretty, so appealing. And, of course, it really does taste fabulous!"

2 tablespoons butter

2 medium-size yellow onions, finely diced

1 medium-size Gala apple, peeled, cored, and
    finely diced

2 large garlic cloves, finely minced

2 pounds ground beef chuck, not too lean

2 tablespoons curry powder

1 teaspoon ground turmeric

2 tablespoons cider or balsamic vinegar

1 tablespoon finely chopped chutney or apricot jam

1½ teaspoons salt, or to taste

½ teaspoon freshly ground black pepper, or to taste

¼ cup dark seedless raisins or sultanas
    (golden raisins)

¼ cup moderately coarsely chopped blanched or
    unblanched almonds

2 slices firm-textured white bread, soaked in
    ½ cup milk, then squeezed dry and mixed with
    1 lightly beaten large egg

3 large fresh bay leaves (see *Note* in Step 3 below)

2 large eggs beaten with 1 cup milk until smooth

2 cups basmati or California long-grain white rice,
    cooked by package directions

1 cup good Indian chutney

1. Preheat the oven to 350°F. Spritz a shallow ovenproof 2- to 2½-quart stoneware, other pottery, ceramic, or heat-resistant glass casserole with nonstick cooking spray and set aside.

2. Melt the butter in a large, heavy skillet over moderate heat, add the onions, apples, and garlic, and sauté lightly, stirring often, for 3 to 4 minutes or just until the onions are translucent.

3. Crumble in the beef, then mix in the next 10 ingredients (curry powder through bay leaves), reduce the heat to low, and cook and stir for 6 to 8 minutes or till the beef is no longer pink. *Note*: For a decorative bobotie, save the

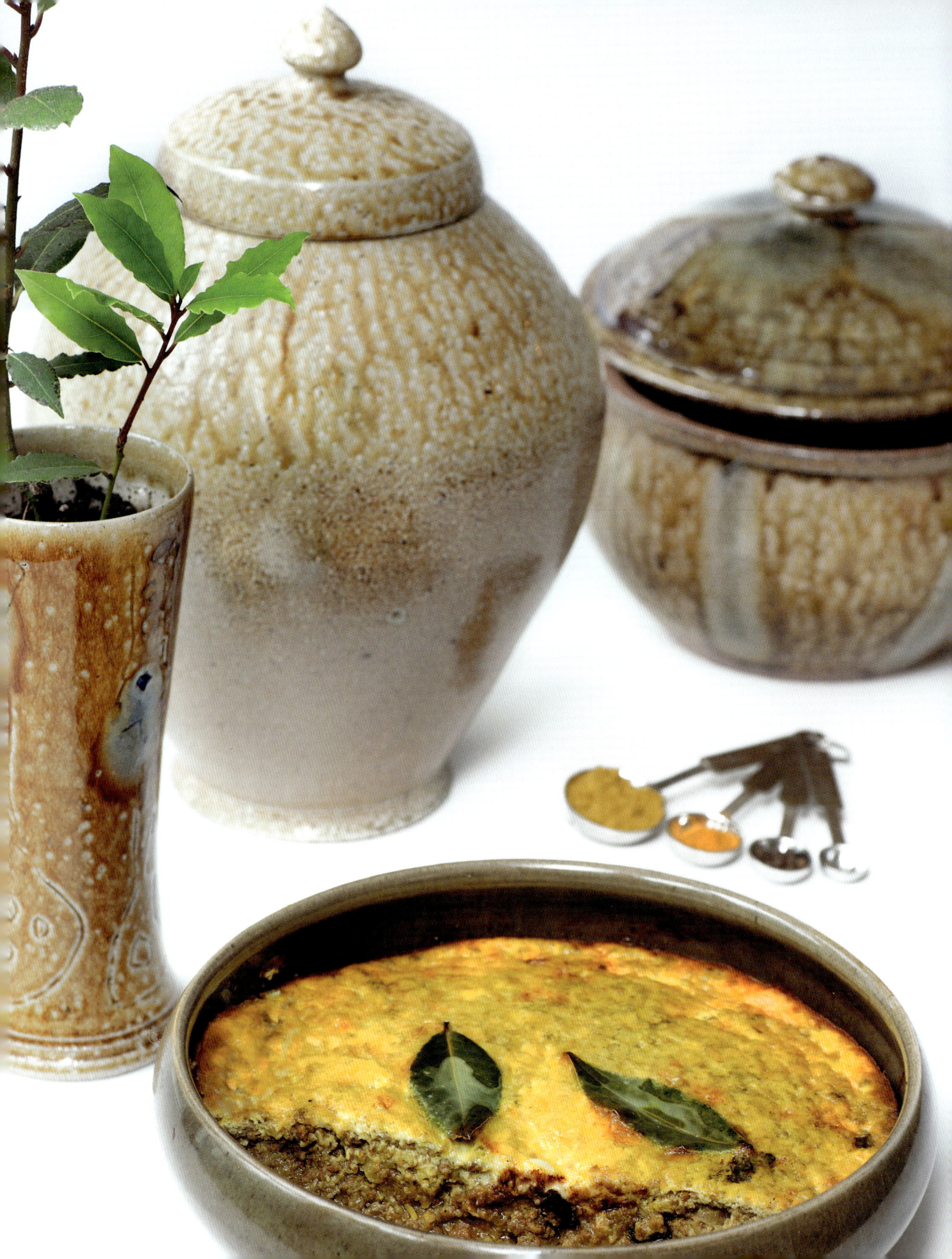

bay leaves and float on the custard at the end of
step 4.

4. Scoop the beef mixture into the prepared
casscrole, spreading to the edge, then pour the
cgg mixture evenly over all.

5. Slide the bobotie onto the middle shelf
of the preheated oven, and bake uncovered for
45 to 50 minutes or just until the custard sets.

6. To serve, carry the steaming casserole to
the table along with a bowl of fluffy cooked
rice and a smaller one of chutney. Lots of good
flavors going on here.

Baked Ham and Chicken Jambalaya

Makes 6 servings

I'd no sooner bought Mark Hewitt's shallow 2½-quart stoneware casserole than it became my go-to baking dish for all manner of recipes, among them this jambalaya adapted from the one in my *From a Southern Oven* (Wiley, 2012) that uses leftovers to best advantage and to the hilt. This is hardly an authentic jambalaya, but it is a perfect one-dish dinner to enjoy with family and friends.

Note: Most high-end groceries sell andouille, and it can also be ordered online (see Sources, page 164).

2 tablespoons bacon drippings or extra-virgin olive oil

½ pound Cajun-style andouille sausage, sliced
    ¼ inch thick (see *Note* above)

1 large yellow onion, coarsely chopped

1 large green bell pepper, cored, seeded, and
    coarsely chopped

2 large garlic cloves, finely chopped

2 teaspoons coarsely chopped fresh thyme or
    ¾ teaspoon crumbled dried leaf thyme

2 large whole bay leaves, preferably fresh

1½ cups diced cooked chicken, a 50–50 mix of
    light and dark meat

1 cup diced cooked ham, preferably country ham

1 cup uncooked long-grain white rice (preferably
    California rice; see page 9)

⅓ cup coarsely chopped fresh Italian parsley

2 cups chicken broth

1 can (14.5 ounces) diced tomatoes, with their liquid

1 teaspoon salt, or to taste

½ teaspoon freshly ground black pepper, or to taste

1. Preheat the oven to 350° F. Spritz a shallow 2½-quart ovenproof stoneware, other pottery, ceramic, or heat-resistant glass casserole with nonstick cooking spray and set aside.

2. Heat the drippings in a heavy 12-inch skillet over moderately high heat for about 1½ minutes or until ripples appear on the pan bottom. Add the andouille and brown, stirring occasionally with a slotted spoon, for 3 to 5 minutes, then lift to the bowl, and reserve.

3. Reduce the burner heat to moderate, add the onions, bell peppers, garlic, thyme, and bay leaves, and cook, stirring occasionally, for 8 to 10 minutes or until limp and lightly browned.

4. Return the andouille and accumulated juices to the skillet, add all the remaining ingredients, and bring to a boil. Taste for salt and pepper and adjust as needed.

5. Transfer to the prepared casserole, making sure that all rice is covered with liquid, then cover with a snug lid or smooth foil tightly over the top of the casserole.

6. Slide the casserole onto the middle shelf of the preheated oven, and bake for about 45 minutes or until the rice is tender and almost all the liquid is absorbed.

7. Serve the jambalaya at table—no accompaniments needed, though a salad of crisp greens tossed with a tart lemon vinaigrette wouldn't be amiss.

Pittsboro Peach and Blue

Makes 6 to 8 servings

"Because they tend to ripen at the same time and taste so good together, peach and blueberry crisps and cobblers are a local classic," says Carol Hewitt, who created this singular crisp that's as easy as pie. Make that easier than pie. "We have a couple of young food entrepreneurs in town who are growing ginger and turmeric," she adds. "Fresh ginger is new to me, and I was an easy convert. So this recipe brings fresh ginger to spice up local peaches and blueberries. I made it gluten-free, but who would ever know?" In fact, Carol mixed rice flour, banana flour, and potato flour—"cuz that's what I had" (see Sources, page 164). She also used turbinado (raw) sugar. "Again," she explains, "that's what I had and I like it better than ordinary sugar."

FRUIT FILLING

3 cups fresh blueberries, stemmed, washed,
   and patted dry on paper toweling

3 large firm-ripe peaches, peeled, pitted, and
   cut into 1/2-inch dice

3 tablespoons gluten-free flour (see headnote)

1 tablespoon finely grated fresh ginger

TOPPING

1 cup old-fashioned rolled oats (oatmeal)

1 cup gluten-free flour combined with 1/8 teaspoon
   each ground cinnamon, ground ginger, and salt

1/2 cup raw sugar

1/2 cup (1 stick) butter, melted

1. Preheat the oven to 350°F. Spritz a shallow 2- to 2 1/2-quart ovenproof stoneware, other pottery, ceramic, or heat-resistant glass casserole with nonstick cooking spray and set aside.

2. *For the fruit filling*: Combine all ingredients, then scoop into the prepared casserole, spreading to the edge.

3. *For the topping*: Toss the dry ingredients (oatmeal through raw sugar) together in a small bowl, drizzle in the melted butter, and toss well again.

4. Scatter the topping evenly over the fruit, once again spreading to the edge.

5. Slide the crisp onto the middle shelf of the preheated oven and bake for about 1 hour or until bubbly and nicely browned. *Tip*: To catch any boilover, place a piece of foil on the oven shelf and center the crisp on top. A 10-inch square is about right.

6. Remove the crisp from the oven, and cool for about 15 minutes on a wire rack.

7. Serve at table accompanied, if you like, with whipped cream, vanilla ice cream, or just a trickle of heavy cream, then bask in the "oohs and aahs" coming your way.

8

Cape Fear Pottery:

Reuben and Ann York

FOR MORE INFORMATION:

info@ncpottery.org

Though their roots run deep in red clay country, neither Reuben nor Ann considered pottery as a profession, let alone felt the call. The two met at NC State University, married in 1986, moved to Lillington some thirty miles southwest of Raleigh, and took over a fast-food restaurant.

"It was a way to make a living," Reuben says. "We cooked, we did everything." But when a new landlord announced that he was tripling the rent, the Yorks bailed out.

They were exhausted after ten years in the restaurant business and ready for a change. Remembering the NC State Crafts Center next door to Reuben's college dorm, the Yorks enrolled in an elementary wheel course, and "were soon addicted to playing with clay."

More lessons followed—everything NC State offered, plus classes at the Pullen Arts Center. In 2003, Reuben and Ann opened the Cape Fear Pottery in Lillington and now exhibit their work every year at thirty-five arts and crafts shows held in Virginia and the Carolinas.

"I do the wheel work and bisque firing," Reuben says, "Ann the slab work and glaze applications."

In the beginning, Cape Fear pottery was decorative— "art-style," Reuben calls it. But functional pieces were what buyers wanted, even such quaint North Carolina classics as chicken cookers and apple bakers. "Customer requests drive our production," Reuben explains.

And keep them mighty busy.

Old Tar Heel Chicken-Cooker Roast Chicken

Makes 4 servings

Some North Carolina potters—Cape Fear among them—still make old-timey stoneware chicken cookers that look like tube pans. The technique of seasoning the bird inside and out, upending it on the central tube, and starting it in a cold oven that slowly reaches 350°F produces a bird of singular succulence. Seasoning? Pretty much up to you, though the Yorks like rosemary and garlic plus wine or beer. We've created a three-herb mix that works well.

Note: Remove the giblets from the chicken and from their packet. Slip into a small plastic zipper bag, press out all the air, then label and date and store in the freezer. Use within three months when making stock, soup, or gravy.

HERB MIX

2½ teaspoons Herbes de Provence or poultry or Italian seasoning

1½ teaspoons salt

¾ teaspoon crumbled dried leaf marjoram

½ teaspoon freshly ground black pepper

CHICKEN

1 (3½- to 3¾-pound) oven-ready chicken (see *Note* above)

4 large garlic cloves, smashed and skins removed

2 large whole bay leaves, preferably fresh

1½ cups dry white wine, such as a Sauvignon Blanc, or a top-quality craft beer

1. *For the herb mix*: Combine all the ingredients with a mortar and pestle, or if you have a little electric spice grinder, buzz several times until almost smooth, and reserve.

2. *For the chicken*: Spritz a 10-inch, 1-quart ovenproof stoneware chicken cooker with non-stick cooking spray, paying particular attention to the central tube; set aside.

3. Rinse the chicken inside and out in cool running tap water, then drain well, and pat dry on paper toweling. Now rub the inside of the chicken with 1½ teaspoons of the herb mix. Carefully insert your fingers underneath the breast skin, rub the breast with ½ of the remaining herb mix, then smooth the breast skin back into place. Finally, rub the outside of the chicken well with the remaining herb mix.

4. Upend the chicken and insert the cooker's central tube deep into the vent so that the drumsticks hang down into the cooker well and the bird doesn't wobble. Drop the garlic and bay leaves into the cooker, and add the wine.

5. Slide the chicken onto the middle shelf of a cold oven, set the thermostat at 350°F, and roast, basting every 30 minutes or so, for 1½ to 1¾ hours or until the bird is golden brown

and an instant-read thermometer, inserted into the meatiest part of a thigh not touching bone, registers 165°F.

6. Remove the chicken from the oven and let rest about 20 minutes before removing from the cooker. Meanwhile, transfer the cooking liquid to a small bowl using a turkey baster, then skim off and discard the fat.

7. Center the chicken on a large platter, spoon about ¼ cup of the reserved cooking liquid on top, then pass the rest in a small gravy boat.

8. Serve the chicken at table, first separating the thighs, drumsticks, and wings from the body, then cutting the breast into thin slices. Or do it the Yorks' way. "We usually use tongs to pull the tender meat off for serving," Reuben says.

Fresh Apple Bread

Makes one 6½- to 7-inch Bundt or tube loaf
(8 servings)

Like many potters, Reuben and Ann York post
a variety of recipes on their website. This, however, isn't one of them and is unique in that it
bakes in their small Bundt pan, in truth a fluted
seven-inch tube pan that holds three cups. Best
apples? We like Galas or Yellow Delicious because of their flavor, also because they don't go
mushy when baked.

Note: The cooled bread will be inverted (upside down). Leave it that way when cutting.

1½ cups sifted all-purpose flour

⅔ cup moderately finely chopped pecans
    or walnuts

½ cup raw sugar

½ teaspoon baking soda

½ teaspoon baking powder

½ teaspoon ground cinnamon

¼ teaspoon salt

1 cup moderately finely chopped peeled and
    cored apple (about 1 medium-size Gala)

½ cup vegetable oil

1 large egg lightly beaten with 1 teaspoon
    vanilla extract

1. Whisk the dry ingredients (flour through
salt) together in the large electric mixer bowl,
and make a well in the middle.

2. Using a hand electric mixer at medium
speed, combine the chopped apple, oil, and egg-
vanilla mixture in a small bowl, then scoop into
the well formed by the dry ingredients.

3. With the electric mixer speed at moderately high speed, beat for about 1 minute or
until a batter almost as thick as cookie dough
forms.

4. Line the bottom of a 6½- or 7-inch ovenproof stoneware, other pottery, ceramic, or heat-
resistant glass Bundt or tube pan with a circle
of baking parchment or nonstick aluminum foil,
then spritz well with nonstick cooking spray,
paying particular attention to the tube and pan
sides.

5. Pack the dough in the prepared pan,
smoothing the top and spreading to the edge.

6. Slide the bread onto the middle shelf of
a cold oven, set the thermostat at 350°F, and
bake for about 1 hour or until nicely browned,
springy to the touch, and a cake tester, inserted
midway between the rim and central tube,
comes out clean.

7. Transfer the bread to a wire rack, setting
right side up, and cool in the pan for 15 to 20
minutes.

8. Carefully run a small thin-blade spatula
around the edge of the bread and central tube
to loosen it, then invert on the wire rack—easy
does it. Cool the bread thoroughly before
cutting.

9. To serve, cut the bread into wedges using
your sharpest serrated knife, and enjoy. No butter needed, no cream cheese, jelly, or jam.

Cape Fear Sour Cream Coffee Cake

*Makes one 6½- to 7-inch Bundt loaf
(6 to 8 servings)*

Another Cape Fear Pottery favorite created especially for their small pottery Bundt pan. And yes, it's easy enough to make for a late Sunday breakfast.

1 cup unsifted all-purpose flour

½ teaspoon ground cinnamon

¼ teaspoon baking powder

¼ teaspoon salt

½ cup (1 stick) butter, at room temperature

1 cup sugar

1 large egg

½ cup firmly packed sour cream (not low-fat)

½ cup golden or dark seedless raisins

½ cup coarsely chopped walnuts or pecans

1. Sift the flour, cinnamon, baking powder, and salt onto a piece of wax paper and reserve.

2. Using a hand electric mixer at moderately high speed, cream the butter and sugar for about 3 minutes or until fluffy and light, pausing midway to scoop the mixture from the sides and bottom of the bowl. Next, beat in the egg.

3. By hand, add the sifted dry ingredients alternately with the sour cream, beginning and ending with the dry and working each in to form a stiff batter—3 additions of the dry ingredients and 2 of sour cream are about right.

4. Finally, fold in the raisins and walnuts, again working in gently but thoroughly to incorporate.

5. Line the bottom of a 6½- or 7-inch oven-proof stoneware, other pottery, ceramic, or heat-resistant glass Bundt or tube with a circle of baking parchment or nonstick aluminum foil, then spritz the pan well with nonstick cooking spray, paying particular attention to the central tube and pan sides.

6. Pack the batter into the pan, smoothing the top and spreading to the edge.

7. Slide the pan onto the middle shelf of a cold oven, set the thermostat at 350°F, and bake the coffee cake for about 50 to 60 minutes or until lightly browned, springy to the touch, and a cake tester, inserted midway between the rim and central tube, comes out clean.

8. Transfer the coffee cake to a wire rack, setting it right-side up, and cool in the pan to room temperature. This may take 1 hour or more.

9. Carefully run a small thin-blade spatula around the edge of the coffee cake and central tube to loosen it, using a poultry pin to free stubborn spots if needed, then invert on a large round plate.

10. Cut the coffee cake into slim wedges and serve. This coffee cake is delicious on its own and needs no accompaniment other than a cup of coffee or a glass of milk.

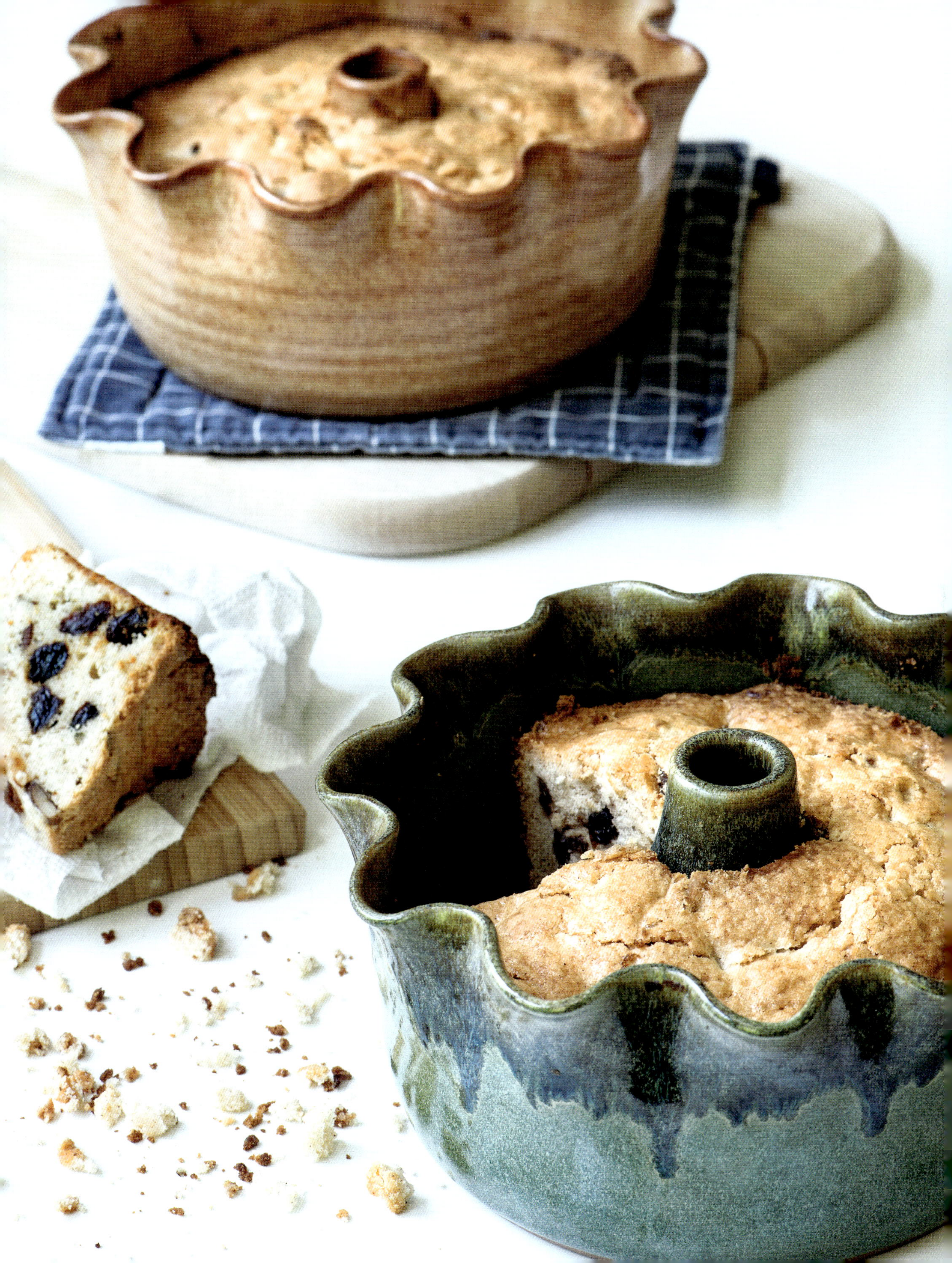

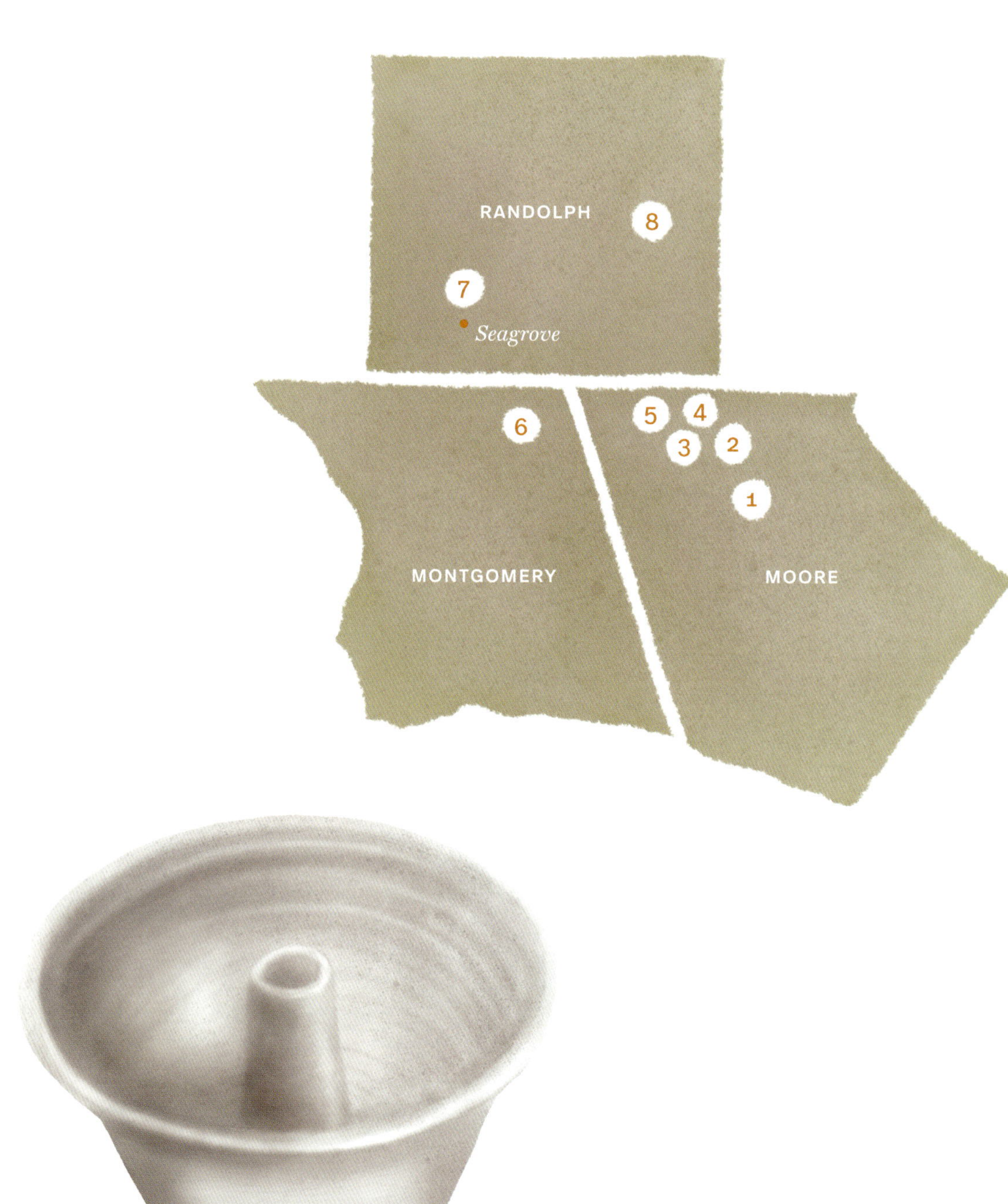

RANDOLPH
8
7
Seagrove
6
5
4
3
2
1
MONTGOMERY
MOORE

Pottery numbers are keyed to the area map opposite.
For an easy-to-follow itinerary, begin at No. 1, or begin at
No. 8 and work your way back to No. 1.

Seagrove-Asheboro Area Potters

1 Jugtown Pottery (Vernon and Pamela Owens)

330 Jugtown Road, Seagrove

Contact: jugtown@mindspring.com

2 Cady Clay Works (Beth Gore and John Mellage)

3883 Busbee Road, Seagrove

Contact: info@cadyclayworks.com

3 Hickory Hill Pottery (Daniel Marley)

4539 Busbee Road, Seagrove

Contact: leanna.hickoryhill@gmail.com

4 Westmoore Pottery (Mary Farrell)

4622 Busbee Road, Seagrove

Contact: westmoore2@gmail.com

5 Ben Owen Pottery

105 Ben's Place, Seagrove

Contact: info@benowenpottery.com

6 Bulldog Pottery
(Bruce Gholson and Samantha Henneke)

3306 U.S. 220 N., Seagrove

Contact: bulldog@bulldogpottery.com

7 Latham's Pottery (Bruce and Janice Latham)

7297 U.S. 220 Alt., just north of Seagrove

Contact: lathamspottery@embarqmail.com

8 New Salem Pottery
(Hal Pugh and Eleanor Minnock-Pugh)

789 New Salem Road, Randleman

Contact: halpugh@northstate.net

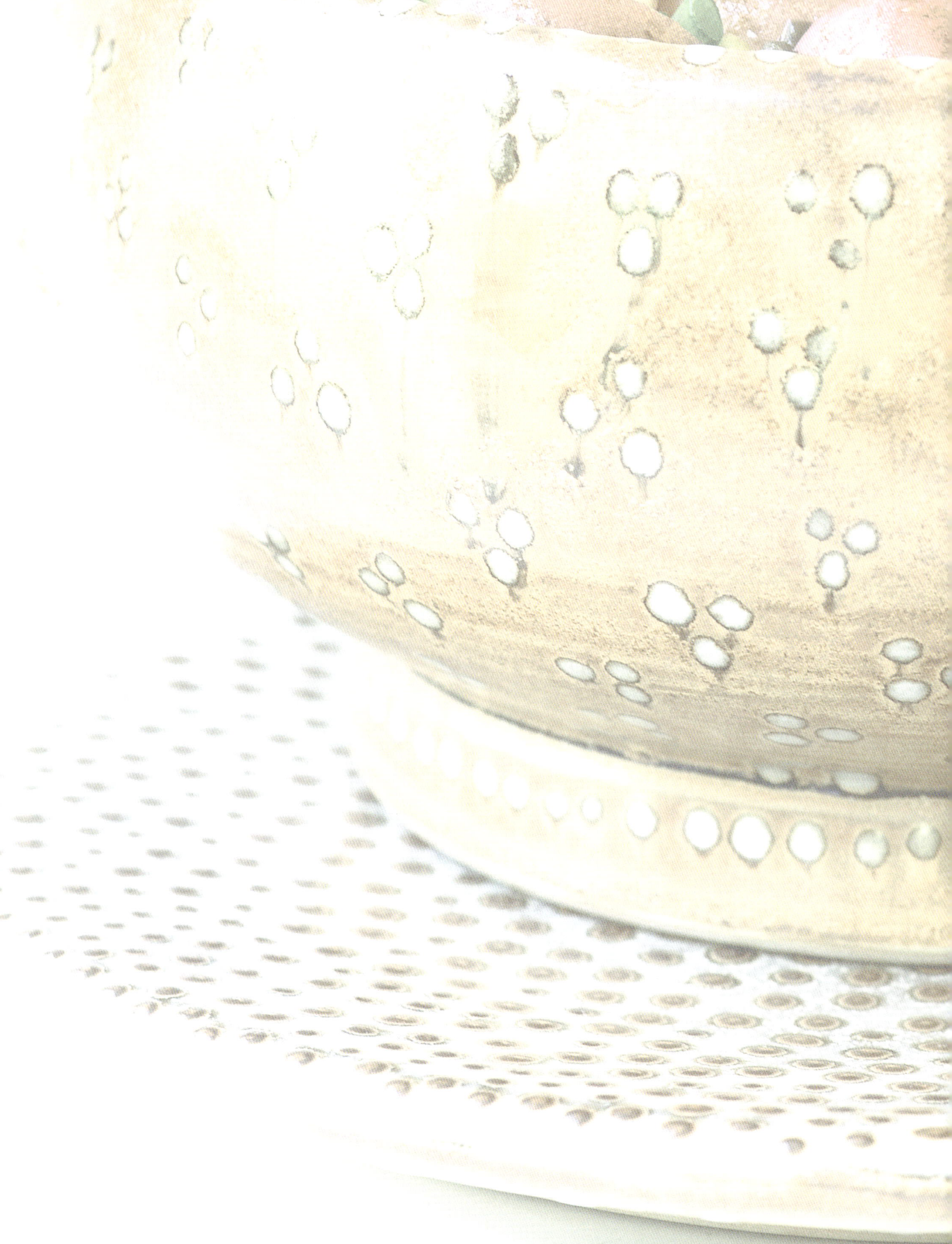

1

Jugtown Pottery:

Vernon and Pamela

Owens

FOR MORE INFORMATION:

jugtownware.com

The one pottery most Tar Heels know? Jugtown, created by a Raleigh couple whose detour from fine art to folk art earned them a historic marker on "The Pottery Highway" (N.C. 705):

JACQUES AND JULIANA BUSBEE

Artists. Ushered old folk pottery tradition into the modern era. Est. in 1922 Jugtown Pottery 3 miles N.E.

Raleigh aristocrats with New York smarts, the Busbees realized that there was money to be made by selling this state's form-follows-function clay casseroles, pie plates, and bowls like the orange "dirt dish" that had captured Juliana's fancy at the Lexington County Fair.

Tracking its source, the Busbees began selling rustic Moore County pots at Juliana's Greenwich Village tea room. Then, eager to vary the designs and replace the old "tobacco spit" glazes with more refined ones, the brand-savvy Busbees moved to Moore County and built Jugtown. They also came up with sleeker designs, many of them decidedly Asian.

"We just pulled men out of the fields," Juliana used to say. And among them was an emerging superstar named Ben Owen, grandfather of today's Ben III.

After Juliana died in 1962, Jugtown, now foundering, was rescued by Massachusetts Yankee Nancy Sweezy, who introduced new shapes and lead-free glazes to veteran potter Vernon Owens (with an "s"). He bought Jugtown in 1983. Today it's a family business with wife Pam (a New Hampshirite and former Owens intern), son Travis, daughter Bayle, and brother Bobby all involved in one way or another making stoneware both decorative and functional.

For me, touring Jugtown's little museum and log sales cabin, not to mention watching an Owens spin a blob of clay into a perfect stoneware pie pan, shows how this gifted family seamlessly melds North Carolina's early pottery designs with the Busbees' modernizing ethic.

Jugtown Pepper Pie

Makes one 10-inch pie (8 servings)

"This is an old family favorite," says Pam Owens. "Cornbread was always a staple in my husband Vernon's family, and this recipe makes a meal of cornbread. We always use organic corn and cornmeal to keep the pie pure and make sure that there are no GMOs."

Notes: Peruvian chili lime seasoning isn't as common as cinnamon, but you can buy it at specialty groceries and online (see Sources, page 164). The chili pepper Pam likes is a Mexi-bell or Hatch, but use your own favorite. Hatch, by the way, is not a species of chili pepper but an umbrella term applied to a variety of chilies grown in New Mexico's Hatch Valley.

Tip: I processor-chop the two red peppers, then add and pulse the canned green chilies, the chili lime seasoning, and half the drained black beans and corn before adding to the heavy-duty mixer along with the remaining ingredients because it produces a slightly finer textured pepper pie that's easier to cut and serve.

½ cup (1 stick) butter

4 large eggs

1 medium-size red chili pepper, cored, seeded, and finely chopped (see *Tip* above)

1 medium size red bell pepper, cored, seeded, and finely chopped

1 (4-ounce) can chopped mild green chili peppers, with their liquid (see *Tip* above)

1½ teaspoons Peruvian chili lime seasoning (see *Notes* above)

1 (15-ounce) can black beans, drained (see *Tip* above)

1 (15-ounce) can organic whole-kernel corn, drained (see *Tip* above)

¼ cup sour cream

½ cup yellow cornmeal

2 teaspoons baking powder

1 teaspoon baking soda

2 cups coarsely shredded sharp Cheddar cheese

¼ teaspoon salt

1. Place the butter in the middle of a 10-inch ovenproof stoneware, other pottery, ceramic, or heat-resistant glass pie plate, slide onto the middle shelf of a cold oven, and set the thermostat at 350°F.

2. Meanwhile, layer the remaining ingredients in the order listed in the large bowl of a heavy-duty mixer equipped with the paddle attachment, add the melted butter, and mix at moderately high speed for about 2 minutes or until combined but still lumpy.

3. Brush the melted butter remaining in the pie plate over the bottom and up the sides. Pour in the pepper mixture, smoothing the top and spreading to the edge.

4. Slide the pie onto the middle shelf of the preheated oven, and bake for about 40 to 45 minutes or until nicely browned and a cake tester inserted midway between the rim and the center comes out clean. *Note*: If at any point the

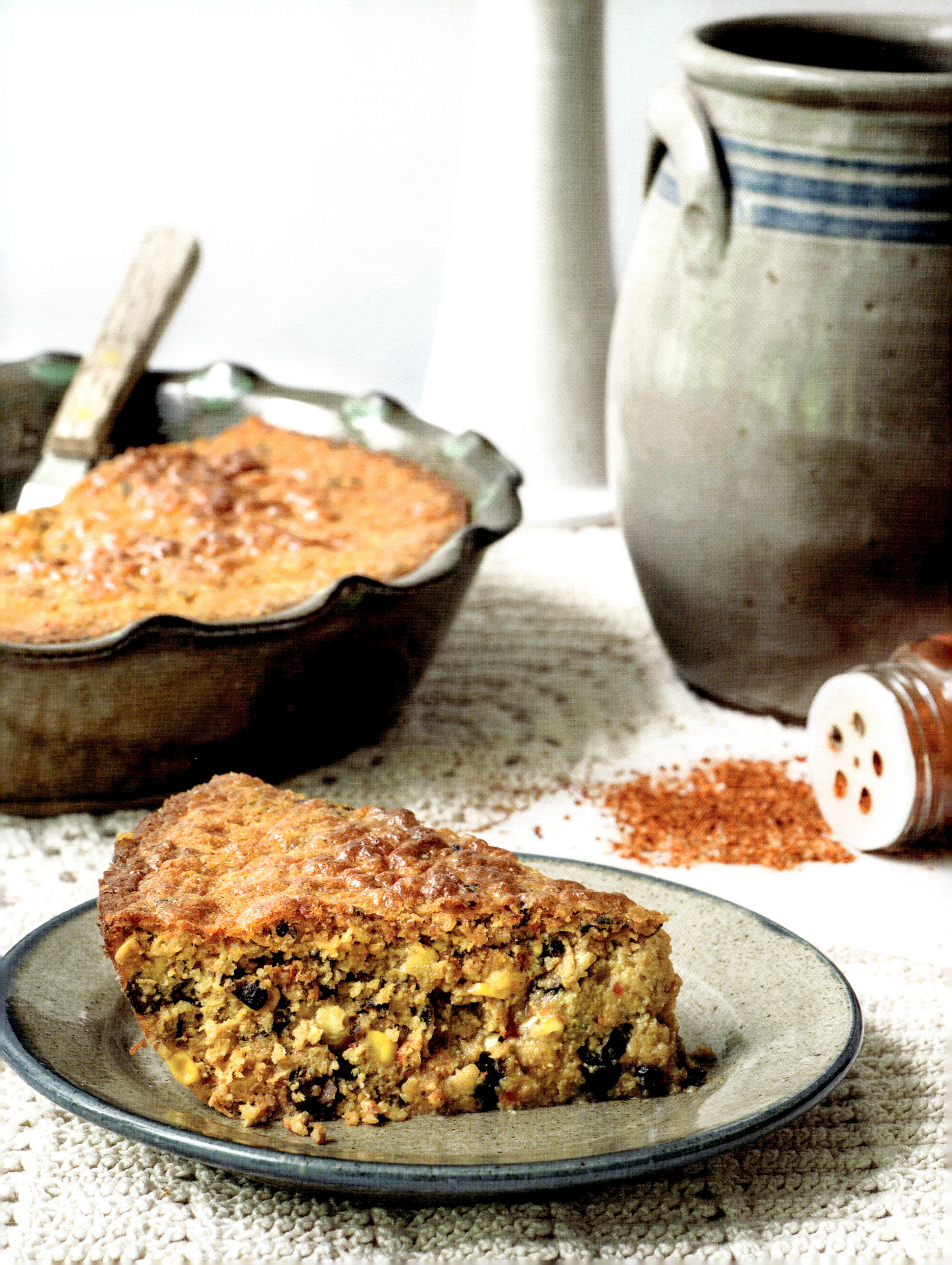

pie threatens to overbrown, cover with aluminum foil.

5. Transfer the pie to a wire rack and cool
to room temperature so it's firm enough to cut
neatly. The pie may sink a bit in the middle as it
cools—no problem.

6. Serve the pie at table, cutting into generous wedges. Accompaniment? Nothing better
than a tartly dressed salad of crisp greens. *Note*:
Pam says the leftovers reheat beautifully (a foil
wrapper and 5 to 7 minutes in a 350°F oven are
all that's needed). And here's more good news.
The cold leftovers are so good a friend thinks
they're picnic-perfect. Just pack them carefully
so they don't crumble in transit.

Jugtown Pumpkin-Chia Pudding

Makes 8 servings

"I created this dish after trying several different chia pudding recipes," says Pam Owens. "It should be served with a spoon because it's the consistency of pumpkin pie filling." Pam uses one of Jugtown's ten-inch handcrafted pie plates when making this easy-as-1-2-3 refrigerator pudding. And to grind the chia seeds? "I use a small electric coffee grinder that's also good for herb seeds and nuts," Pam says. She mixes the filling with an electric mixer, but if you have a food processor, simply pulse all ingredients quickly to combine.

Note: You can buy chia seeds at health food stores or online (see Sources, page 164).

Tip: Use pure maple syrup for this pudding, preferably Grade B, which has deep maple flavor (see Sources, page 164).

PUDDING

2 (13.66-ounce) cans unsweetened coconut milk (full-fat, not "light")

1 (15-ounce) can solid-pack pumpkin (not pumpkin pie filling)

¾ cup chia seeds, half of them finely ground (see *Note* above)

¾ cup maple syrup (see *Tip* above)

2 teaspoons pumpkin pie spice

2 tablespoons unsweetened cocoa powder

TOPPINGS

1 cup heavy cream, whipped to soft peaks with 2 tablespoons confectioners' (10X) sugar

1 (1-ounce) square semisweet chocolate, shaved into curls with a swivel bladed vegetable peeler

¾ teaspoon ground cinnamon

1. *For the pudding*: Using an electric mixer at medium speed or pulsing in a food processor, mix all ingredients well.

2. Pour into an ungreased 10-inch stoneware, other pottery, ceramic, or heat-resistant glass pie plate, cover snugly with foil, and chill for at least 4 hours. Overnight is even better.

3. To serve, spoon the pudding onto colorful medium-size plates (Pam would use Jugtown's own), then drift each portion with the whipped cream, and top with a few chocolate curls and a light sprinkling of ground cinnamon.

2

Cady Clay Works:

Beth Gore and

John Mellage

FOR MORE INFORMATION:

cadyclayworks.com

"One of our favorite things about having a pottery, " Beth says, "is the support we've received from our customers over the past thirty years. We now have second-generation customers."

You've only to stroll through Cady Clay Works to understand why. There are stoneware casseroles in myriad designs, colors, and sizes, bowls galore, and dinnerware so beautiful a Bavarian friend of mine bought an entire set and had it shipped back home.

John, it turns out, was born in Bendorf, Germany, an ore-rich Rhine town "a stone's throw from a village that's been producing stoneware for six hundred years." After World War II when John was just an infant, a job at Thomasville Industries brought his father, a cabinet-maker, and the German Mellage family to High Point practically within hollerin' distance of Seagrove.

Much later, on semester break from UNC Greensboro, John visited friends studying pottery at Montgomery Tech. They were having such fun he decided to take the course and "felt such rapport with clay" that he switched his UNC major from engineering to ceramics.

A thousand miles away, University of Wisconsin art ed major Beth also made a life-changing shift—from teaching grammar-school art classes to becoming a decorator, then company books handler at Rowe Pottery Works in Cambridge, Wisconsin. John was also there.

"I've had some kind of art project in the works since the day I was old enough to hold my first crayon," Beth continues. And the biggest—no question—was moving to North Carolina in 1987 and opening Cady Clay Works with husband John. "We are continuously amazed and grateful that we can earn a living creating functional stoneware of thoughtful design in this throw-away society," she says. "We like the organic, asymmetrical, often serendipitous forms that start with a simple slab of clay."

Beth's Zucchini, Mushroom, Brown and Wild Rice Casserole

Makes 6 servings

"If you don't have zucchini growing in your garden," Beth says, "your neighbor probably does." Her original recipe called for canned sliced mushrooms, but with so many now processed in Asia and frequent recalls, we've substituted the sliced fresh mushrooms sold at supermarkets.

Note: For the latest information about brown rice and wild rice and their arsenic content, in particular, see page 9.

4 cups thinly sliced tender young zucchini

½ teaspoon salt

2 tablespoons extra-virgin olive oil

½ pound presliced cremini or white mushrooms (see headnote)

1 small yellow onion, coarsely chopped

1 (10.75-ounce) can cream of mushroom soup blended with ½ cup cold water and ¼ teaspoon freshly ground black pepper

⅓ cup uncooked wild rice mixed with ⅓ cup uncooked brown rice, cooked by brown rice package directions (see *Note* above)

¾ cup coarsely shredded sharp Cheddar or Monterey Jack cheese

1. Place the sliced zucchini in a large colander, set in the sink, sprinkle with the salt, toss well, and allow to drain while you proceed with the recipe.

2. Spritz a 3-quart ovenproof stoneware, other pottery, ceramic, or heat-resistant glass casserole well with nonstick cooking spray and set aside.

3. Heat the olive oil in a large, heavy skillet for 1½ to 2 minutes over moderately high heat until ripples appear on the skillet bottom. Add the mushrooms and onions and cook, stirring often, for about 5 minutes or until the mushrooms are limp.

4. Add the mushroom soup mixture to the skillet and bring to a boil, stirring often. Now layer the ingredients into the prepared casserole this way: ⅓ of the sliced zucchini, ½ of the cooked rice, ⅓ of the hot mushroom mixture, and ⅓ of the shredded cheese.

5. Repeat the layers once, top with the remaining zucchini and mushroom mixture, then scatter the remaining shredded cheese evenly over all.

6. Cover the casserole with oiled aluminum foil, slide onto the middle shelf of a cold oven, set the thermostat at 375°F, and bake for about 40 minutes.

7. Uncover the casserole and bake for about 20 minutes or until bubbling around the edge and an instant-read thermometer inserted in the center registers 170°F.

8. Serve as an accompaniment to roast chicken, roast pork, or baked ham. Or serve as the main dish of a light lunch or supper with sliced sun-ripened tomatoes.

Aunt Annie's Calico Beans

Makes 6 to 8 servings

"This recipe looks like fall," Beth says. Wholly vegetarian, it comes from her Aunt Annie, her mother's youngest sister in a family of eight children who grew up on a small farm in northern Wisconsin during the Depression. "They weren't ashamed of being poor," Beth says, "because all of their neighbors were poor, too. Of course, living on a farm meant they had enough to eat. Later as adults, their meals were always wholesome and home-cooked— like these Calico Beans." Beth often makes a double batch because "these beans taste great reheated." Shhhhh! She sometimes cooks Calico Beans all day in a crock-pot.

Note: These baked beans are fairly sweet, so if you like them less sweet, halve the amount of brown sugar.

1 (28-ounce) can baked beans, with their liquid

1 (15-ounce) can dark red kidney beans, well drained

1 (15.5-ounce) can baby lima beans (butter beans), well drained, or 2 cups frozen baby limas, thawed and well drained

1 medium-size yellow onion, moderately coarsely chopped

½ cup tomato ketchup

¼ cup firmly packed light brown sugar (see *Note* above)

2 tablespoons cider vinegar

1 tablespoon Dijon mustard

½ teaspoon freshly ground black pepper

½ teaspoon salt, or to taste

1. Spritz a 2½-quart ovenproof stoneware, earthenware, ceramic, or heat-resistant glass casserole well with nonstick cooking spray. Add all the ingredients except the salt and mix well.

2. Cover the casserole, slide onto the middle shelf of a cold oven, set the thermostat at 350°F, and bake for about 2 hours, stirring every half hour, until the flavors have married and an instant-read thermometer, inserted between the rim and the center of the casserole, registers 160°F.

3. Taste for salt, add as needed, then serve as the main dish of a light lunch or supper accompanied by a tartly dressed salad of crisp, mixed greens. Nothing more needed.

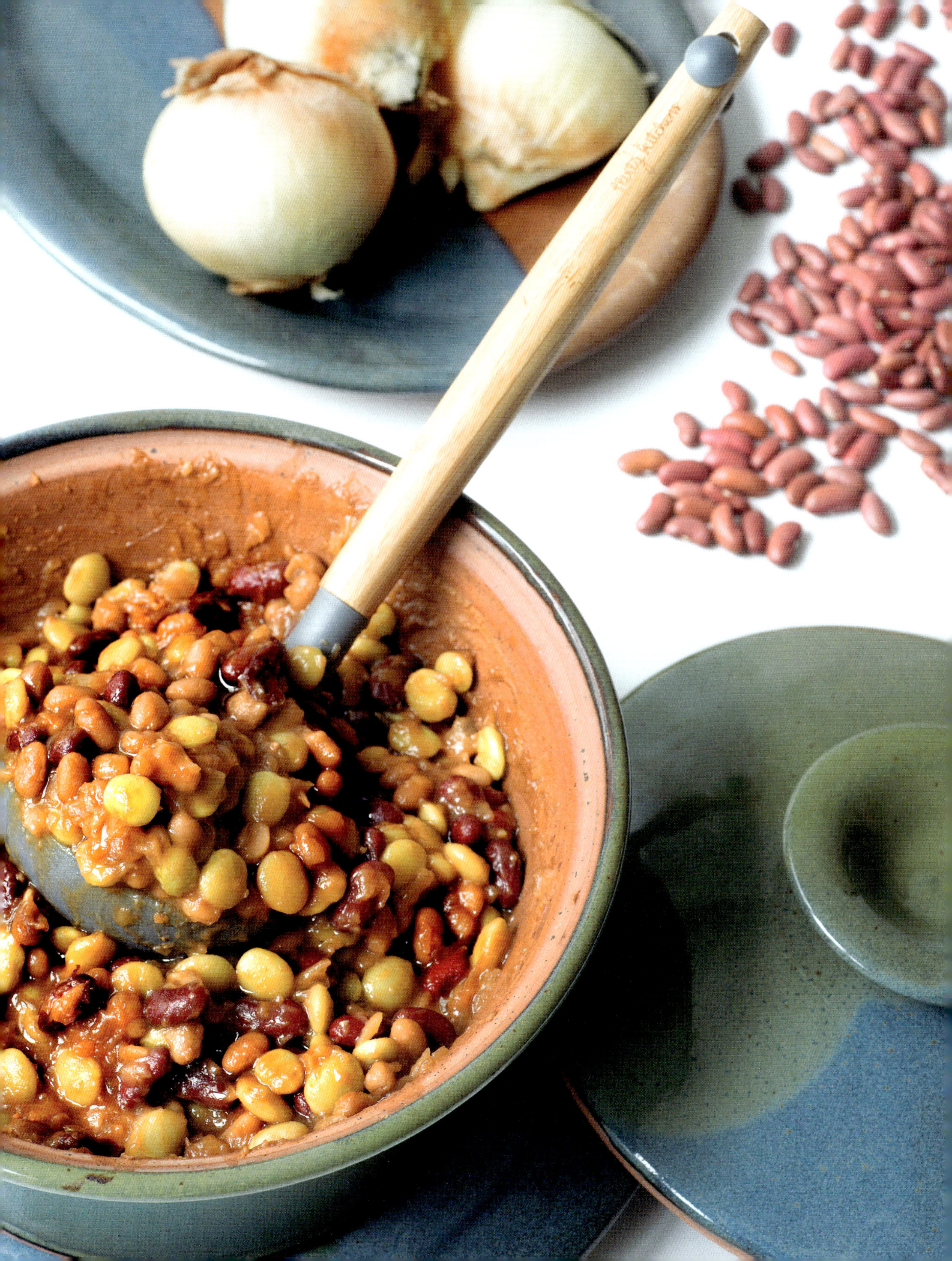

Four Corners Casserole

Makes 6 servings

"I made this one up one cold day," Beth says. "Think comfort food." Why Four Corners? It's where Arizona, New Mexico, Utah, and Colorado meet—the very soul of the Southwest. So, too, this casserole made with two kinds of beans, bell pepper, and corn.

Tip: If canned mixed pinto and great northern beans are unavailable, buy a 16-ounce can of each bean, drain well, then use 1 scant cup of each in the recipe. Use the leftover beans in soup or chili.

2 tablespoons extra-virgin olive oil

1 medium-size yellow onion, moderately coarsely chopped

3 medium-size celery ribs, trimmed and moderately thinly sliced

1/2 medium-size red bell pepper, cored, seeded, and moderately coarsely chopped

3 large garlic cloves, finely minced

1/2 pound ground beef chuck

1 (16-ounce) can mixed pinto and great northern beans, well drained (see *Tip* above)

1 (8.75-ounce) can whole-kernel corn, well drained

1 (10.5-ounce) can cream of celery soup (use low-fat, if desired)

1 cup cooked long-grain white rice (preferably California rice; see page 9)

1/2 cup water

2 tablespoons Worcestershire Sauce

1 teaspoon lemon pepper

1/2 teaspoon salt, or to taste

ACCOMPANIMENTS

1 (13-ounce) package restaurant-style tortilla chips

2 cups coarsely grated sharp Cheddar cheese

1 1/2 cups sour cream (low-fat or fat-free, if desired)

1 1/2 cups bottled salsa (red or green, tepid or torrid)

1 cup coarsely chopped pitted Kalamata olives

1. Spritz a 2-quart ovenproof stoneware, other pottery, ceramic, or heat-resistant glass casserole well with nonstick cooking spray and set aside.

2. Heat the olive oil in a very large, heavy skillet for 1½ to 2 minutes over moderately high heat until ripples appear on the pan bottom. Reduce the heat to moderate, add the onion, celery, bell pepper, and garlic and cook, stirring often, for about 4 minutes or until limp.

3. Crumble in the ground beef and cook, stirring often, for about 5 minutes or until lightly browned. Mix in the remaining ingredients, taste for salt, adjusting as needed, then bring to a boil. Spoon all into the prepared casserole, spreading to the edge.

4. Slide the casserole onto the middle shelf of a cold oven, set the thermostat at 350°F, and bake uncovered for 15 minutes. Stir the casserole mixture well, then bake for 15 minutes more or until bubbling around the edge.

5. To serve, mound each accompaniment in a separate bowl and bring to the table along with the casserole. Tell everyone to crumble some tortilla chips on their dinner plates before spooning on some of the hot casserole mixture, then to top with whatever other accompaniments they fancy—none, any, or all. It's their choice.

3

Hickory Hill Pottery:

Daniel Marley

FOR MORE INFORMATION:

hickoryhillpottery.blogspot.com

"Made by hand on historic Busbee Road in Seagrove, North Carolina."

That's the slogan that greets you when you open Hickory Hill's website. What it doesn't suggest is the pottery's gripping back story.

Though surrounded by potteries, the Marleys were full-time chicken farmers with a Townsend Farms contract to raise broilers. When they lost that contract some ten years ago, they scrambled to make ends meet. So when a local village mayor asked if they'd appear on a CBS feature on poverty, they agreed, unaware that it would air coast-to-coast, and to quote Leanna, "become the opened door we were looking for." It brought them business.

Then while interning at Westmoore Pottery down the road, Danny got a grant from the National Endowment for the Arts "to study the rich tradition and techniques" of the Seagrove potteries. More important, a kid who'd grown up among them had found his life's calling.

Today, whenever New York colleagues head this way, we hit Seagrove's pottery trail, and it was during one of Sara Moulton's visits that I spotted a makeshift Hickory Hill sign on Busbee Road between Jugtown and Westmoore. I slowed, peered up the unpaved drive to a tiny, tin-roofed log cabin. Was this new pottery worth a stop? We agreed that it was.

Inside, floor-to-ceiling walls of shelves greeted us, each stacked with casseroles, bowls, dinnerware, spoon holders, and tube pans with pound cake recipes tucked inside.

We bought ourselves silly (as do other "visiting firemen" in need of pottery bakeware and tableware), so Hickory Hill is now stop number three on my Seagrove itineraries.

To quote their website, the Marleys are "committed to keeping the pottery tradition alive" by making utilitarian pieces that "reflect the traditional shapes of the area." And how!

Chili-Cheese Dip

"This recipe was given to me by a neighbor," Leanna says, "and our kids think it's the best appetizer ever." She bakes it in Danny's 8-inch stoneware ring baker.

Note: When testing Leanna's recipe, we found that it's better if the cream cheese is melted and suggest that you do so via microwave at a moderately low power to minimize the risk of cracking the pottery. Microwave wattages vary significantly, so it's best to follow the manufacturer's directions.

Tip: We also suggest using top brands—like Newman's Own salsa and Eden Foods organic chili beans (no meat, no soy, and preferably low-sodium).

1 (8-ounce) package cream cheese, at room temperature (see *Note* above)

1 (15-ounce) can low-sodium chili beans, with all liquid (see *Tip* above)

1 (16-ounce) can medium-hot salsa, with all liquid

½ pound organic Pepper Jack cheese, coarsely shredded

2 (13-ounce) packages restaurant-style tortilla chips

1. Warm an ovenproof shallow 2-quart stoneware, other pottery, ceramic, or heat-resistant glass baking dish under the hot water tap, wipe dry, then press the cream cheese over the bottom. Slide into the microwave, then heat on low or moderately low power just until the cheese is puffed, bubbly, and melted.

2. Meanwhile, combine the chili beans and salsa in a medium-size nonreactive saucepan and cook and stir over moderately high heat for about 5 minutes or until the mixture begins to bubble.

3. Remove from the heat and pour over the cream cheese, spreading to the edge. Finally, sprinkle the shredded Pepper Jack evenly over all.

4. Slide the dip onto the middle shelf of a cold oven, set the thermostat at 350°F, and bake for about 25 to 30 minutes or until the cheese melts and browns.

5. Remove from the oven, cool for about 10 minutes, then serve with tortilla chips and the beverages of your choice.

Danny's Zucchini Bake

Makes 4 to 6 servings

"We call this Danny's Zucchini Bake because Danny made up the recipe," Leanna Marley says of her husband's quick-and-easy one-dish dinner. She bakes it in one of Danny's large, shallow fluted stoneware baking dishes. For this smaller version, a 9- to 10-inch deep-dish pie plate is perfect. Living as she does on a farm, Leanna is more likely to use home-canned tomatoes than store-bought.

Note: The mozzarella you need for this recipe is a firm one that can be sliced or shredded for pizza and lasagna, not the soft, fresh one immersed in brine.

Tip: For 3 cups canned tomatoes, you'll need two (14.5-ounce) cans diced tomatoes; save the extra ⅔ cup for soup or pasta sauce.

**2 medium-size zucchini, trimmed and sliced
   1 inch thick**
1 pound ground beef (not too lean)
1 medium-size garlic clove, crushed
1½ teaspoons Italian seasoning
1 teaspoon salt, or to taste
½ teaspoon freshly ground black pepper, or to taste
2 small yellow onions, thinly sliced
**3 cups canned diced tomatoes, drained well and
   mixed with 2 teaspoons sugar (see *Tip* above)**
¼ cup freshly grated Parmigiano-Reggiano cheese
**1 cup coarsely shredded mozzarella cheese
   (see *Note* above)**

1. Bring a medium-size saucepan half full of lightly salted water to a boil over moderate heat, add the zucchini, and cook uncovered for 5 to 7 minutes or until firm-tender.

2. Drain the zucchini well, and arrange in a single layer in the bottom of an ungreased 9-inch, 1½-quart ovenproof stoneware, other pottery, ceramic, or heat-resistant glass casserole or deep-dish pie plate, and set aside.

3. Brown the ground beef in a medium-size heavy skillet for 4 to 6 minutes over moderate heat, stirring and breaking up the meat until it is no longer pink.

4. Mix in the garlic, Italian seasoning, and salt and pepper to taste, then spread the meat mixture evenly over the zucchini.

5. Arrange the sliced onions on top, then add the sweetened tomatoes, smoothing and spreading to the edge. Finally, sprinkle with the Parmigiano-Reggiano.

6. Cover with aluminum foil, venting one side to prevent boilovers, then stand the casserole on a rimmed baking sheet.

7. Slide the casserole and baking sheet onto the middle shelf of a cold oven, set the thermostat at 350°F, and bake for about 1 hour or until bubbling around the edge.

8. Remove the foil, sprinkle the shredded mozzarella evenly on top, and bake uncovered for 15 minutes more or just until the cheese melts and browns lightly.

9. Serve at once with garlic bread and get ready for recipe requests.

Hickory Hill Pound Cake

*Makes one 6½- to 7-inch tube cake
(8 to 10 servings)*

The first time I visited Hickory Hill Pottery, some twenty-five years ago, I bought a 10-inch stoneware tube pan and found Leanna Marley's pound cake recipe tucked inside. And what a good cake it made. Then came the new transfat-free vegetable shortenings and howls of leaden pound cakes. So I've created this smaller, all-butter version, which I'm pleased to say fits in the smaller 6½- to 7-inch, 8-cup Hickory Hill stoneware tube pan.

Note: Pottery tube pans vary slightly in size because each is individually shaped on a potter's wheel.

Tips: Use pure extracts only. The artificial ones taste—well—artificial. Also, spray the tube pan with nonstick cooking spray just before you add the batter, otherwise it will puddle in the bottom.

2¼ cups sifted all-purpose flour

1 teaspoon baking powder

¼ teaspoon salt

1 cup (2 sticks) butter, at room temperature
    (no substitute)

2 teaspoons vanilla extract (see *Tips* above)

¾ teaspoon finely grated lemon zest or ¾ teaspoon
    lemon extract

1½ cups sugar

4 large eggs, at room temperature

½ cup milk, at room temperature

1. Combine the flour, baking powder, and salt by whisking briskly in a large bowl and reserve.

2. Cream the butter, vanilla, and lemon zest in the large electric mixer bowl at medium-high speed for about 1 minute or until light. Reduce the mixer speed to medium, and add the sugar in a slow, steady stream. Raise the mixer speed to high and beat for about 2 minutes or until fluffy and almost white.

3. With the mixer at low speed, add the eggs one by one, beating after each addition only enough to incorporate.

4. With the mixer still at low speed, add the combined dry ingredients alternately with the milk, beginning and ending with the dry, and beat after each addition just till combined. *Note*: 3 additions of the dry and 2 of milk is about right.

5. Line the bottom of a 6½- to 7-inch, 8-cup ovenproof stoneware, other pottery, ceramic, or heat-resistant glass tube with a circle of baking parchment or nonstick aluminum foil, then coat the pan well with nonstick cooking spray, paying particular attention to the central tube and pan sides.

6. Pour the batter into the pan, smoothing to the edge, then set the pan on a rimmed baking sheet (to catch any boilovers).

7. Slide the cake onto the middle shelf of a cold oven, set the thermostat at 350°F, and bake for about 1 hour and 10 minutes or until the cake pulls from the sides of the pan, is nicely browned, and a cake tester inserted midway between the rim and the central tube comes out clean. *Note*: If the cake is browning too fast, cover loosely with foil. You might also move the cake to a shelf in the lower third of the oven because the upper heating elements in today's

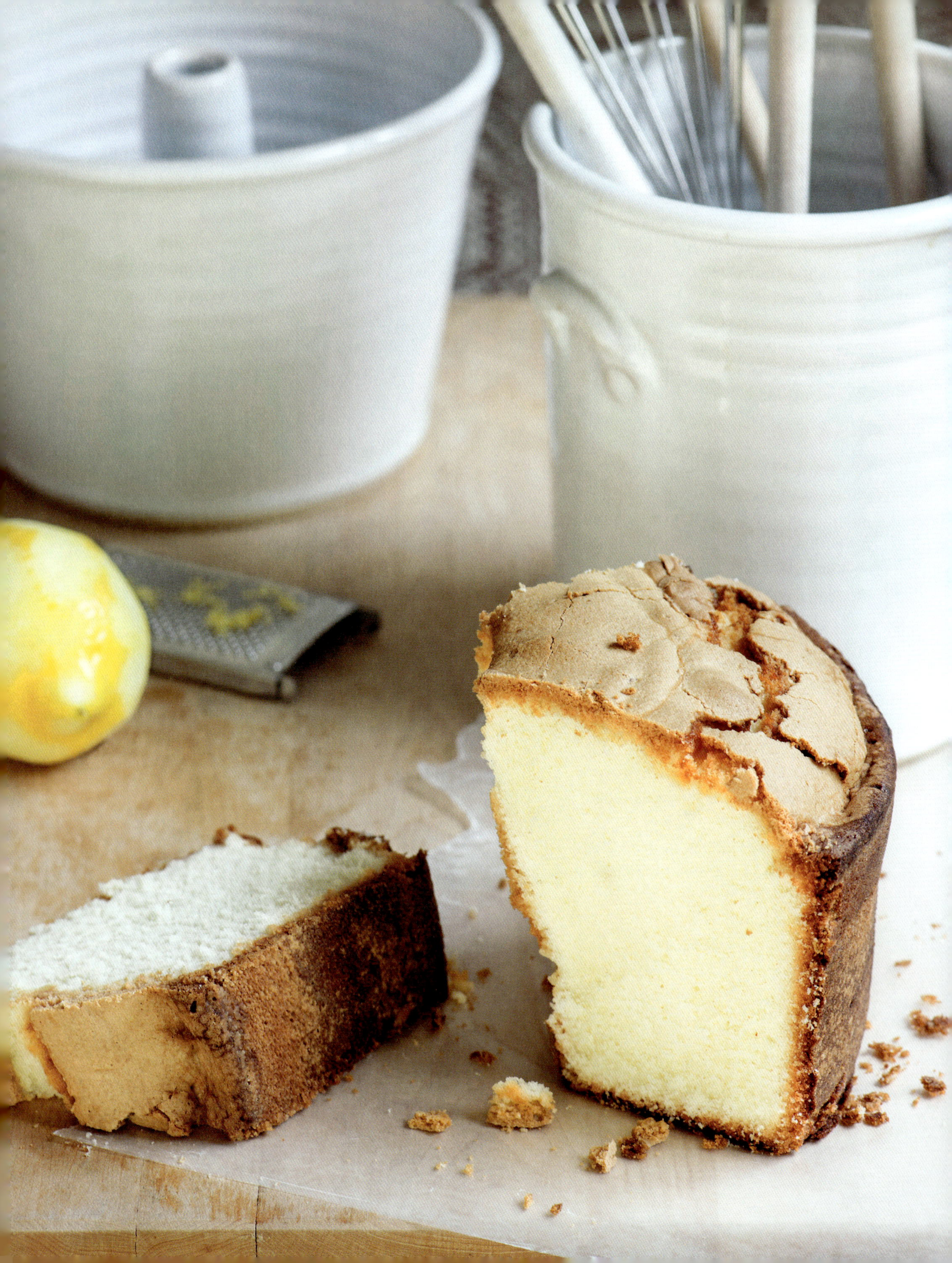

ovens are often intense. Leanna says she sometimes cuts the oven temperature back to 325°F
"once the cake begins to rise."

8. Transfer the cake to a wire rack and cool
in the upright pan for 20 minutes. Using a small
thin-blade spatula, carefully loosen the cake
around the edge and the central tube. Invert
the cake on the wire rack and cool to room
temperature.

9. To serve, cut the cake into slim wedges
using a sharp serrated knife.

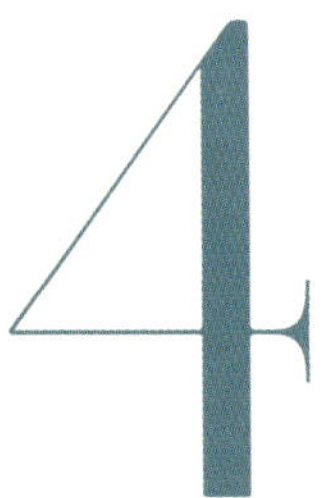

Westmoore Pottery:

Mary Farrell

FOR MORE INFORMATION:

westmoorepottery.com

Hard to believe that Westmoore, a pottery known for its decorated and undecorated redware, its salt- and green-glazed pieces, is forty years old, and even harder to believe that "the entire staff consists of one person. Me, Mary Farrell."

Mary was about eight when she announced that she was going to be a potter. The daughter of a Duke professor, she grew up near Durham and, thanks to her mom's passion for pottery, tagged along on jaunts to the A. R. Cole Pottery in Sanford as well as the J. B. Cole and Ben Owen Sr. potteries near Seagrove.

Mary began her pottery training as a teenager, "with a neighbor giving me my first instruction," then continued her studies at Wesleyan as future husband David did at SUNY Plattsburgh. Mary and the young Upstate New Yorker met while apprenticing at Jugtown. They opened Westmoore in 1987 and, to honor Mary's love of history, made lead-free replicas of functional eighteenth- and early nineteenth-century pottery, some of it redware of Moravian design.

About ten years ago, David left pottery to teach math at a local community college.

"He's an excellent teacher," Mary says. "But let's face it, I love being my own boss. Pottery has been important throughout history and it's rewarding to be able to pass that history on to others," she adds, noting that she's created pottery for some hundred museums and historic sites around the country, most of them east of the Mississippi.

"Occasionally I make pottery for educational programs and exhibits. And more than fifteen (probably closer to twenty) historical films or TV series have used my work."

For collectors, however, the best place to check out Mary's imposing gallery of work is at Westmoore's little "gingerbread house" on Busbee Road. No appointment needed.

Pimento Cheese Pinwheels

Makes eight 3-inch biscuits

Mary Farrell tops her shrimp casserole (recipe follows) with these colorful biscuits. But you can also bake and serve them separately. Make the pimento cheese a day or two in advance, if you like. No matter if you get twice what you need for the pinwheels; save the rest for sandwiches. Or spread on crackers and serve with cocktails.

PIMENTO CHEESE (MAKES ABOUT 1 CUP)

1 (4-ounce) jar diced pimientos, with their liquid

6 ounces sharp Cheddar cheese, coarsely shredded

1½ tablespoons mayonnaise (about)

PINWHEELS

1½ cups sifted unbleached all-purpose flour

1½ teaspoons baking powder

4 tablespoons cold salted butter, cut into
   ¼-inch dice

¾ cup milk

½ cup Pimento Cheese

1. *For the pimento cheese*: Fork all ingredients together in a small bowl, adding only enough mayonnaise for good spreading consistency. Cover the bowl with plastic food wrap and refrigerate until needed.

2. *For the pinwheels*: Sift the flour and baking powder into a medium-size bowl, scatter the diced butter on top, then using a pastry blender, cut in until the texture of lentils.

3. Forking the mixture briskly, drizzle in the milk and continue forking to form a soft but manageable dough. Shape into a ball, wrap loosely in foil, and refrigerate until needed.

4. When ready to proceed, knead the chilled dough lightly on a floured surface, then roll into a rectangle 9 inches long, 8 inches wide, and ¼ inch thick. Skim-coat the dough with the pimento cheese, leaving a ⅛-inch margin at the far 9-inch end. Roll up jelly-roll style into a log 8 inches long, moisten the far end, and press firmly to seal.

5. Lay the log seam-side down on a piece of aluminum foil, wrap snugly, and store in the refrigerator until ready to bake or to use as a topper for Mary's Shrimp Casserole (recipe follows).

6. *To bake as biscuits*: Preheat the oven to 425°F. Lightly rub a baking sheet with cooking oil.

7. Unwrap the pimento cheese log, then slicing crosswise at 1-inch intervals, divide into 8 pinwheels. Arrange the slices an inch apart on the prepared baking sheet.

8. Bake the pinwheels in the upper third of the oven for 15 to 17 minutes or until golden brown.

9. Serve at once.

Mary's Shrimp Casserole with Pimento Cheese Pinwheels

Makes 6 servings

This may seem like a fussy casserole. Not at all, because it can be made in stages. Mary bakes it in her eleven-inch, 1½-quart redware pie plate. Glazed inside only, it can go into a preheated oven. This pottery shape, often referred to simply as a "dish," was popular from the seventeenth through the nineteenth centuries. It's 1¾ inches deep and hugely versatile.

1 recipe Pimento Cheese Pinwheels
   (recipe precedes)
4 tablespoons extra-virgin olive oil
1 medium-size yellow onion, sliced very thin
1 small garlic clove, sliced very thin
1½ pounds medium-size fresh raw shrimp,
   shelled and deveined
2 tablespoons lightly rounded all-purpose flour
1½ teaspoons sweet paprika
1½ teaspoons salt, or to taste
1 teaspoon freshly ground black
1½ cups milk

1. Prepare the Pimento Cheese Pinwheels as directed through step 5.

2. When ready to proceed, preheat the oven to 350°F. Spritz a 1½-quart Westmoore redware pie plate or a same-size ovenproof stoneware, earthenware, or heat-resistant glass casserole that can go into a preheated oven with nonstick cooking spray and set aside. Also remove the foil-wrapped pimento cheese log from the refrigerator and set aside while you proceed with the recipe.

3. Heat 2 tablespoons of the olive oil in a large, heavy skillet over moderate heat for 1½ to 2 minutes until ripples appear on the pan bottom. Add the onion and garlic, and sauté, stirring often, for 3 to 5 minutes or until limp and golden.

4. Add the shrimp and cook, stirring often, for 3 to 4 minutes or until pink and translucent. Scoop the shrimp mixture onto a chopping board, cut the shrimp into ½-inch chunks, and reserve.

5. Add the remaining 2 tablespoons olive oil to the skillet, reduce the heat to low, then blend in the flour, paprika, salt, and pepper. Whisking briskly, add the milk in a slow, steady stream, and cook and stir for 5 to 6 minutes or until the sauce thickens and reduces slightly.

6. Fold in the reserved shrimp mixture, taste for salt and adjust as needed, then scoop into the prepared casserole, and set aside.

7. Unwrap the pimento cheese log, then slicing crosswise at 1-inch intervals, divide into 8 pinwheels. Arrange the pinwheels decoratively on top of the shrimp mixture.

8. Slide the casserole onto the middle shelf of the preheated oven, and bake uncovered about for about 45 to 50 minutes or until the shrimp mixture is bubbly and the pinwheels are light golden brown.

9. Serve at once. Best accompaniments? Steamed asparagus or broccoli or, if you prefer, a tartly dressed salad of mixed greens.

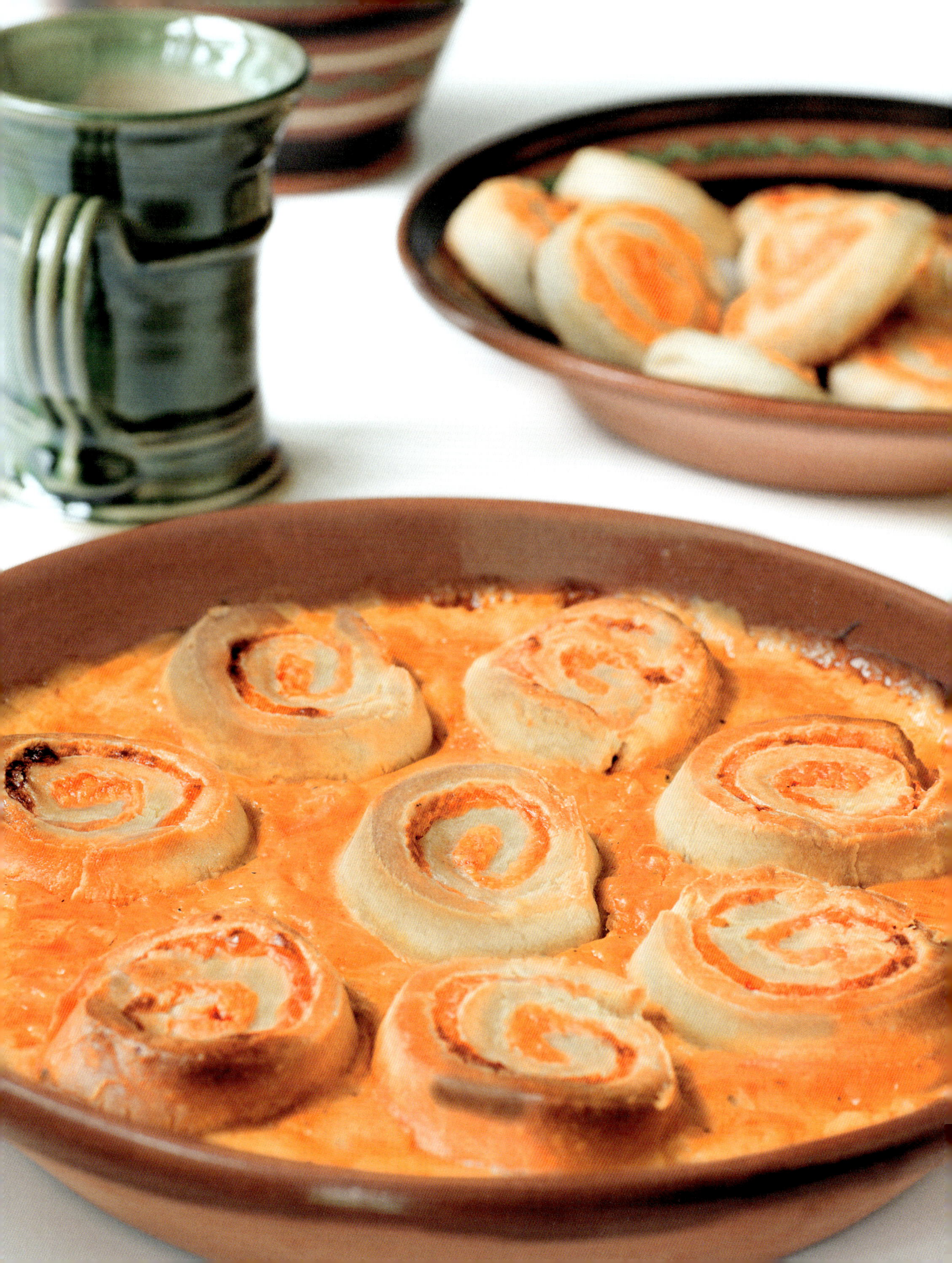

Mary Farrell's Easy Chicken Roll-Ups

Makes 8 servings

Have leftover cooked chicken or turkey? Then try this entirely original main dish. Mary likes to use green spinach tortillas (also called spinach wraps) that come eight to the package; most supermarkets carry one brand or another.

Note: Unlike some handcrafted pottery that must go into a cold oven, Mary's redware can take the shock of a preheated oven. "It has always been important to me to be able to put the earthenware I make into a preheated oven because so many recipes call for that," Mary explains.

2 cups moderately finely chopped leftover chicken or turkey (light and dark meat)

1 (15-ounce) can organic lentils, drained

1⅓ cups firmly packed plain fat-free yogurt

1 medium-size red, orange, or yellow bell pepper, stemmed, cored, and moderately coarsely chopped

1 cup thinly sliced pitted black olives

3 tablespoons pesto (homemade or store-bought)

1 teaspoon salt, or to taste

½ teaspoon freshly ground black pepper, or to taste

8 (7½- to 8-inch) green tortillas (see headnote)

1½ cups coarsely shredded sharp Cheddar cheese

1. Preheat the oven to 350°F (see *Note* above). Grease a 15 × 10 × 1½-inch Westmoore redware baking dish or a similar-size ovenproof stoneware, other pottery, or heat-resistant glass baking dish that can go into a preheated oven well with extra-virgin olive oil and set aside.

2. Place the first 8 ingredients (chicken through black pepper) in a large mixing bowl, then alternately fold and stir until well combined.

3. Working with one tortilla at a time, spread with the chicken mixture, leaving a ¼-inch border all around, then roll up jelly-roll style into a little log. Lay the tortilla log crosswise and seam-side down in the prepared baking dish.

4. Spread and roll the 7 remaining tortillas the same way, then arrange shoulder-to-shoulder in the baking dish.

5. Scatter the shredded Cheddar evenly on top, then slide the chicken roll-ups onto the middle oven shelf of the preheated oven, and bake for about 20 minutes or until bubbly and tipped with brown.

6. Serve oven-hot as the main dish of a casual supper. Accompaniment? How about kale or turnip salad stir-fried in olive oil, then drizzled with cider vinegar?

Lemon Meringue Pie

Makes one 10- or 11-inch pie (8 servings)

"When my boys were young," Mary says, "one of them announced that there were only two foods that I could make well—Lemon Meringue Pie and gravy (and I do make good gravy). Lemon meringue is one of my favorite pies, and this one, a combination of the best attributes of several recipes, has great lemon flavor, a thick filling, and an adequate but not over-high meringue."

Note: There are five eggs yolks in the filling but only four whites in the meringue. No problem. Add the fifth white to scrambled eggs or an omelet.

Tip: Your meringue will less apt to weep if you use a 50–50 mix of granulated and confectioners' (10x) sugar.

CRUST

1½ cups sifted all-purpose flour

¾ cup (1½ sticks) cold unsalted butter, diced

1 tablespoon finely grated lemon zest

2 tablespoons fresh lemon juice

2 tablespoons milk (about)

FILLING

2 cups minus 2 tablespoons granulated sugar

⅔ cup unsifted cornstarch

1 tablespoon finely grated lemon zest

2 cups water

½ cup fresh lemon juice

5 large egg yolks (see *Note* above)

2 tablespoons unsalted butter

MERINGUE

4 large egg whites (see *Note* above)

⅔ cup granulated sugar mixed with ¼ teaspoon cream of tartar or ⅓ cup each granulated sugar and confectioners' (10x) sugar (see *Tip* above)

1. *For the crust*: Place the flour in a medium-size bowl, scatter the butter and lemon zest on top, then using a pastry blender, cut the butter into the flour mixture until the texture of lentils. Forking briskly, drizzle in the lemon juice, then enough milk to make a soft but manageable dough. Shape the dough into a disk, wrap in aluminum foil, and refrigerate until needed. This can be done a day in advance.

2. *For the filling*: Combine the sugar, cornstarch, and lemon zest in a medium-size, heavy nonreactive saucepan. Whisk in the water and lemon juice, set over moderate heat, and cook, whisking constantly, for 3 to 5 minutes or until the mixture thickens. Never boil because the cornstarch will break down and your filling will be soupy.

3. Beat the egg yolks well in a medium-size bowl, then whisking nonstop, add the hot lemon mixture in a slow, steady stream. When

smooth, stir back into the pan, set over low heat and simmer (never boil), stirring constantly, for about 5 minutes or until the yolks thicken. Remove from the heat, add the butter, and stir until melted. Set the filling aside and stir occasionally to keep it from skinning over.

4. *To finish the pie*: Preheat the oven to 375°F. Turn the dough onto a lightly floured surface, and roll into a circle 1 inch larger all around than your pie pan. Mary uses her shallow 11-inch Westmoore redware baking dish, but a 10- or 11-inch ovenproof stoneware, other pottery, or heat-resistant glass pie pan that can go into a preheated oven works equally well.

5. Ease the pastry circle into the pie pan, trim the overhang as needed, and crimp into a high fluted edge. Also prick the bottom of the pastry with a dinner fork. Line the pie shell with aluminum foil, and fill with pie weights or dried navy beans.

6. Slide the pie shell onto the middle shelf of the preheated oven, and bake for about 20 minutes or until the crimped edge begins to brown. Carefully remove the pie weights and the foil, then bake the pie shell 10 minutes longer or until lightly browned.

7. *Meanwhile, prepare the meringue*: Beat the egg whites at moderate speed in the large electric mixer bowl for about 2 minutes or until foamy. With the mixer speed at moderately high speed, add the sugar mixture in a slow, steady stream, then continue beating for about 4 minutes or until the meringue is soft and billowing. *Note*: If you beat the meringue to stiff peaks, it may shrink as it bakes and weep.

8. Remove the baked pie shell from the oven, add the lemon filling, smoothing the top and spreading to the edge. Finally, swirl the meringue on top of the filling, making sure that it touches the crust all around. This helps keep it from shrinking.

9. Slide the pie onto the middle oven shelf, and bake for 5 to 7 minutes or until tipped with brown.

10. Remove the pie from the oven and cool to room temperature before serving. Cover leftovers—not that there'll be any—and refrigerate.

5

Ben Owen Pottery:

Ben Owen III

FOR MORE INFORMATION:

benowenpottery.com

Watching Ben aboard a backhoe gouging clay out of a steep bank is an eye-opener. The clay he's after is not the red-as-iron-rust mud for which the Piedmont is famous but a pale tannish layer several feet below that may contain the proper mix of feldspar minerals.

He pinches a bit of it together, rolls it into a little ball, and grins. Is it sticky enough to hold together on his wheel? Resilient enough to withstand kiln temperatures that soar past 2000°F? Sturdy enough to endure daily household use? Time will tell.

Few people know clay more intimately than Ben Owen III, whose English forefathers settled in Moore County two centuries ago to make whatever pots the colonists needed.

Mentored by his late grandfather, Jugtown master potter Ben Owen, young Ben spent after-school hours and summers at Ben Sr.'s shop and, by the time he was twelve, had decided to follow the family tradition and become a professional potter.

But his career path was different. First a BFA from East Carolina University, then two pivotal trips across the Pacific, first a ceramic workshop in Tokoname, Japan, then twelve years later, an ambassadorial trip to China with visits to museums and pottery villages.

Ben came home with a greater understanding of the Asian designs and glazes that had also intrigued his grandfather. Today, his skilled melding of traditional Carolina styles with the more refined Oriental ones are hallmarks of his own evolving designs—from fiery Chinese red bowls to carved frogskin-glazed Edo jars to shimmering tea dust vases.

Given the number of accolades and commissions he's won over the years, the myriad exhibits organized, the ongoing educational programs and television appearances, is it any wonder that Ben Owen III has been named "North Carolina's Living Treasure"?

Lucille's Brunswick Stew

Ben says that on the coldest winter evenings, his grandfather, the Jugtown master potter for whom he is named, "could smell the aroma of this stew floating out to the potter's wheel. His wife, Lucille, never had to call him—he just knew when the stew was ready." Also that it would be accompanied by "a big black skillet of hot cornbread."

Notes: Frozen limas, frozen whole-kernel corn, and frozen sliced okra can be substituted for the fresh. So, too, home canned. Some chickens have giblets, some don't. No problem. Stew's delicious with or without.

1 (4-pound) oven-ready chicken (see *Notes* above)

Chicken giblets, if any, well rinsed

1 quart water (about)

2 teaspoons salt, or to taste

1 small chili pequin (dried hot pepper pod; see Sources, page 164)

1 large clove garlic, smashed and skin removed

2 medium-size celery ribs, trimmed and sliced about 1 inch thick

1 medium-size green bell pepper, cored, seeded, quartered, and each quarter thickly sliced

2 large bay leaves, crumbled

2 cups shelled lima beans (see *Notes* above)

2 cups whole-kernel corn (see *Notes* above)

2 cups thickly sliced, stemmed small okra (see *Notes* above)

1 quart tomatoes, preferably home-canned

½ teaspoon freshly ground black pepper, or to taste

1. Place the chicken, giblets, if any, water, salt, chili pequin, garlic, celery, bell pepper, and bay leaves in a deep, heavy nonreactive 3½- to 4-quart soup pot, set over moderately high heat, and bring to a simmer.

2. Adjust the heat so the water barely ripples, cover, and simmer for about 1 hour or until the chicken is fork-tender.

3. Lift the chicken to a large cutting board, then strain the cooking liquid into a large fine sieve set over a medium-size bowl. Discard the solids in the sieve.

4. Return the strained broth to the soup pot, add all the remaining ingredients, cover, and bring to a simmer.

5. Meanwhile, when the chicken is cool enough to handle, tear the meat from the bones in bite-size pieces, and return to the pot.

6. Cover, and continue simmering for 30 to 40 minutes or until the flavors meld. *Note*: If at any point the stew seems too thick, add another cup of water or enough to thin the stew to the consistency of chowder. When the stew is done, taste for salt and pepper and adjust as needed.

7. To serve, ladle the steaming stew into heated pottery soup bowls, and accompany with fresh-baked cornbread.

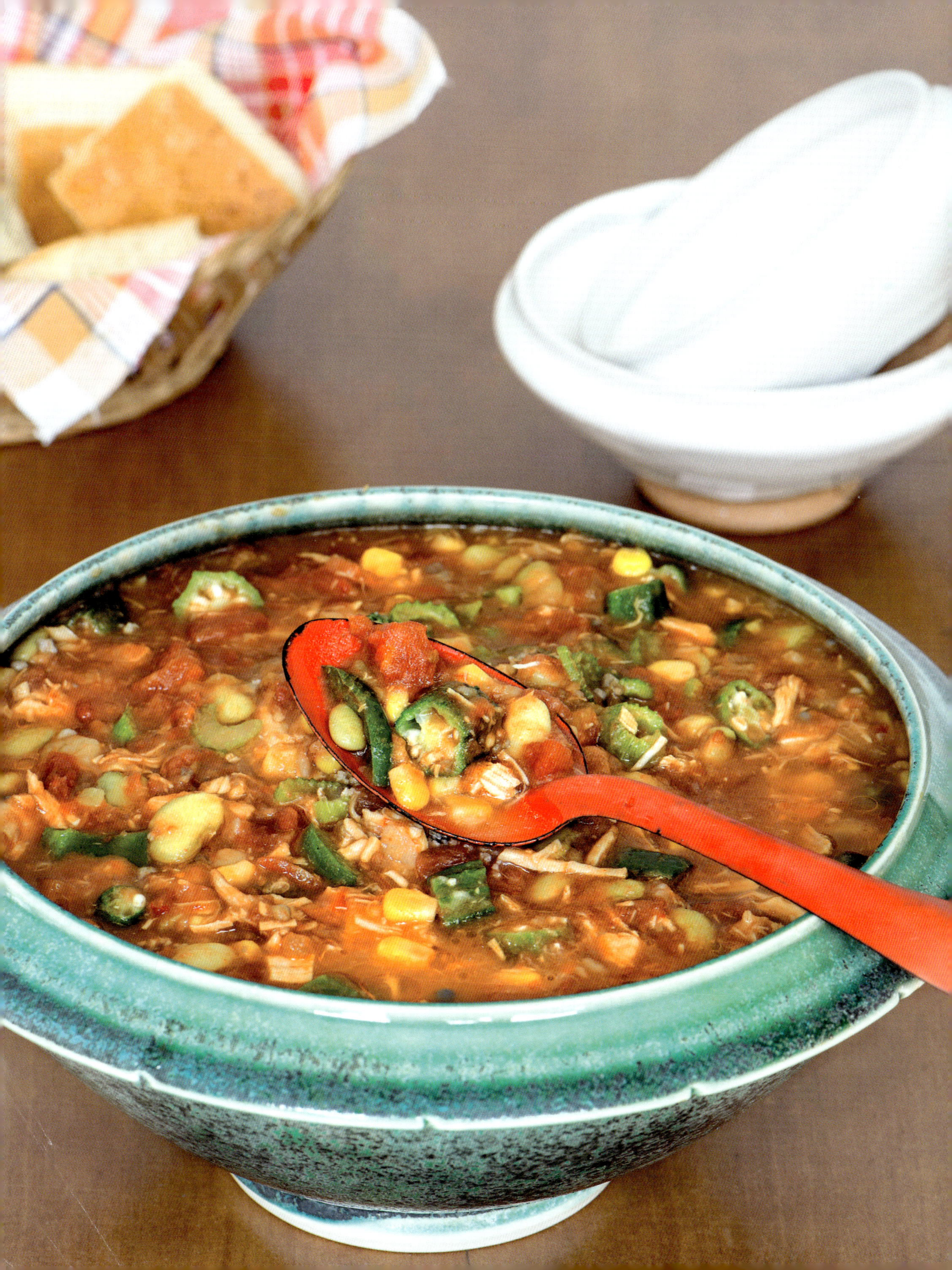

Lucille's Whole-Wheat Biscuits

Makes eight 2¾-inch biscuits

Ben's grandmother Lucille Owen would bake these biscuits for daily meals as well as for special occasions. "She could whip up a large pan of these biscuits in no time," he says. "They always went to the table so hot that the butter melted and guests would almost burn their fingers." A friend who tried Lucille's biscuits confessed that they were so delicious "I could not keep my hands off them."

Note: Lard is rendered hog fat, the only shortening many southerners use for biscuits.

Tip: It's easier to cut the ¾ cup cold lard into the dry ingredients if you add it in three ¼-cup measures and distribute them evenly in the sifted dry ingredients before beginning your pastry-blender attack.

1 cup sifted all-purpose flour

1 cup unsifted whole-wheat flour

1 tablespoon baking powder

1 teaspoon salt

**¾ cup firmly packed refrigerator-cold lard
(see *Note* and *Tip* above)**

½ cup milk (about)

1. Preheat the oven to 450°F.

2. Sift the two flours, baking powder, and salt into a large mixing bowl.

3. Add the lard, distributing it evenly, then using a pastry blender, cut in until the texture of lentils or small peas.

4. Forking briskly, drizzle in just enough of the milk to make a soft but manageable dough. Turn onto a lightly floured surface, then using a light touch, knead briskly 5 to 7 times.

5. With a lightly floured rolling pin, roll the dough into a circle ½ inch thick, then cut into rounds using a lightly floured 2¾-inch round biscuit cutter.

6. Space the biscuits about 1 inch apart on an ungreased baking sheet, then slide onto the middle oven shelf of the preheated oven, and bake for 12 to 14 minutes or until puffed and nicely browned.

7. Serving hissing hot with lots of butter—make that lots of room-temperature butter.

Lucille's Wild Persimmon Pudding

Makes 8 to 10 servings

Back in the 1970s when Vice President Walter Mondale's wife, Joan, visited Ben III's grandfather's pottery, she and her secret service tasted this old North Carolina delicacy for the first time. They loved it, so Ben Sr.'s wife willingly shared her recipe for this "true taste of the South." Now, thanks to her grandson, we can also enjoy this beloved Owen family recipe.

Wild persimmon trees are indigenous to the South, and yet they grow as far north as Indiana. Honey-sweet and no bigger than Ping-Pong balls, ripe persimmons drop from the trees "after first frost," old-timers say. When fully ripe, wild "simmons" are as orange as apricots but lightly hazed with purple.

With suburbia running amok, persimmon trees have become so scarce that cooks rarely share the locations of their secret groves.

Note: Fortunately, wild persimmon pulp shows up at farmers' markets in the fall and can be bought online (see Sources, page 164).

PUDDING

2 cups unsweetened wild persimmon pulp or purée
  (see *Note* above)
1 cup buttermilk
1 cup sugar
¼ cup (½ stick) melted butter or margarine
2 large eggs
¼ cup milk
½ teaspoon vanilla extract
1½ cups sifted all-purpose flour blended with
  ½ teaspoon each baking soda and ground
  cinnamon

OPTIONAL TOPPING

1 cup heavy cream, softly whipped

1. *For the pudding*: Preheat the oven to 300°F. Lightly butter a 9 × 9 × 2-inch heat-resistant glass or ovenproof ceramic baking dish or spritz with nonstick cooking spray and set aside.

2. Place all the pudding ingredients in a large mixing bowl in the order listed, then using a whisk or a hand electric mixer set at moderate speed, beat just long enough to combine, no longer or you may toughen the pudding.

3. Gently scoop the pudding batter into the prepared baking dish, smoothing the top and spreading to the corners.

4. Slide the dish onto the middle shelf of the preheated oven and bake for about 1 hour and 15 minutes or until the pudding begins to pull from the sides of the pan, is springy to the touch, and a cake tester inserted midway between the rim and the center comes out clean.

5. Transfer the pudding to a wire rack and cool for about 30 minutes or just until it firms up a bit.

6. To serve, cut the pudding into squares, arrange on bright pottery dessert plates, and if you like, top with softly whipped cream. *Tip*: This is such a soft pudding I find that it's easier to lift the individual portions from the baking dish if I use a small offset spatula.

6

Bulldog Pottery:

Bruce Gholson and

Samantha Henneke

FOR MORE INFORMATION:

bulldogpottery.com

Scientist? Explorer? There's no denying that Bruce Gholson is an artist, but scientist? Explorer? Absolutely.

Of all the potters who've settled in North Carolina, Oklahoma-born Bruce, arriving after gigs at the University of Georgia (BFA ceramics); College of Ceramics, Alfred, New York (MFA); and Berea, Kentucky (apprenticeship), is assessing the potential of our love-it-or-hate-it red clay.

Switching from porcelain to stoneware to red clay or combining specific qualities of them, he believes, "stimulates ideas." One that he's tried and liked: firing red clay at 2000°F plus (stoneware temperatures) with contrasting white slip or marbled with porcelain clay.

"Red clay provides me with a whole new palate of color and surface texture for the glazes I'd previously developed for porcelains," Bruce explains.

Both he and Virginia-born wife Samantha Henneke (Virginia Tech, then BFA Alfred) grew up in small towns and in 1997 "planted their artistic roots in the pottery community of Seagrove" because they wanted a quiet life "in a rural setting."

Their dream was to pursue their passion for clay by opening their own studio "in a state that appreciates art." Mission accomplished in 2000 with the founding of the pottery they named for their two American Staffordshire bull terriers.

Whenever I visit Bulldog, I see Bruce and Samantha working side by side on another exploratory voyage of "evolving ideas, techniques, clays, and glazes" as they create new pieces for their repertoire of "psychedelic studio art pottery," many of them inspired by nature.

Their little studio-cum-shop showcases sophisticated jugs, bowls, and vases unlike anything made in North Carolina. And dazzling new pieces emerge from each kiln firing.

Bulldog's Thai Curry

Makes 4 to 6 servings

"We have developed this recipe over time," Samantha says. It calls for a few odd ingredients, but all can be found in specialty groceries or online (see Sources, page 164). Samantha uses the newly trendy small, cucumber-slim, bright purple Japanese eggplants. Use them, if you can find them. Otherwise, substitute the bigger, more widely available supermarket eggplant, and cut it into wedges so it's easier to sear in a skillet. And those no-heat jalapeños that Samantha grows? Called Fooled-You Peppers, they look and taste like jalapeños, but, she says, "they have no heat." As for the Panang curry paste, "You could use red curry paste," Samantha says, "but it is hotter."

Tip: Samantha adds that this curry can also be made ahead and frozen.

6 dried shiitake mushrooms

3 tablespoons extra-virgin olive oil

3 (8-ounce) whole Japanese eggplants or

1 (1½-pound) eggplant, stemmed and cut lengthwise into 6 or 8 wedges but not peeled (see headnote)

½ large Vidalia or other sweet onion, coarsely chopped

1 tablespoon Panang curry paste, or to taste (see headnote)

2 tablespoons Asian fish sauce, or to taste

½ pound no-heat jalapeño peppers or equal parts regular jalapeños and mini sweet peppers, seeded and coarsely chopped, or to taste (see headnote)

1 tablespoon fresh lime juice, or to taste

1 tablespoon coarsely chopped fresh Thai basil or 1 teaspoon crumbled dried leaf basil

1 (13.66-ounce) can unsweetened coconut milk

1¼ cups basmati or organic long-grain white rice, cooked by package directions

1. Put the dried mushrooms in a medium-size heatproof bowl, cover with boiling water, and soak for 20 to 30 minutes or until soft.

2. Meanwhile, heat 1 tablespoon of the olive oil in a very large, heavy skillet over moderately high heat for 1½ to 2 minutes until ripples appear on the pan bottom.

3. Add the eggplant, cover, and sear, turning occasionally, for about 15 minutes or until soft. Remove the eggplant from the skillet, cool, then cut into 1-inch chunks and reserve.

4. Drain the shiitakes well, coarsely chop, and set aside.

5. Add the remaining 2 tablespoons of olive oil to the skillet along with the chopped onion and sauté, stirring occasionally, for about 5 minutes or until tender.

6. Add the curry paste and fish sauce to the skillet, and cook and stir for 30 to 40 seconds. Add the chopped peppers and reserved mushrooms, and cook for about 3 minutes or until the peppers are tender.

7. Mix in lime juice to taste, the chopped Thai basil, and the reserved eggplant, and stir-fry for 2 to 3 minutes over moderate heat.

8. Add the coconut milk, bring to a soft boil, then simmer uncovered for about 5 minutes or until the curry flavors mingle and marry.

9. To serve, ladle the curry over the hot cooked rice using your most colorful hand-crafted pottery plates.

MJ's Greek Potato Salad

Makes 6 to 8 servings

This recipe comes from Bruce's sister Mary Jane. It's best at room temperature and, Samantha adds, "superb" when made with first-crop or immature green garlic. A scallion look-alike, it's sweet and mild compared to the mature heads of garlic we know so well. If six cloves of green garlic are too much for you, simply use whatever you like.

Note: Bruce and Samantha do not bake anything in their museum-piece pottery, but if company's coming, they turn their decorative bowls and plates into—dare I say it?—"tableware."

6 large redskin potatoes, scrubbed but not peeled

6 large green garlic cloves, finely minced
   (see headnote)

2 to 3 medium-size scallions, thinly sliced (include
   some of the green tops)

3 canned pepperoncini, drained, seeded, and
   finely chopped

2 teaspoons pepperoncini liquid

1 generous tablespoon capers, well drained

⅓ cup extra-virgin olive oil

2 tablespoons fresh lemon juice

¼ teaspoon salt, or to taste

¼ teaspoon freshly ground black pepper,
   or to taste

1. Boil the potatoes in enough water to cover in a large, heavy saucepan over moderate heat for 30 to 35 minutes or until fork-tender in the center.

2. Drain the potatoes, cool enough to handle, then without peeling the potatoes, cut into ¾-inch cubes, letting the pieces fall directly into a large bowl. Add the garlic, scallions, pepperoncinis, pepperoncini liquid, and capers and toss lightly to mix.

3. Quickly whisk the olive oil, lemon juice, salt, and pepper until smooth, drizzle evenly over the potato mixture, and toss lightly. Taste for salt and pepper and adjust as needed and toss lightly once more.

4. Serve at once or, if you prefer, cover and refrigerate until needed.

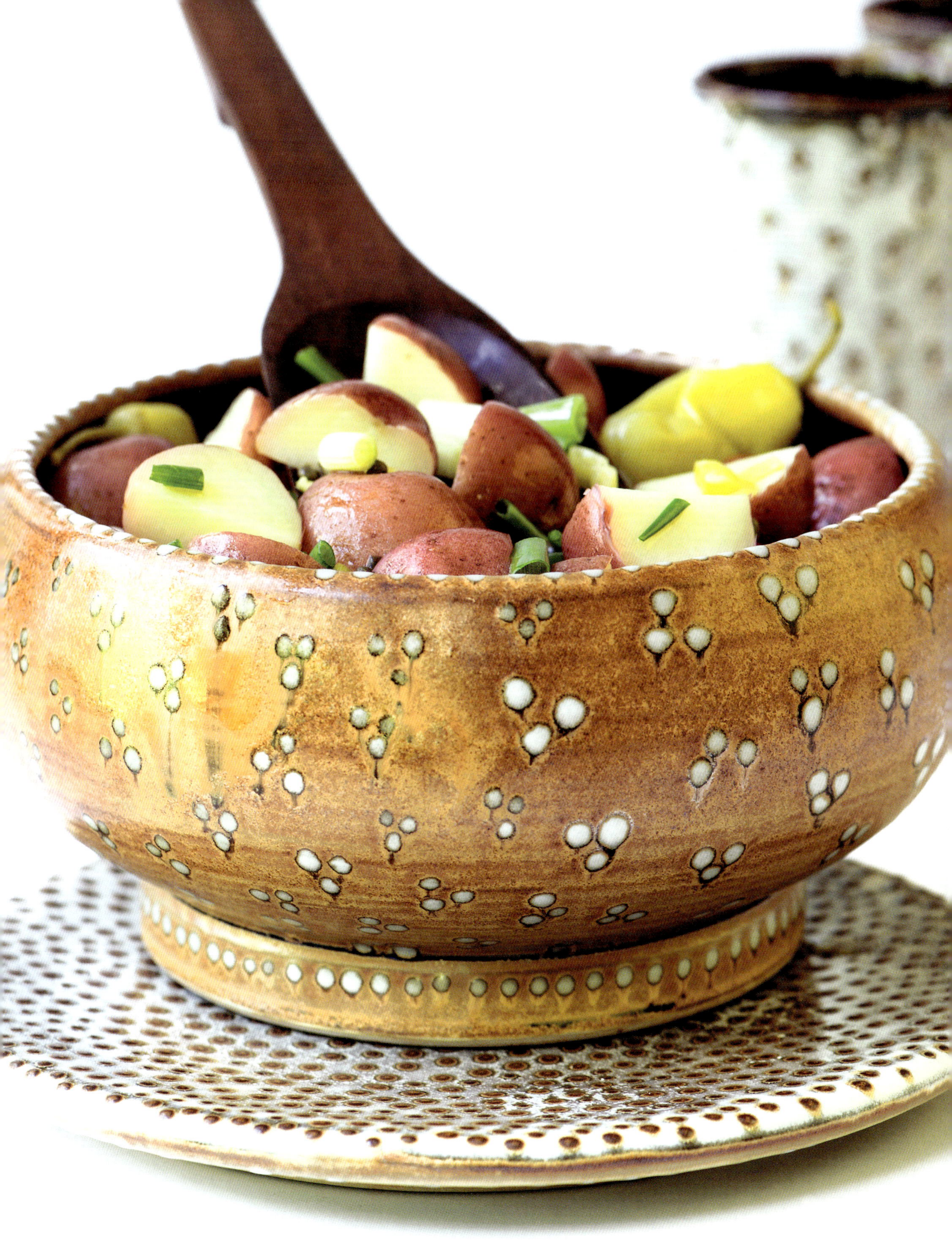

Cousins Granola

Makes 8½ cups (about 16 servings)

Samantha's mom, Gloria, created this granola for Cousins in Clay, a two-day event that Samantha, Bruce, and Bakersville potter Michael Kline host every weekend after Memorial Day. "We invite two potters from outside North Carolina that we admire to sell pottery along with us at Bulldog," Samantha explains. "On Sundays we host a potluck lunch that's open to everyone, and it's become one of our favorite parts of Cousins in Clay." Collectors get to chat with their favorite potters and buy pieces on display.

Note: Use pure maple syrup for this recipe (see Sources, page 164).

2¾ cups old-fashioned rolled oats (oatmeal)

½ cup wheat germ

½ cup sesame seeds or an equal-parts mixture of sesame, flax, and sunflower seeds

1 cup coarsely chopped pecans, walnuts, hazelnuts, or sliced almonds

1 cup unsweetened coconut chips

⅓ cup pumpkin seeds (not toasted)

1½ teaspoons kosher salt

½ cup firmly packed light brown sugar

⅓ cup pure maple syrup (see *Note* above)

⅓ cup extra-virgin olive oil

½ cup halved, pitted dried tart cherries

1. Preheat the oven to 300°F. Line a 14 × 10 × 1-inch baking sheet with baking parchment and set aside.

2. Place the first 7 ingredients (rolled oats through kosher salt) in a large bowl and toss well to mix.

3. Warm the brown sugar, maple syrup, and olive oil in a small, heavy saucepan over low heat 3 to 4 minutes or until the sugar has dissolved. Pour at once over the oats mixture, turning and tossing until the dry ingredients are nicely coated.

4. Spread the dry mixture evenly in the prepared baking pan, pushing to the corners, then slide onto the middle oven shelf of the preheated oven, and bake uncovered for about 40 minutes, stirring every 10 minutes, or until lightly golden. *Note*: Pay attention to the granola around the edges, which browns faster than that in the middle of the pan.

5. Remove the granola from the oven and mix in the dried tart cherries.

6. Cool the granola, then spoon into an airtight container, seal, and store in a cool, dry spot. Samantha uses a big glass jar because "it keeps the granola crisp."

7. To serve, mound the granola into a colorful pottery bowl (preferably one of Bulldog's) so that party guests can help themselves. *Note*: A friend who tried this recipe commented, "Pretty tasty for granola! And none better if you use toasted pecans. Perfect for breakfast with a big dollop of plain yogurt on top."

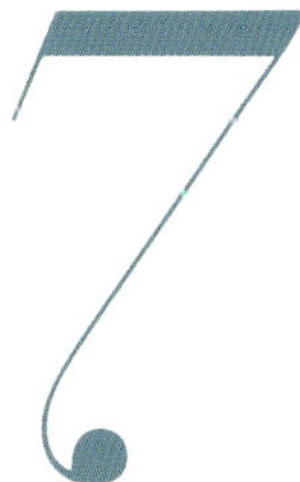

Latham's Pottery:

Bruce and Janice

Latham

FOR MORE INFORMATION:

lathamspottery.com

Less than ten miles north of the Bulldog Pottery (Map #6) on N.C. 220 Alternate, Latham's classic Carolina pots are polar opposites of Bulldog's blazingly contemporary ones.

And why not? Latham's an old North Carolina name and the Lucks (Bruce's maternal forebears) are pottery "nobility," listed as eighteenth-century founders of Seagrove's pottery industry on Historic Marker number K-52 along with the Chriscoes, Coles, Cravens, McNeills, Owens, and Teagues.

Bruce and Janice Latham's website states that they make "functional, traditional stoneware that can be used in the microwave, dishwasher, and oven." There are bean pots, pie plates, Brie pans, casseroles large and small—all hand-turned and lead-free.

But here's a surprise. Though descended from Seagrove pottery aristocracy, Bruce didn't get into pottery until the early 1990s, when he bought his wife a potter's wheel and "took off with it" himself. He is a completely self-taught potter and proud of it.

Bruce and Janice opened Latham's Pottery in 1993 next door to their home on the northern fringe of Seagrove and have won fans among the travelers who drop in and stock up.

Though known for their adaptations of early Carolina pots, the Lathams have also introduced festive new glazes: "Mystery Blue" that's as intense as cobalt . . . lacey "Blue Monday" . . . a sunny yellow . . . a wine-dark burgundy . . . even rose spongeware.

They're also creating new signature pieces best described as giftware: hand-shaped pottery baskets in several sizes, even earring trees and birdhouses.

But it's their functional ovenware and tableware—microwave-, oven-, and dishwasher-safe—that have put Latham's Pottery on the map.

Janice Latham's Buttermilk Cornbread

Makes one 7- to 7½-inch loaf (6 to 8 servings)

Many southern cooks insist upon white stone-ground cornmeal. Not Janice Latham, whose jiffy cornbread uses the self-rising yellow meal supermarkets sell. After hours shaping pottery, she's not up for hours in a hot kitchen, and this four-ingredient cornbread helps her get supper on the table fast. The verdict of a friend who tried Janice's cornbread? "Nice texture and taste. An excellent accompaniment to the big pot of soup I'm making."

Note: Janice bakes it in her skillet-shaped ovenproof stoneware pan, but a small ovenproof other pottery, ceramic, or heat-resistant glass pie pan works equally well.

1¾ cups unsifted self-rising yellow cornmeal (see headnote)
¾ cup buttermilk
⅓ cup vegetable oil
2 large eggs

1. Spritz a 7- to 7½-inch ovenproof stoneware, other pottery, ceramic, or heat-resistant glass pie pan or shallow round casserole well with nonstick cooking spray and set the pan aside.

2. Place the cornmeal in a medium-size mixing bowl and make a well in the center.

3. Place the buttermilk, vegetable oil, and eggs in a second medium-size mixing bowl and whisk for 15 to 20 seconds or until smooth.

4. Pour the buttermilk mixture into the well in the cornmeal and whisk just enough to combine. No matter if a few floury specks show; they will disappear as the cornbread bakes and prove that you haven't overbeaten the batter, which tends to make the cornbread tough.

5. Pour the mixture into the prepared pie pan, smoothing the top and spreading to the edge. Slide the pan onto the middle shelf of a cold oven, set the thermostat at 350°F, and bake for 30 to 35 to 40 minutes or until the cornbread begins to pull from the sides of the pan and a cake tester, inserted halfway between the rim of the pan the center, comes out clean.

6. Remove the cornbread from the oven and cut at once into wedges. Put out plenty of butter—room-temperature butter is best so that it melts the instant it's spread on the split wedges of cornbread.

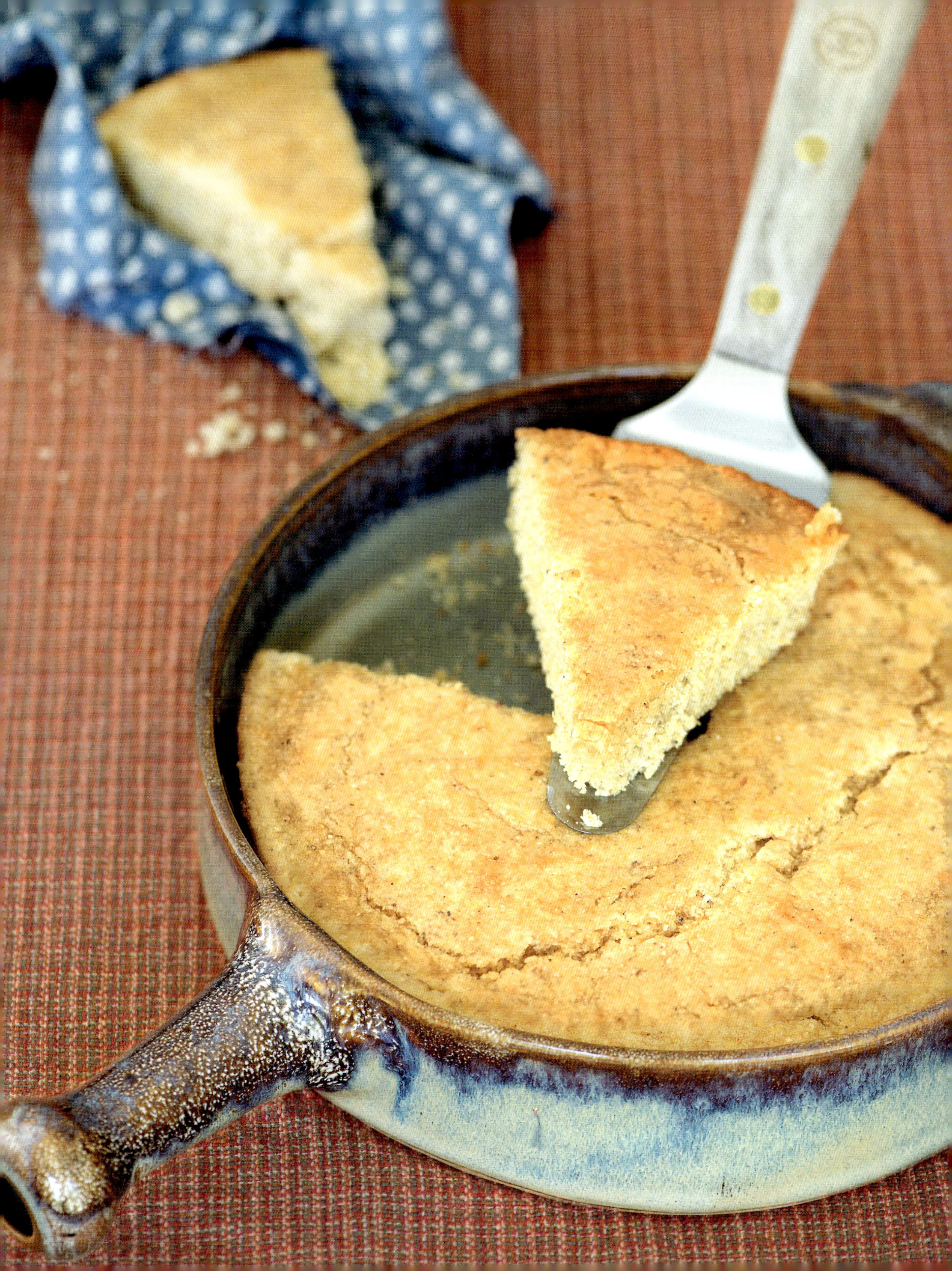

Easy Sausage and Cheddar Quiche

Makes 6 servings

Like many busy cooks, Janice Latham takes short-cuts, but only if those short-cut recipes are good. The idea for this quiche, she admits, is a back-of-the-box one, but she's improvised and made it her own.

Tip: The sausage to use is a southern bulk sausage meat like Neese's. Janice likes peppery sausage, but go for tepid if you prefer (see Sources, page 164). Just make sure the sausage is cooked, drained, and crumbled before you sprinkle it on top of the unbaked quiche.

1½ cups milk, at room temperature

¼ cup (½ stick) butter, melted

3 large eggs

½ cup biscuit baking mix (every supermarket
   carries them)

⅛ teaspoon freshly ground black pepper

6 ounces sausage meat, cooked, drained, and
   crumbled fairly fine (see *Tip* above)

¾ cup coarsely shredded sharp Cheddar cheese

1. Spritz a 9-inch ovenproof stoneware, other pottery, ceramic, or heat-resistant glass pie pan well with nonstick cooking spray and set aside.

2. Quickly pulse the milk, melted butter, and eggs in an electric blender. Add the baking mix and pepper and buzz for about 5 seconds until creamy, pulsing once midway.

3. Pour the batter into the prepared pan, and scatter the sausage meat, then the shredded cheese, evenly on top.

4. Slide the quiche onto the middle shelf of a cold oven, set the thermostat at 350°F, and bake uncovered for 40 to 45 minutes or until a cake tester, inserted between the rim and center, comes out clean.

5. Remove the quiche from the oven, set upright on a wire rack, and cool for 15 minutes.

6. To serve, cut into wedges and accompany with a tartly dressed salad of crisp greens. Nothing more needed.

Variation: Jalapeño-Cheddar Quiche: Prepare steps 1 and 2 as directed, then using a rubber spatula, mix in 1 well-drained 4-ounce can diced fire-roasted green chilies. Pour into the prepared pie pan as directed in step 3. Omit the sausage, but scatter the shredded cheese evenly on top of the quiche. Proceed as the recipe directs in steps 4 through 6. Makes 6 servings.

One-Fourth Chocolate Pound Cake

Makes one 6- to 6½-inch cake (4 to 6 servings)

Must every pound cake be big enough to feed an army? "No," says Janice Latham. "This one is great for two people." There's even enough for seconds, maybe thirds. She bakes the cake in her smallest stoneware tube pan. And always, always starts it in a cold oven.

1 cup sifted cake flour

⅓ cup unsweetened cocoa powder (not a mix)

⅛ teaspoon baking powder

⅛ teaspoon salt

¾ cup sugar

¼ cup (½ stick) butter, at room temperature

2 tablespoons canola or other vegetable oil

1 teaspoon vanilla extract

2 large eggs

¼ cup milk

1. Sift the flour, cocoa, baking powder, and salt onto a piece of wax paper and reserve.

2. Using a hand electric mixer at moderate speed, cream the sugar, butter, oil, and vanilla together in a medium-size mixing bowl for about 2 minutes or until well blended, then switch to high speed and beat about 2 minutes longer or until light and fluffy.

3. Add the eggs one by one, beating well after each addition.

4. By hand, add the sifted dry ingredients alternately with the milk, beginning and ending with the dry and mixing only enough to combine after each addition. *Note*: 3 additions of the dry ingredients and 2 of milk work well.

5. Line the bottom of a 6- or 6½-inch oven-proof stoneware, other pottery, ceramic, or heat-resistant glass Bundt or tube pan with a circle of baking parchment or nonstick aluminum foil, then spritz well with nonstick cooking spray, paying particular attention to the tube and pan sides.

6. Scoop the batter into the prepared pan, smoothing the top and spreading to the edge.

7. Slide the pan onto the middle shelf of a cold oven, set the thermostat at 350°F, and bake for 40 to 45 minutes or until the cake begins to pull from the sides of the pan and a cake tester, inserted halfway between the rim and the central tube, comes out clean with just a few crumbs attached.

8. Remove the cake from the oven, set upright on a wire rack, and cool for 15 minutes. Using a small thin-blade spatula, carefully loosen the cake around the edge and the central tube, then invert and turn out on a small round plate.

9. Cool the cake to room temperature, then cut into wedges and serve.

8

New Salem Pottery:

Hal Pugh and Eleanor

Minnock-Pugh

FOR MORE INFORMATION:

newsalempottery.com

Hal Pugh's passion? How early Quakers influenced this state's earthenware tradition, hardly surprising for a college anthropology and decorative arts major. And where better to open a pottery than on the woodsy tract the Dennis family and other Pennsylvania Quakers settled in 1766?

Its location astride an old Indian trading path plus the presence of "large beds of earthenware clay made it ideally suited for a pottery," Hal says, adding that William Dennis (b. 1760) and his son Thomas (b. 1791) were Randolph County's first documented potters.

In 1832, the Dennis family sold their pottery to a Quaker businessman from nearby New Salem, who sold it forty years later to another potter. The Pugh family, whose North Carolina roots reach back into the 1750s, bought the place in 1939.

Today the William Dennis Pottery Kiln and House Site appears on the National Register of Historic Places, thanks to the painstaking research of Hal and his wife, Eleanor (a North Shore Long Island ed major whom he met in the flu-shot line at Appalachian State in Boone).

While in college, Hal reminisces, "I made the mistake of getting on a potter's wheel one day, fell in love with the art form, and started taking classes in the Industrial Arts Department."

Ever since they founded the New Salem Pottery in 1972 (with Eleanor working elsewhere till 1987), the Pughs have been turning the red clay they dig into replicas of early local earthenware, with eighteenth–nineteenth-century slip-decorated redware their specialty. Years at the wheel have also meant a subtle fusion of Pugh originality and tradition—hallmarks of their style.

Historians and authors as well as potters, the Pughs are busy consultants whose faithful reproductions are displayed at museums, universities, historic sites, even in movies. But for me nothing beats an over-the-back-roads-into-the-woods trip to New Salem's doorstep.

The Spanish Dish

Makes 4 to 6 servings

Hal says that his mother got the recipe for this cornbread-topped one-dish hamburger-tomato-and-rice dinner from a friend. Over the years, Hal and his wife, Eleanor, have spiced up the old recipe. Hal uses lean ground beef, and a can of diced tomatoes with green chilies adds a welcome "touch of heat." More liquid than traditional cornbread batters, Eleanor's cornbread topping is also thinner. The result, both agree, "is a moist, warm, and spicy" dinner in a dish. Though Hal uses a cast-iron skillet to make this recipe, he serves it on his colorful New Salem plates.

Tip: To save time, Hal cooks the rice while the skillet mixture simmers.

1 tablespoon corn or other vegetable oil

1 pound lean ground beef chuck

1 medium-size yellow onion, cut into ¼-inch dice

1 medium-size green bell pepper, cored, seeded,
    and cut into ¼-inch dice

1 medium-size garlic clove, crushed

1 teaspoon chili powder

½ teaspoon salt, or to taste

⅛ teaspoon freshly ground black pepper, or to taste

1 (10-ounce) can diced tomatoes with green chilies,
    with their liquid

½ cup long-grain white rice (preferably California
    rice; see page 9), cooked by package directions

TOPPING

⅞ cup unsifted stone-ground yellow cornmeal
    (see Sources, page 164)

2 tablespoons all-purpose flour

2 teaspoons baking powder

½ teaspoon salt

¾ cup milk blended with 1 large egg and
    1½ tablespoons corn or other vegetable oil

1. Preheat the oven to 425°F.

2. Heat the vegetable oil in a 10-inch cast-iron skillet with an ovenproof handle over moderately high heat for about 1½ minutes or until ripples appear on the pan bottom.

3. Add the beef, breaking up the large clumps, the onion, bell pepper, and garlic, and cook, stirring and turning, for about 3 minutes or until the beef is no longer pink.

4. Mix in the chili powder, salt, pepper, and canned tomatoes with green chilies and cook, stirring now and then, for 8 to 10 minutes or just until the flavors meld.

5. Fold in the cooked rice, taste for salt and pepper, adjusting as needed, then set off-heat while you prepare the topping.

6. *For the topping*: Whisk the cornmeal, flour, baking powder, and salt together in a medium-size mixing bowl and make a well in the center. Pour the milk mixture into the well, and stir only enough to incorporate—no matter if a few floury specks show.

7. Pour the cornbread batter evenly over the meat mixture, slide the pan onto the middle shelf of the preheated oven, and bake uncovered for 15 to 20 minutes or until the cornbread is golden brown and springy to the touch.

8. Serve at once, accompanied, if you like, by lightly sautéed kale, collards, or other greens or, easier still, a tartly dressed crisp salad.

Hal's Gingerbread

"This gingerbread is one I developed from a 150-year-old Quaker recipe," Pugh says, adding that his aim was "to create a lighter gingerbread cake that could be enjoyed by itself or with a simple icing"—like the limoncello one below. He mixes the batter by hand but to save a bit of time uses self-rising flour. He bakes the gingerbread in a metal pan but showcases it on one of his own decorative pottery plates.

Note: Since this recipe calls for self-rising flour, which contains leavening, I've reduced the amount of baking soda to ¼ teaspoon. I've also reduced the amount of molasses and water slightly. The baked gingerbread cracks a bit as it bakes, but you'll find the loaf moist and fine-textured. And oh, my, the flavor.

GINGERBREAD

2½ cups unsifted self-rising flour

¼ teaspoon baking soda

1¼ teaspoons ground cinnamon

1¼ teaspoons ground ginger

½ teaspoon ground cloves

¼ cup granulated sugar

¼ cup firmly packed vegetable shortening
    melted with ¼ cup (½ stick) margarine

1 large egg

¾ cup unsulfured medium-brown molasses

¾ cup hot water

ICING

2 cups unsifted confectioners' (10X) sugar

1 tablespoon plus 1 teaspoon softened margarine

1 tablespoon limoncello liqueur

1½ to 2 tablespoons milk (about)

1. Preheat the oven to 350°F. Spritz a 9 × 9 × 2-inch metal baking pan with nonstick cooking spray and set aside.

2. *For the gingerbread*: Sift the flour, baking soda, cinnamon, ginger, and cloves together onto a large piece of wax paper and reserve.

3. Using a large wooden spoon, stir the sugar and melted shortening mixture in a large mixing bowl until smooth, then mix in the egg and molasses all at once.

4. Now add the sifted dry ingredients alternately with the hot water, beginning and ending with the dry and beating after each addition only enough to combine.

5. Pour the batter into the prepared pan, smoothing the top and spreading to the corners.

6. Slide the pan onto the middle shelf of the preheated oven and bake for about 30 minutes or until the gingerbread begins to pull from the sides of the pan, is springy to the touch, and a cake tester, inserted in the middle of the gingerbread, comes out clean.

7. Transfer the pan to a wire baking rack and cool the gingerbread to room temperature.

8. *For the icing*: Whisk the confectioners' sugar, margarine, and limoncello together until smooth, then beat in the milk, tablespoon by tablespoon, until the consistency of sour cream.

9. Spread the icing over the cooled gingerbread, and allow to harden for 25 to 30 minutes.

10. To serve, cut the gingerbread into 12 pieces and serve on your most decorative plate or platter.

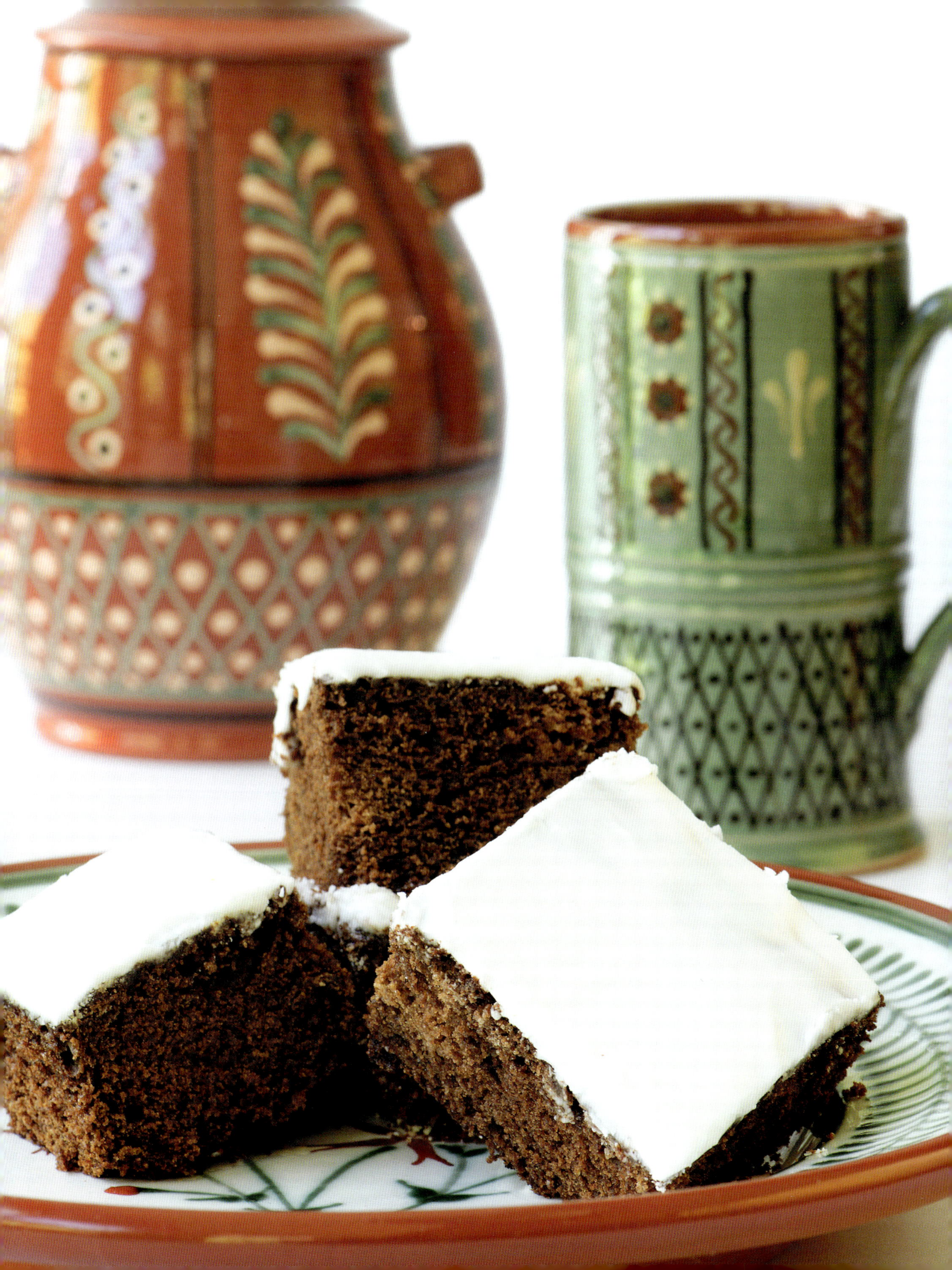

New Salem Peach and Blueberry Cobbler

Makes 4 to 6 servings

This family recipe came from Missouri with Hal's mother, Velda McCurdy, in 1945, when she married Hal's father, Ewart Pugh. "A simple recipe, with basic staple ingredients, baked in the dirt pie dish found in most farm homes during this time," Hal says. A better shape for this cobbler, he finds, is an eight-inch-square Pyrex-type baking dish. "We have our own blueberry bushes," he adds, "so we have lots of blueberries in the freezer."

2 tablespoons melted butter or margarine

FRUIT MIXTURE

3 cups moderately thinly sliced peeled and pitted firm-ripe peaches (about 4 medium-size) or thawed and drained frozen sliced peaches

1 cup stemmed fresh or solidly frozen blueberries

1 cup water

½ cup sugar

CAKE BATTER

1 cup sifted all-purpose flour

½ cup sugar

1½ teaspoons baking powder

1 teaspoon ground cinnamon

¼ teaspoon ground ginger

¼ teaspoon salt

¾ to 1 cup milk (enough to make batter pouring consistency)

OPTIONAL ACCOMPANIMENT

1 cup heavy cream, whipped to soft peaks, or 1 pint vanilla or dulce de leche ice cream

1. Preheat the oven to 375°F.

2. Spoon the melted butter into an 8 × 8 × 2-inch heat-resistant glass baking dish (see headnote), then tilt from side to side so that the bottom and sides are nicely coated. Set the baking dish aside.

3. *For the fruit mixture*: Place all ingredients in a medium-size nonreactive saucepan, bring to a boil over moderate heat, then adjust the heat so the fruit simmers gently, and cook uncovered for 3 to 5 minutes or until the fruit begins to soften. Set off the heat and reserve.

4. *For the cake batter*: Whisk the dry ingredients (flour through salt) together in a medium-size mixing bowl and make a well in the middle.

5. Whisking gently, add the milk slowly, stopping the instant the batter is thin enough to pour. *Note*: The batter should be lumpy and specks of flour visible.

6. Pour half of the batter into the prepared baking dish, then using a slotted spoon, scoop the warm fruit mixture on top, making sure that it touches the sides all around. Finally, squiggle the remaining batter on top.

7. Slide the cobbler onto the middle shelf of the preheated oven, and bake for about 40 minutes or until bubbling and lightly browned.

8. Transfer the cobbler to a wire rack and cool in the baking dish for 30 minutes.

9. Serve at table on colorful pottery plates with or without whipped cream or ice cream. "Years ago when we bought a cow from a neighbor," Hal says, "my mom would skim off the top milk and drizzle it on top of the warm cobbler." Perfect.

Coconut Pecan Pie

Makes one 9 inch pie (6 to 8 servings)

Hal and Eleanor developed this recipe back in their college days when they couldn't afford enough nuts for a proper pecan pie. Both disliked corn syrup, integral to most southern pecan pies, so you'll find none in this recipe. The Pughs both bake and serve this pie in reproductions of eighteenth- and nineteenth-century North Carolina Quaker plates for which New Salem is famous.

Note: To save time, use one of the unroll-and-use pastry circles supermarkets sell; look for them near the refrigerated biscuits. Press the pastry over the bottom of a 9-inch ovenproof stoneware, other pottery, ceramic, or heat-resistant glass pie pan, crimping into a high fluted edge to reduce the risk of boilovers.

5 tablespoons (½ stick plus 1 tablespoon) butter, at room temperature

1 cup sugar

1 teaspoon vanilla extract

2 large eggs

¼ cup milk

1 cup firmly packed sweetened flaked or shredded coconut

¾ cup coarsely chopped pecans

1 (9-inch) unbaked pie shell (see *Note* above)

1. With your electric mixer at high speed, cream the butter, sugar, and vanilla in the small mixer bowl for 2½ to 3 minutes or until light and fluffy.

2. With the mixer speed at medium, beat in the eggs and milk. Using a rubber spatula, fold in the coconut, then the pecans, and scoop the filling into the pie shell, spreading to the edge.

3. Slide the pie onto the middle shelf of a cold oven and set the thermostat at 450°F.

4. As soon as the oven reaches 450°F, reduce the temperature to 350°F, and bake the pie for about 30 minutes or until puffed, golden brown, and a cake tester inserted midway between the rim and the center comes out clean. *Note*: If at any point the pie seems to be browning too fast, cover loosely with aluminum foil.

5. Transfer the pie to a wire rack and cool to room temperature before cutting. *Note*: The pie will fall slightly as it cools, but this is typical of pecan pies.

6. To serve, cut the pie into slim wedges and arrange on your most colorful dessert plates. Resist the temptation to top with whipped cream or ice cream. No need here "to cut the richness," as southerners would say.

Pottery numbers are keyed to the area map opposite.
For an easy-to-follow itinerary, begin at No. 1, or begin at
No. 8 and work your way back to No. 1.

1 **B. R. Hilton Pottery
   (Bob Hilton, Heather Hilton, and
   Linda Hilton Long)**

   4026 Old State Road, Newton
   Contact: info@hiltonpottery.com

2 **Ellington Pottery (Kim Ellington)**

   7110 West N.C. 10, Vale
   Contact gke@ellingtonpottery.com
   Open by appointment only.

3 **Beckett Pottery (Robin Beckett)**

   1884 Fonta Flora Drive, Nebo
   Contact: playsinclay55@yahoo.com
   Open by appointment only.

4 **Melting Mountain Pottery (Joey Sheehan)**

   Phil Mechanic Studios
   109 Roberts Street, Asheville
   Contact: joey@meltingmountainpottery.com

5 **East Fork (Alex Matisse)**

   82 N. Lexington Avenue, Asheville
   Contact: Subscribe to the East Fork newsletter
   at https://eastfork.com

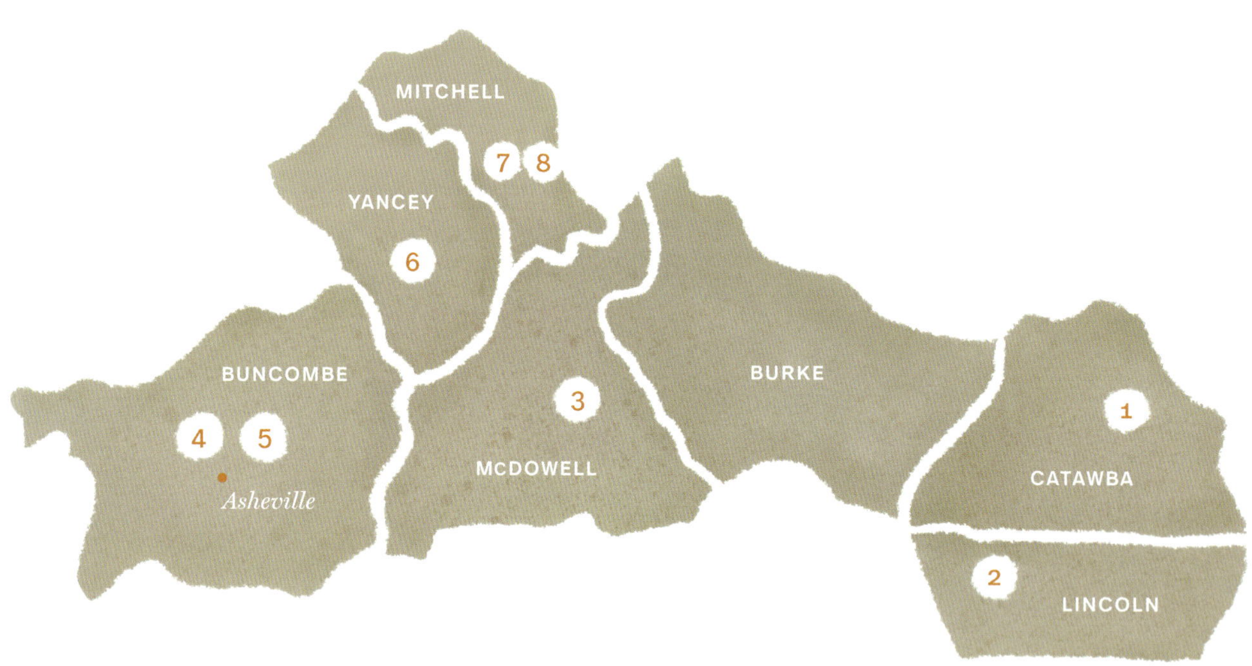

6 **Rutkowsky Pottery**
   (Michael Rutkowsky and
   ** Ruth Fischer Rutkowsky)**
   1489 Cane Branch Road, Burnsville
   Contact: www.rutkowskypottery.com
   Fill out and submit the "contact us" form,
   then make an appointment.

7 **Barking Spider Pottery**
   (Jon Ellenbogen and Rebecca Plummer)
   1446 Conley Ridge Road, Penland
   Contact: potters@barkingspiderpottery.com

8 **Bandana Pottery**
   (Michael Hunt and Naomi Dalglish)
   3385 N.C. 80, Bakersville
   Contact: huntdalglish@gmailcom

Catawba Valley, Foothills & Mountain Potters

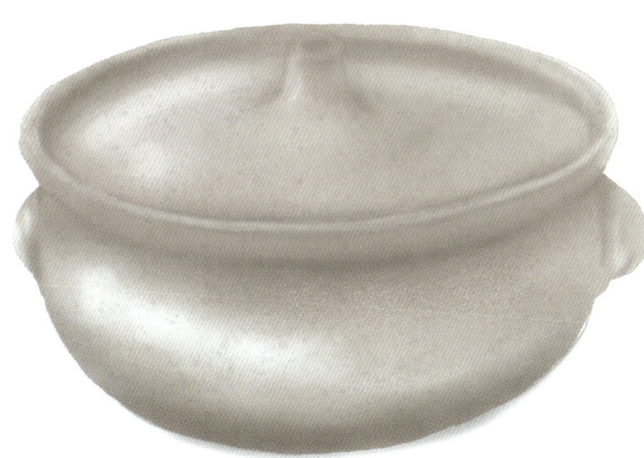

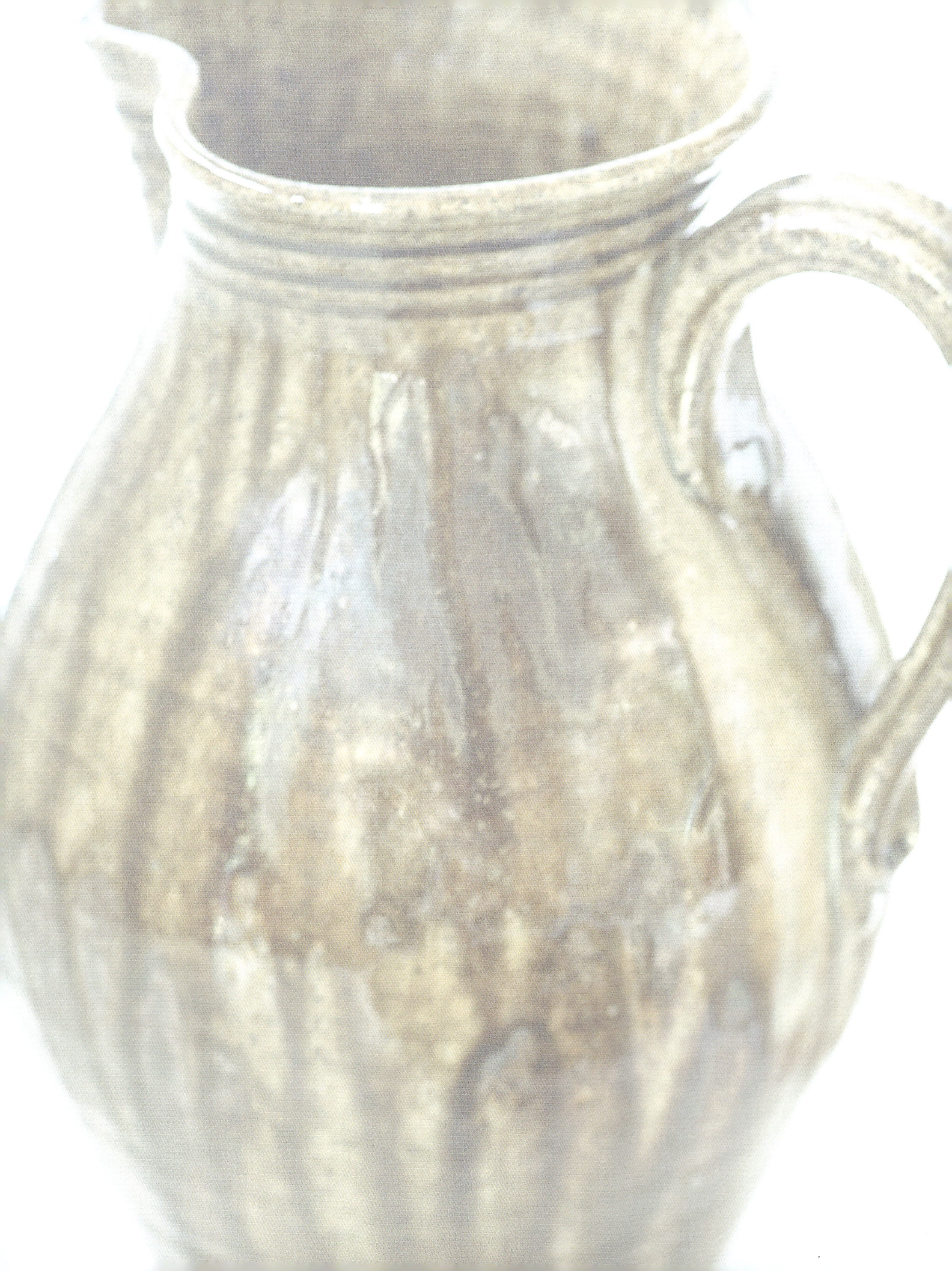

1

B. R. Hilton Pottery:

Bob Hilton,

Heather Hilton, and

Linda Hilton Long

FOR MORE INFORMATION:

hiltonpottery.com

When it comes to functional pottery, Hilton's a name known throughout the Catawba Valley for more than 150 years, and the two at their wheels today are Bob (B. R.) Hilton (fourth generation) and his daughter, Heather (fifth generation).

Catawba's first potters were farmers of German heritage who settled in the valley in the 1820s and turned the local clay into whiskey jugs, butter churns, and other must-haves.

The first Hilton potter (spelled Helton then) was John Wesley Hilton, who came home to his farm after the Civil War and began making the alkaline-glazed stoneware for which Catawba County is synonymous today.

Then, as successive generations of Hiltons carried the family tradition forward (Boyd Shuford Hilton, Bob's father, being one of the most prominent), they began to modify the old glazes, the shapes, and added some decorative pieces.

Early last century, when mass-produced tableware replaced the handmade, many "functional" potters became folk art potters and supplemented their incomes by making whimsical (some say hideous) face jugs. Tourists loved them. And the uglier, the better.

The Hiltons, however, continued making the utilitarian stoneware that's the family hallmark, though Bob does make an occasional face jug. He calls himself a "studio potter" and is noted for the "blue edge drippy" glazes he applies to fluted pie plates, bowls, and such.

Use these pottery pieces as the Hiltons do for the recipes in the *Hilton Homeplace Cookbook*, written by Bob's sister Linda Hilton Long "to honor our family, our heritage, and to document the stories and recipes for the next generation before they are lost."

Aunt Dotti's Crab Meat au Gratin

Makes 6 servings

This casserole from family friend Tamara Lancaster's West Palm Beach Aunt Dotti Morse and the three that follow are adapted from the *Hilton Homeplace Cookbook* by Linda Hilton Long, whose father was the legendary Catawba Valley potter Boyd Shuford Hilton. For details about the cookbook, e-mail Linda@LHLtextile solutions.com.

3 tablespoons butter

½ medium-size green bell pepper, cored, seeded, and moderately finely chopped

1 small yellow onion, moderately finely chopped

3 tablespoons all-purpose flour

2 cups milk

1 pound coarsely flaked fresh lump or backfin crab meat, bits of shell and cartilage removed

½ teaspoon salt, or to taste

½ cup moderately coarsely shredded mild Cheddar cheese

1 cup fairly fine soft white bread crumbs mixed with 1½ tablespoons melted butter

1. Lightly spritz a 1½- to 2-quart ovenproof stoneware, other pottery, ceramic, or heat-resistant casserole with nonstick cooking spray and set aside.

2. Melt the butter in a large, heavy skillet over moderately high heat, add the bell pepper and onion, and cook, stirring often, for about 5 minutes or until the pepper and onion are limp.

3. Blend in the flour, then add the milk, and cook, stirring constantly, 3 to 4 minutes until thickened. Fold in the crab meat, taste for salt, and adjust as needed.

4. Scoop the crab mixture into the prepared casserole, spreading to the edge. Scatter with the shredded cheese, then sprinkle the bread crumbs evenly over all.

5. Set the casserole on a rimmed baking sheet (to catch boilovers), then slide onto the middle shelf of a cold oven, and set the thermostat at 350°F. Bake for about 45 to 50 minutes or until bubbling and tipped with brown.

6. Serve as the main dish of an elegant dinner and accompany as Aunt Dotti does with a mixed green salad and a rice pilaf (or, even easier, California long-grain white rice cooked by package directions).

Judith's Rich Blend Meatloaf

Makes 6 servings

"My cousin Judith remembers her mother at the old wooden table mixing this meatloaf with her hands," says Linda Hilton Long. Using three different meats (traditionally beef, veal, and pork) added to the flavor of meatloaves, but with ground veal and ground raw pork rarely available today, we've substituted ground beef and ground turkey.

1 pound ground beef chuck or sirloin (see headnote)

½ pound ground turkey

1 cup coarsely crumbled toast (about 2 slices
    firm-textured white bread) soaked about 5 minutes
    or until mushy in 1 (5-ounce) can evaporated milk
    (use low-fat, if you like)

¾ cup tomato ketchup, divided

1 large egg

1 medium-size yellow onion, moderately coarsely
    chopped

1 medium-size green bell pepper, cored, seeded,
    and moderately coarsely chopped

1 medium-size celery rib, trimmed and moderately
    coarsely chopped

1 teaspoon salt

½ teaspoon freshly ground black pepper

1. Butter a 2-quart ovenproof stoneware, other pottery, ceramic, or heat-resistant glass casserole well or spritz with nonstick cooking spray, and set aside.

2. Using your hands, mix all the ingredients (except ¼ cup of the ketchup) together thoroughly in a large mixing bowl, then pat firmly into the prepared casserole, pushing to the edge. Drizzle the remaining ketchup decoratively over all.

3. Slide the casserole onto the middle shelf of a cold oven, set the thermostat at 400°F, and bake uncovered for 1 hour and 10 minutes or until richly browned and an instant-read thermometer inserted between the edge and the center registers 165°F.

4. Remove the meatloaf from the oven, and cool 10 to 15 minutes to firm it up and allow the juices to settle.

5. To serve, cut into wedges or squares and serve with mashed or boiled potatoes and a mixed green salad.

Mama's Sweet Potatoes

Makes 6 to 8 servings

"My mother always made this dish for holiday family gatherings," says Linda Hilton Long. "It's quick, easy, and nutritious!" She adds that her mother would buy sweet potatoes when they were on sale, cook up a batch, then peel and freeze them so that she could make this family favorite quickly. What's unusual about the recipe is that the potatoes are partially cooked, then peeled, cut into medallions, stood on end, and baked in one of the Hilton casseroles.

Tip: Choose sweet potatoes that are 2 to 2½ inches in diameter. If you refrigerate the cooked, peeled sweet potatoes for about 30 minutes, they'll slice cleanly.

6 large sweet potatoes of uniform size and shape, scrubbed but not peeled (see *Tip* above)

¼ cup (½ stick) butter

¾ cup firmly packed dark brown sugar

¾ cup fresh orange juice

1 tablespoon medium-brown unsulfured molasses

½ teaspoon ground cinnamon

¼ teaspoon salt

1 teaspoon vanilla extract

1 cup coarsely chopped pecans (optional)

1. Parboil the sweet potatoes in enough water to cover in a large, heavy pot for 20 to 25 minutes or until not quite tender. Drain well, then slip into a large plastic zipper bag and refrigerate for at least ½ hour.

2. Meanwhile, spritz a 2½ quart ovenproof stoneware, other pottery, ceramic, or heat-resistant casserole with nonstick cooking spray and set aside.

3. When ready to proceed, melt the butter in a small nonreactive pan over low heat, then mix in the brown sugar, orange juice, molasses, cinnamon, and salt, and cook and stir about 4 minutes or just until the sugar is thoroughly dissolved. Remove from the heat, mix in the vanilla, and set aside.

4. Meanwhile, peel the chilled sweet potatoes, and cut crosswise into slices about ½ inch thick.

5. Lay the sweet potato end slices flat in the bottom of the prepared casserole, arranging some pointy sides down, others cut-sides down so that they fit together smoothly without overlapping. Now stand the remaining slices on

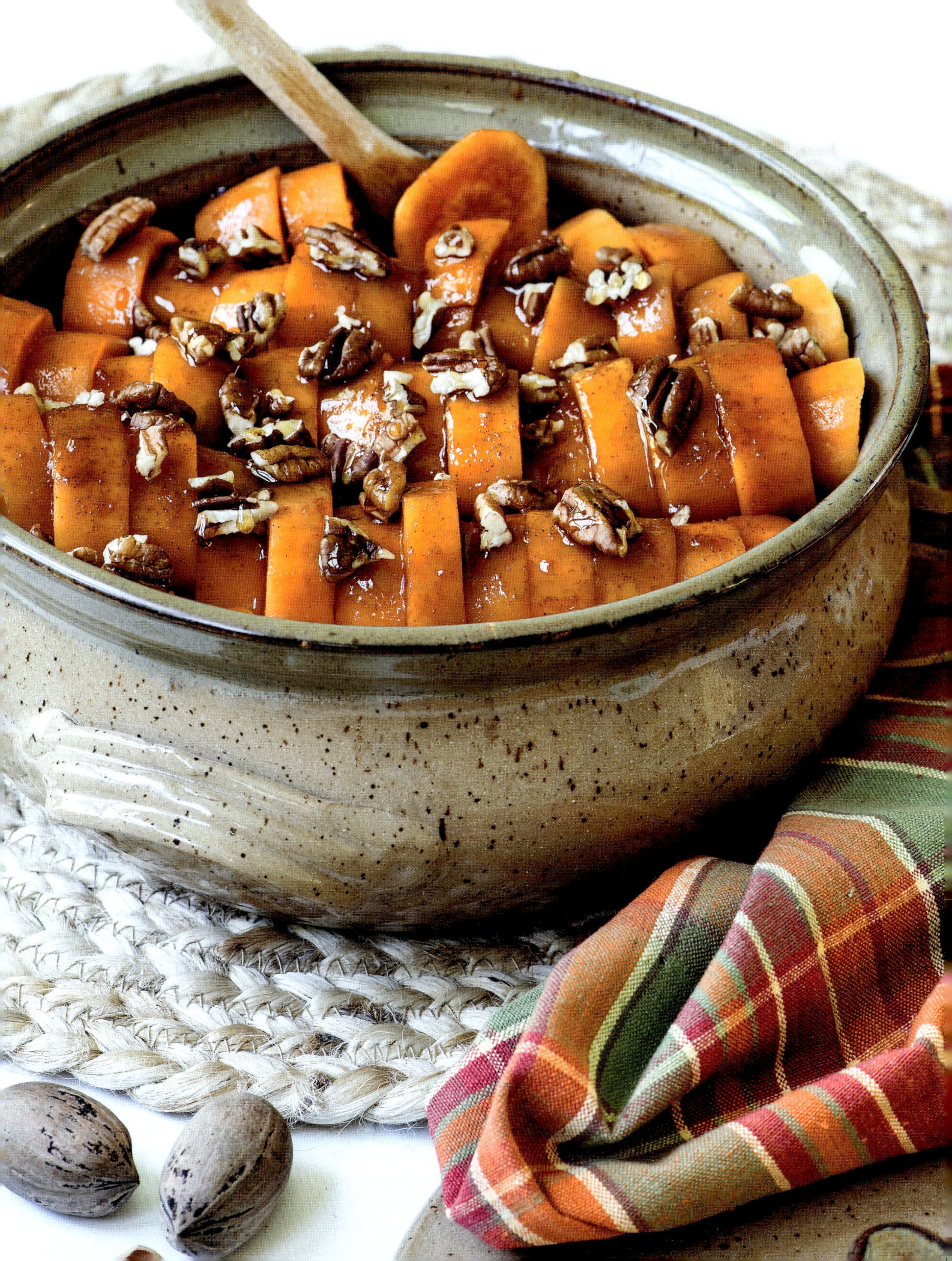

end and in rows on top of the bottom layer, each touching its neighbors so that none will topple. Finally, pour the reserved brown sugar sauce evenly over all.

6. Set the casserole on a rimmed baking sheet (to catch boilovers), then slide onto the middle shelf of a cold oven, and set the thermostat at 350°F.

7. Bake the sweet potatoes uncovered for 45 minutes, basting every 20 minutes with the sauce that bubbles up. *Note*: It's easier to distribute the sauce evenly if you use a turkey baster.

8. Add the pecans, if you like, sprinkling evenly over the sweet potatoes, and bake 15 minutes longer or until the potatoes are fork-tender.

9. Serve at once as an accompaniment to roast turkey, chicken, or pork. Delicious, too, with baked ham.

Cousin John's Strawberry Sonker Pie

John Hilton, grandson of John Wesley Hilton, who started a pottery business after the Civil War, was known for this old family favorite. These jiffy pies, unique to Surry County, can be made with any fruit, but Cousin John liked spring strawberries best. "It's so easy to make," says Linda Hilton Long, "and heavenly with a big scoop of vanilla ice cream."

1 cup sugar

¾ cup unsifted self-rising flour

1 cup milk

**1⅔ cups moderately thinly sliced, hulled
    red-ripe strawberries**

1 tablespoon melted butter

1. Grease a 9-inch ovenproof stoneware, other pottery, ceramic, or heat-resistant glass pie pan well and set aside.

2. Combine the sugar and flour in a medium-size mixing bowl, then whisking briskly, drizzle in the milk, and continue whisking until smooth. Fold in the strawberries and pour into the prepared pie pan. The strawberries will float to the top.

3. Slide the sonker onto the upper shelf of a cold oven, set the thermostat at 400°F, and bake uncovered for about 35 to 40 minutes or until lightly browned.

4. Remove from the oven, drizzle the melted butter on top, then serve warm or at room temperature with vanilla ice cream or, if you prefer, with plain yogurt or unsweetened whipped cream. *Note*: Sonker cuts better at room temperature but tastes better warm.

2

Ellington Pottery:

Kim Ellington

FOR MORE INFORMATION:

ellingtonpottery.com

. . . .

Kim's first pot?

"I was ten-ish," he says, "and made it out of creek mud near our house in Hickory." It wasn't what you'd call an "ah-hah" moment, but the feeling of having crafted something with his own hands stuck with Kim.

So much so that, when discharged from the army, he enrolled in the pottery program at Haywood Community College in the Smokies just west of Asheville. A disciple of the legendary Catawba Valley folk potter Burlon Craig, Kim immersed himself in the Catawba tradition of making functional stoneware.

"Having grown up in a household using Blue Willow Spode every day and fine china for special occasions," Kim says, "I fell in love with the first bowl and mug I made at Haywood." More important, he decided that pottery would be his life's work.

Now living in Vale, a town where potters have been digging, shaping, and turning the local clay since the early nineteenth century, Kim's not only known for his rich wood-fired, alkaline-glazed stoneware rooted in the Catawba River Valley tradition but also for his skillful modernizing.

"The clay, the groundhog kiln, and the glaze we still use," Kim says, "make us only one of a few continuously surviving pottery traditions in the whole country," including this state's Catawba River Valley and Seagrove in addition to the Southwest's Native Americans.

Though not a potter herself, Kim's wife, Betsy, is deeply involved in the Ellington pottery. She handles the mailing lists and correspondence; serves home-cooked food at the kiln firings; and not least, organizes, publicizes, and sets up each pottery sale.

Summer Marinara Sauce

Makes 3½ cups (4 to 6 servings)

"I've never been to Italy," says Betsy Ellington, "so this marinara sauce is my own creation. I used to grow and can my own Roma tomatoes," she adds, "but now buy them from local organic growers. I roast and freeze the Romas for winter and consider them 'gold.'" Betsy's favorite way to use Summer Marinara Sauce? On a 50–50 mix of whole-wheat and semolina spaghettis mounded on one of husband Kim's decorative rimmed platters.

Note: A New York friend who tried Betsy's marinara raved, "The best and simplest recipe yet."

ROASTED ROMA PURÉE

3 pounds medium-size, firm-ripe Roma tomatoes, halved the long way but not peeled

2 tablespoons extra-virgin olive oil

1 tablespoon sea salt

1 teaspoon freshly ground black pepper

MARINARA SAUCE

2 tablespoons extra-virgin olive oil

1 medium-size yellow onion, finely chopped

2 medium-size garlic cloves, crushed

1 recipe roasted Roma purée (above)

1 large whole bay leaf (preferably fresh)

1 tablespoon finely chopped fresh basil

¾ teaspoon crumbled dried leaf oregano

½ teaspoon sea salt, or to taste

½ teaspoon freshly ground black pepper, or to taste

1 tablespoon coarsely chopped fresh Italian parsley

1. *For the roasted Roma purée*: Preheat the oven to 450°F. Arrange the tomatoes cut-sides-up and shoulder-to-shoulder on a rimmed baking sheet. Drizzle the olive oil evenly over all, then sprinkle with the salt and pepper.

2. Slide the tomatoes onto the middle oven shelf and roast uncovered for 25 to 30 minutes or until the juices begin to concentrate and the tomatoes begin to caramelize.

3. Remove the tomatoes from the oven and cool for 15 minutes, then scoop into a food processor (preferably a large, heavy-duty one) fitted with the metal chopping blade, and alternately pulse and churn until smooth—about 5 seconds.

4. Spoon the tomatoes into 1-pint freezer cartons, snap on the lids, then date, label, and store in the coldest part of your freezer. *Note*: If not making the marinara sauce immediately, refrigerate the Roma purée, and use within 3 days. Keeping time for the frozen purée: 3 to 4 months.

5. *For the marinara sauce*: Heat the olive oil in a medium-size, heavy nonreactive skillet over moderately high heat for 1½ minutes or until ripples appear on the pan bottom.

6. Add the onion and garlic and cook, stirring constantly, for 2 to 3 minutes or just until translucent. Add all but the final sauce ingredient (parsley), reduce the heat to low, cover, and simmer, stirring occasionally, for 15 minutes.

7. Mix in the parsley, cover, and simmer for about 10 minutes more or until the flavors are well blended. Stir well, then remove and discard the bay leaf.

8. Serve at once over your favorite pasta or use when making lasagna, ravioli, or other recipe that requires a deeply flavorful marinara sauce.

Betsy's Baked Ratatouille

Makes 4 to 6 servings

For this recipe, Betsy Ellington layers fresh summer vegetables into one of her husband's wood-fired fluted 9-inch stoneware deep-dish pie pans. "This dish works great with a single layer of everything," she says, but two, we found, were perfect. She prefers Asian eggplants for this ratatouille—the thin-skinned Shikou Hybrid or Black Beauty that don't have to be peeled—but uses whatever's available. The best tomatoes? "Fresh Romas or Better Boys," but again, Betsy, recommends "whatever you have in your garden." Or failing that, whatever you find at your farmers' market, as long as it's ripe and full of flavor. Betsy likes to serve fried okra with her ratatouille, "but," she adds, "it's fine with bread only."

Note: A friend who tried Betsy's recipe pronounced it "delicious. A great summer side dish that's easy to prepare without going to all the trouble of making a traditional ratatouille."

2 smallish elongated purple eggplants, stemmed
  and sliced about ¼ inch thick, but not peeled
  (see headnote)
1 large red onion, moderately thinly sliced
4 large garlic cloves, sliced about ⅛ inch thick
1 medium-size poblano, green, or red bell pepper,
  stemmed, halved, seeded, and each half cut
  crosswise, then sliced ¼-inch thick
1 tablespoon coarsely chopped fresh basil
1½ teaspoons coarsely chopped fresh oregano
1¼ teaspoons salt
½ teaspoon freshly ground black pepper
6 small firm-ripe Roma tomatoes, cut into rounds
  ¼ inch thick
2 tablespoons extra-virgin olive oil
½ cup freshly grated Parmigiano-Reggiano cheese

1. Lightly rub a 9-inch ovenproof deep-dish stoneware, other pottery, ceramic, or heat-resistant glass pie pan with extra-virgin olive oil.

2. Now layer the ingredients into the prepared pan in the order listed, using only enough of each to cover the previous layer—for example, one layer of eggplant, one of onion, one of garlic, and so forth, ending with the tomatoes.

3. Drizzle the olive oil over the tomatoes, then sprinkle the grated cheese evenly on top—enough of it to cover the tomatoes.

4. Slide the ratatouille onto the middle shelf of a cold oven, set the thermostat at 350°F, and bake uncovered for 60 to 65 minutes or until nicely browned.

5. To serve, carry the ratatouille to the table, spoon onto luncheon plates, and accompany with chunks of crusty or chewy country bread and little dipping bowls of extra-virgin olive oil. Accompaniments? Excellent with simply sautéed meat or fish.

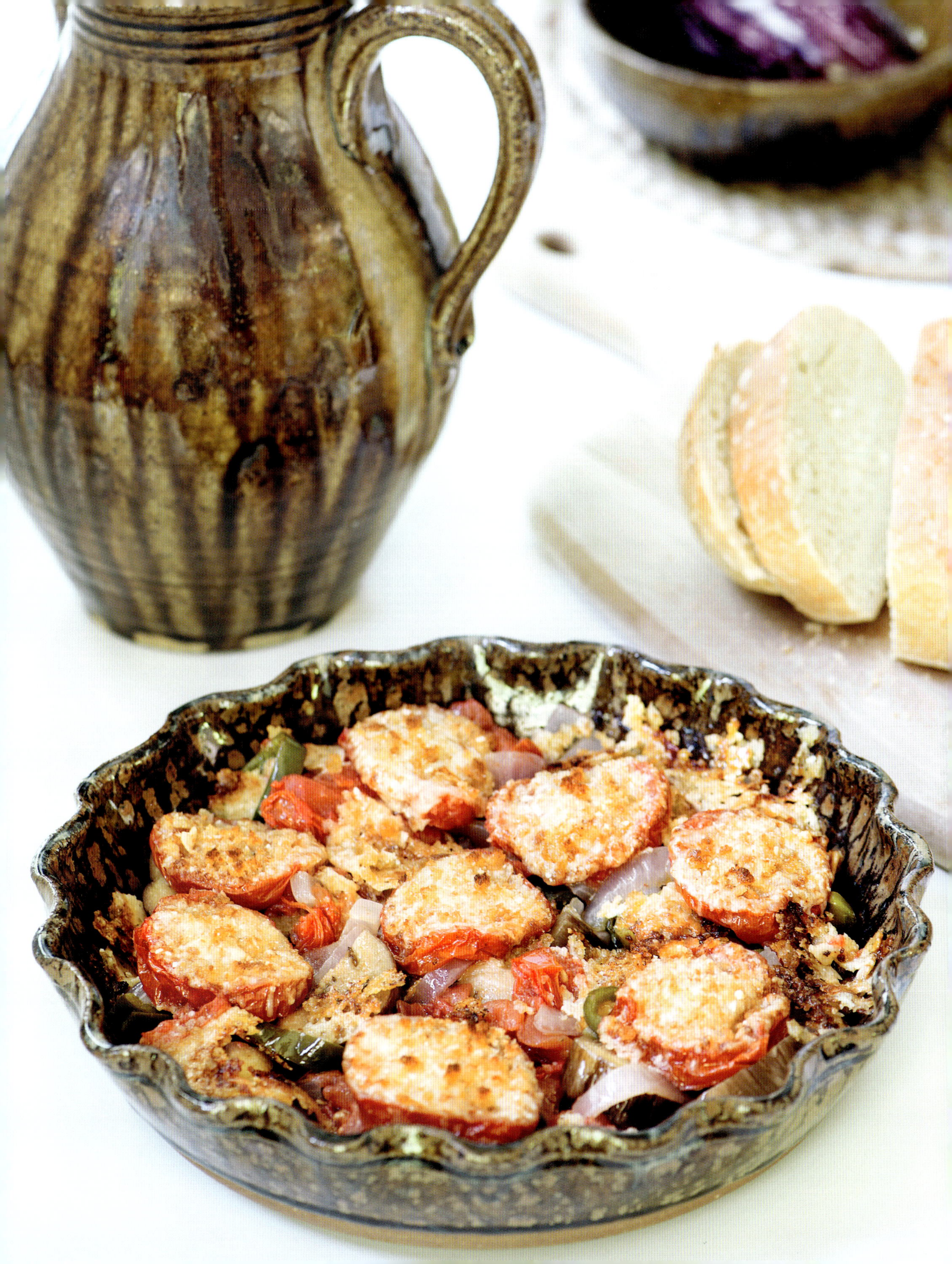

Kiln Beans a.k.a. Funeral Beans

Makes 6 to 8 servings

"We serve these beans with barbecue to Kim's kiln crew during the annual summer and fall kiln firings," says Betsy, explaining that they are also frequently served after a funeral either at church or at the home of the bereaved.

2 (15.5-ounce) cans pork and beans, with all liquid

1 (15.5-ounce) can dark or light red kidney beans, well drained

1 medium-size yellow onion, moderately finely chopped

1 medium-size green bell pepper, cored, seeded and moderately finely chopped

¼ cup firmly packed dark brown sugar mixed with 3 tablespoons each warm water and tomato ketchup plus 1 teaspoon each Worcestershire sauce and Dijon mustard

Salt and freshly ground black pepper to taste

4 slices hickory-smoked bacon, halved crosswise

1. Mix all but the final ingredient (bacon) in a large bowl, then scoop into an ungreased 9½- to 10-inch ovenproof deep-dish stoneware, other pottery, ceramic, or heat-resistant glass pie pan pushing to the edge, then lay the bacon strips on top.

2. Slide the pie pan onto the middle shelf of a cold oven, set the thermostat at 350°F, and bake uncovered for 60 to 70 minutes or until the beans are bubbly and the edges of the bacon are curled and crisp. "The beans," Betsy adds, "should look glazed, almost caramelized."

3. Serve hot as an accompaniment to barbecue and coleslaw.

3

Beckett Pottery:

Robin Beckett

FOR MORE INFORMATION:

beckettpottery.blogspot.com

. . . .

What inspires Robin Beckett? It might be a rock splotched with green lichen. Pink lady's-slippers tiptoeing about the Linville Gorge Wilderness. A red gecko streaking across the rafters of her new studio in Glen Alpine. In a word, Robin's inspiration is Nature.

Its twists and turns, its kaleidoscopic palette have sustained, indeed reinforced, Robin's imagination ever since she was growing up in Winston-Salem and Greensboro. Back then her love of make-believe could turn a simple forest path into the Yellow Brick Road.

It was no fantasy, however, when eight-year-old Robin was mesmerized by the sight of "a ball of clay growing into a beautiful vase" in the hands of a Florida potter. Though her own home was decked with Jugtown, thanks to an aunt who promoted it, watching a potter work his magic clinched her dream of becoming one herself.

That very year Robin took a turn at the wheel, felt the miracle of clay taking shape, and began pursuing her dream in earnest. She took pottery in high school and was so smitten she hung around the classroom wheel after hours.

After graduating from Appalachian State in 1978 with a major in ceramics technology and a gig making little terra-cotta pots for a dried flower company, Robin hung out her shingle.

She recently created two dramatically different lines of stoneware, and credits Carolina Clay Matters, a motivational guild to which she belongs, for the inspiration.

Her Fiesta line's a collection of stoneware reminiscent of the Crayola-bright Fiestaware our grandmothers loved—only Robin's colors are refreshingly muted.

And her Earthy Pot Gallery? Functional red stoneware swirled in the down-home rusts, creams, and greens that entranced an aspiring young Carolina potter long ago.

Lemon Chicken Baked in a Sauerkraut Nest

Makes 4 to 6 servings

Inspired by a recipe in Sherill and Gil Roth's *Country Gourmet Cookbook* (Workman, 1981), this casserole bakes perfectly in Robin's heavy oval baker. The Roths, she says, "moved to my hometown and promoted their book at the local art gallery." Robin's version not only substitutes the oregano she grows for rosemary and lemon zest for juice but also adds garlic.

Note: Remove the giblets from the chicken and from their packet. Slip into a small plastic zipper bag, press out all the air, then label and date and store in the freezer. Use within 3 months when making stock, soup, or gravy.

2 pounds (4 cups) fresh sauerkraut, rinsed in
    cool water and drained well

2 tablespoons coarsely chopped fresh oregano
    or 2 teaspoons crumbled dried leaf oregano

2 large garlic cloves, finely chopped

1 teaspoon finely grated lemon zest

⅛ to ¼ teaspoon dried red chili flakes (depending
    on how hot you like things)

¾ teaspoon salt

¼ teaspoon freshly ground black pepper

1 (3½- to 4-pound) oven-ready chicken
    (see *Note* above)

1 tablespoon extra-virgin olive oil

1. Spritz a 3½-quart shallow oval ovenproof stoneware, other pottery, or ceramic casserole or a heat-resistant 13 × 9 × 2-inch glass baking dish well with nonstick cooking spray, then add the sauerkraut.

2. Combine the oregano, garlic, lemon zest, and chili flakes, add ½ of this mixture to the sauerkraut, and toss well. Mix the salt and black pepper into the remaining oregano mixture and reserve.

3. Using poultry shears, cut along each side of the chicken backbone, lift the bone out, and discard. Arrange the bird skin-side up on a cutting board like an open book, and press hard with both hands to crack the breastbone so that the chicken will lie flat.

4. Rub both sides of the chicken and under the breast skin with the olive oil, then with the reserved oregano mixture, and place skin-side up in the sauerkraut.

5. Slide the baking dish onto a shelf in the upper third of a cold oven, set the thermostat at 375°F, and bake the chicken uncovered for about 65 minutes or until lightly browned and an instant-read thermometer, inserted in the meatiest part of a thigh not touching bone, registers 165°F.

6. Remove the baking dish from the oven, then as soon as the chicken is cool enough to handle, cut it into pieces just as you would for frying—drumsticks, thighs, wings, backs, and breasts, then halve each breast crosswise.

7. To serve, lift pieces of chicken to the plates, honoring guests' wishes for light or dark meat, then top with plenty of the sauerkraut.

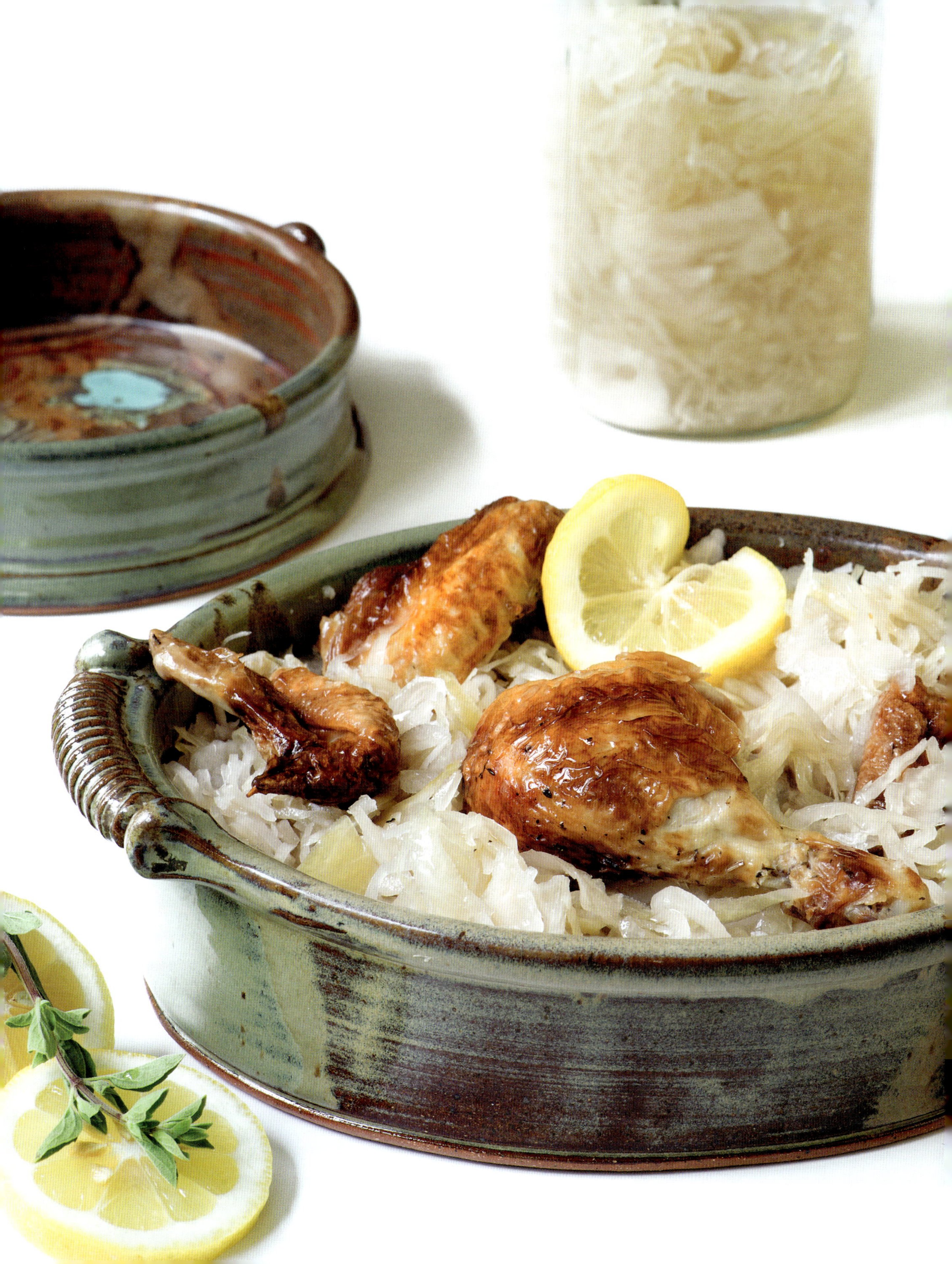

Robin's Salmon Ring

Makes 6 servings

"I'm a pretty casual cook," Robin admits. She bakes her salmon loaf in one of her mini–tube pans, but it's so good we've doubled the recipe to serve more people. Robin says that she treats her stoneware "like any commercial bakeware unless the food requires a cold oven start as an extra-cautious move." A good idea here.

Note: Because of the saltiness of the crackers and the salmon, this recipe isn't likely to need additional salt. But taste and adjust as needed.

SALMON RING

1 (14.75-ounce) can pink Alaska salmon, drained, flaked, bits of dark skin removed, and the liquid reserved

1 cup moderately coarse soda cracker crumbs (see page 11)

1 (5-ounce) can evaporated milk blended with the reserved salmon liquid (about 1 cup total liquid; add a little cold water, if necessary)

2 large eggs

1 medium-small yellow onion, coarsely chopped

¼ cup moderately finely chopped fresh parsley

1 tablespoon fresh lemon juice

1 tablespoon coarsely chopped fresh dill or 1 teaspoon dill weed

½ teaspoon freshly ground black pepper

Salt, if needed, to taste (see *Note* above)

SAUCE (MAKES ABOUT 1 ⅔ CUPS)

1½ cups solidly packed mayonnaise mixed with ⅓ cup well-drained dill pickle relish

1. Using your hands, combine all of the salmon ring ingredients thoroughly in a large mixing bowl.

2. Line the bottom of a 7-inch, 4½- to 5-cup ovenproof stoneware, other pottery, ceramic, or heat-resistant glass tube pan with a circle of nonstick aluminum foil, then spritz well with nonstick cooking spray, paying particular attention to the central tube and the sides of the pan.

3. Pack the salmon mixture in the pan, mounding it slightly in the center.

4. Slide the pan onto middle shelf of a cold oven, set the thermostat at 325°F, and bake for about 1 hour or until the loaf begins to pull from the sides of the pan, is nicely browned, and is moist but firm to the touch.

5. Transfer the salmon ring to a wire rack, setting the pan right-side up, and cool to room temperature.

6. Carefully loosen the salmon ring around the edge and the central tube using a small thin-blade spatula, then rap the pan gently on the counter, and invert the salmon loaf on a plate.

7. To serve, slice the salmon ring about 1 inch thick, and overlapping the slices, fan them into a ring on a medium-size colorful round pottery platter. Spoon a little of the sauce decoratively on top of the slices, and pass the rest in a small sauceboat. The perfect accompaniment? Steamed asparagus spears or broccoli florets.

4

Melting Mountain Pottery:

Joey Sheehan

FOR MORE INFORMATION:

meltingmountainpottery.com

"I love to cook and am always experimenting," Joey says, "so my recipes are always changing." So, too, his pottery.

"Life," Joey continues, "is beautiful, inspiring, and unpredictable," the very qualities he expresses in ceramics that manage to combine functional glaze ware and sculpture.

"I not only continue to search for new ideas outside the studio," Joey explains, "but also to push the existing boundaries of what my clay and hands can do inside the studio." For proof, you've only to scroll through the photographs on Joey's website.

With a fine arts degree in ceramics from Virginia Tech, not to mention his participation in exhibits and workshops near and far, Joey's up for any challenge.

He and his wife, Mandy McKee Shechan, both Virginians, settled just north of Asheville in a village that promotes itself as "the epitome of a picturesque mountain town with the French Broad River at its feet and the steep rocky edge of a mountain at its back." Small wonder Marshall's become a magnet for artistic families like the Sheehans seeking crisp mountain air and a patch of ground big enough for a few chickens and maybe a goat or two.

Joey's a force here known for his fashion-forward pottery as well as for support of other artists in the River Arts District.

Is there another Sheehan potter in our future? Maybe. Baby Thea "couldn't wait to get her hands dirty" in her dad's studio. So what does little Thea, now a toddler, look forward to? Going to work with Daddy. Otherwise, why so many shots on his website of the two at Joey's wheel?

Some-Are-Hot-Some-Are-Not Stuffed Peppers

Makes 2 dozen (4 to 6 servings)

During his wood firings, these make-ahead finger foods are one of Joey's favorites "to share with friends around the kiln."

Note: Thumb-size peppers are the ones to use, a 50–50 red-yellow-green mix of the sweet and peppery. Joey grows his own—jalapeños plus others both sweet and hot. Look for them at your farmers' market. Or grow your own.

Tips: For this recipe, think thumb shape as well as thumb size so that all the peppers are done at the same time. Many supermarkets sell packaged mini sweet peppers (about 15 per bag), and that's what we used here. Can you use a grill pan instead of a charcoal grill? Absolutely. Spritz the pan with nonstick cooking spray, set over moderately high heat, and when a drop of water sputters when it hits the pan, add the stuffed peppers, and reduce the heat to moderate. Grill the peppers for about 5 to 7 minutes on each side, but watch carefully and reduce the heat and/or cooking time as needed. The burner heat should not be so hot that the stuffing oozes out.

1 (8-ounce) package cream cheese, at room temperature

8 ounces finely chopped provolone cheese, at room temperature

8 ounces moderately coarsely shredded sharp Cheddar cheese, at room temperature

4 medium-size garlic cloves, crushed

½ cup crumbled crisply cooked bacon or cooked peppery southern country-style sausage (see headnote, White Chicken Chowder Chili, page 135)

12 thumb-size sweet peppers, halved lengthwise and seeded but the stems left intact (see *Note* and *Tips* above)

12 thumb-size jalapeño peppers, halved lengthwise and seeded but the stems left intact

1. Combine the cream cheese, provolone, Cheddar, garlic, and bacon in a large mixing bowl until well blended and stiff enough to mold.

2. Pack about 1 tablespoon of the cheese mixture into each half pepper, then gently pinch the cut edges of the peppers together to keep the filling from oozing out as the peppers grill. *Note*: At this point, the peppers can be covered and refrigerated until ready to grill. But let them stand at room temperature for at least ½ hour first.

3. Arrange the stuffed peppers on their sides and not touching on a charcoal grill preheated to medium low. *Note*: For extra-smoky flavor, Joey tosses some smoking wood chips onto the grill.

4. Grill the stuffed peppers slowly for 15 to 20 minutes, turning them gently with tongs midway, so both sides are charred and the filling's hot and bubbly.

5. Arrange the grilled peppers on a large stoneware or other heatproof platter, serve, and, as Joey says, "Enjoy and beware . . . !" These peppers may be blisteringly hot.

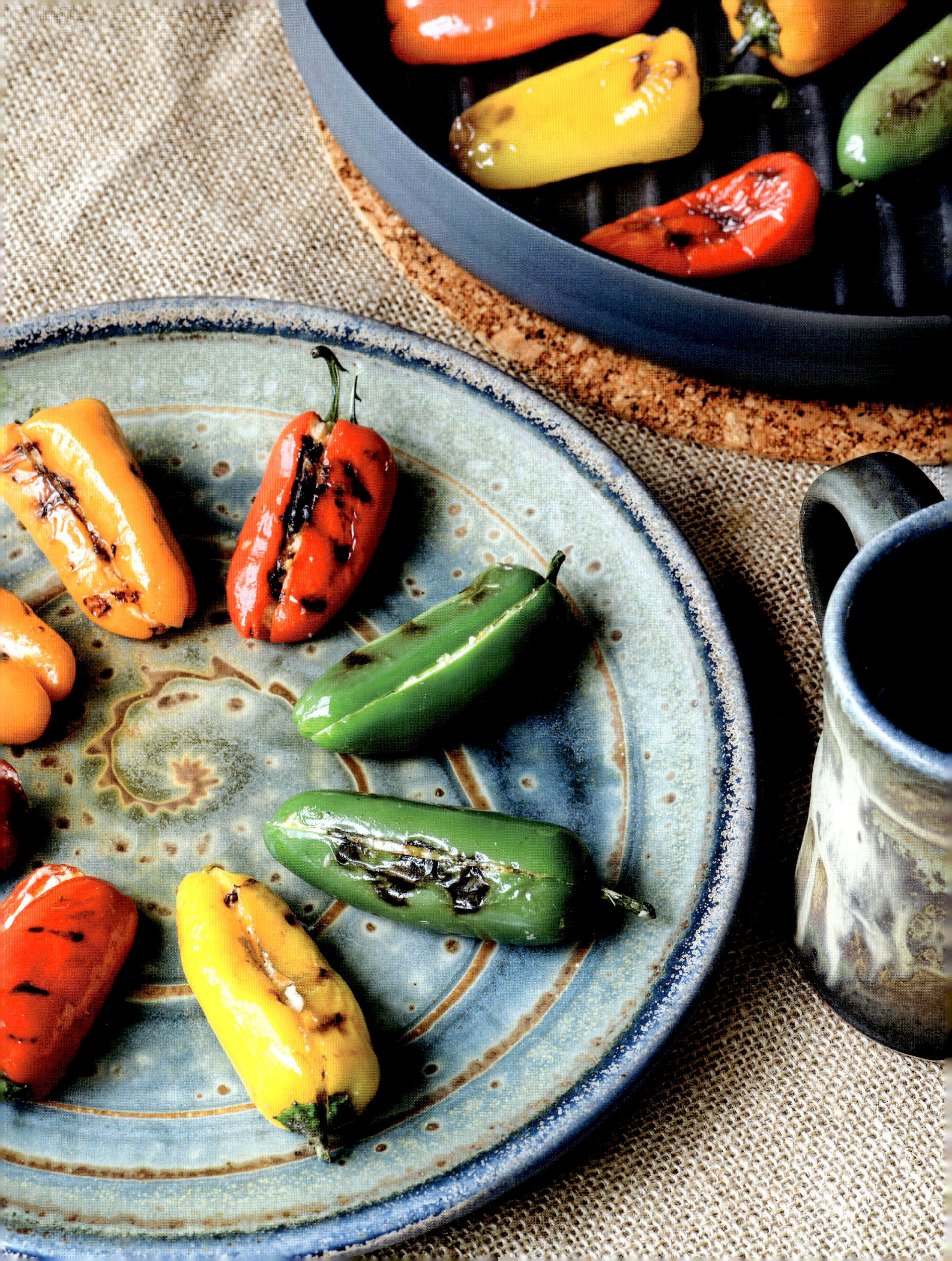

Holiday Crab and Shrimp Mac 'n' Cheese

Makes 16 servings

"I am a mac and cheese junky," Joey Sheehan admits, "and this is one of my favorites. It'll feed the gang at your holiday gatherings!"

Note: Do not substitute fresh shrimp for frozen, but look for American shrimp. The Asian may have been farmed in polluted waters.

8 slices thick-cut bacon (about 1 pound), sliced crosswise into strips about ¼ inch wide

1 pound medium-size frozen shelled and deveined raw shrimp, thawed for 20 minutes, then cut into ½-inch dice (see *Note* above)

2 tablespoons butter

2 medium-size garlic cloves, finely minced

1 teaspoon Old Bay Seasoning

1 teaspoon salt, or to taste

½ teaspoon freshly ground black pepper

½ pound lump crab meat, bits of shell and cartilage removed

3 tablespoons all-purpose flour

3 cups heavy cream (no substitute)

½ pound coarsely chopped mozzarella cheese

¼ pound coarsely shredded Vermont Cheddar cheese

¼ pound coarsely shredded sharp English Cheddar cheese

¼ pound coarsely shredded Monterey Jack cheese

2 (16-ounce) boxes medium-size pasta shells, cooked and drained by package directions

TOPPING

¼ to ½ pound mozzarella cheese, cut into slices ⅛ inch thick

¾ cup panko crumbs

1 tablespoon extra-virgin olive oil

1. Spritz a shallow 4½- to 5-quart ovenproof stoneware, other pottery, ceramic, or heat-resistant glass casserole with nonstick cooking spray and set aside.

2. Sauté the bacon in an extra-large, broad, heavy saucepan over moderate heat for about 10 minutes or until it begins to crispen. Add the next 7 ingredients (shrimp through crab), and simmer for about 3 minutes or just until the shrimp turn pink.

3. Blend in the flour, then cook and stir for 2 minutes. Slowly add the cream, stirring all the while, then cook and stir for 6 to 8 minutes or until thickened and smooth.

4. Add the chopped and shredded cheeses (mozzarella through Monterey Jack), and simmer, stirring often, on moderately low heat for 5 to 6 minutes or until all of the cheeses have melted and the sauce is smooth.

5. Remove the pan from the heat, mix in the cooked, drained pasta shells, and scoop into the prepared casserole, spreading to the edge. *Note*: If your saucepan is too small to hold the cooked pasta shells, scoop the pan mixture into the prepared casserole, add the pasta shells, and mix well with gloved hands.

6. *For the topping*: Arrange the sliced mozzarella on top of the pasta mixture, scatter the panko crumbs evenly over all, then drizzle with the olive oil.

7. Slide the casserole onto the middle shelf of a cold oven, set the thermostat at 375°F, and bake for about 1 hour or just until bubbling and touched with brown.

8. Carry the casserole to the dining table and dish up at once. Accompaniment? Keep it simple—a big bowl of arugula, radicchio, and other bitter salad greens tossed with a lemon vinaigrette.

White Chicken Chowder Chili

Makes 6 to 8 servings

"One of my favorites," says Joey Sheehan, adding that he and his crew wolfed it down on the overnight shift of his last firing. "The chili's warmth and spice hit the spot during those cold nights. And it's an awesome dish to eat out of my special handled soup bowls!"

Notes: Joey's recipe feeds an army, so I've halved it here. I've also tempered the chilies' fire for those who don't like it so hot. Southern country-style sausage? Ground pork (two parts lean to one part fat) seasoned with sage, salt, and pepper (black or red or both). Neese's sells it in one-pound loaves. It's distributed throughout the South and can now be ordered online (see Sources, page 164).

Tips: For ¾ cup fresh whole-kernel corn, you'll need about one medium-large ear. For moister chicken, use dark meat (thighs) only.

½ pound sliced hickory-smoked bacon

6 ounces Yukon Gold potatoes, cut into ½-inch dice but not peeled

4 tablespoons reserved bacon drippings, divided

2 tablespoons vegetable oil (about)

¾ pound boneless skinless chicken breasts, cut into 1-inch chunks

¾ pound boneless skinless chicken thighs, cut into 1-inch chunks (see *Tips* above)

1 medium-size yellow onion, coarsely chopped

⅓ cup coarsely chopped cored and seeded poblano peppers

¼ cup coarsely chopped cored and seeded jalapeño peppers

1 small red bell pepper, cored, seeded, and coarsely chopped

1 small yellow bell pepper, cored, seeded, and coarsely chopped

3 medium-size garlic cloves, finely minced

¼ pound uncooked southern country-style bulk sausage (not peppery; see *Notes* above)

1½ teaspoons ground cumin

1 teaspoon chili powder

½ teaspoon salt, or to taste

½ teaspoon freshly ground black pepper

¼ teaspoon smoked paprika

⅛ teaspoon ground hot red pepper (cayenne)

1¾ cups heavy cream

¾ cup fresh or thawed frozen whole-kernel corn (see *Tips* above)

1 (15.5-ounce) can great northern beans, drained

1¼ cups chicken broth, or as needed to thin the chili to the consistency of chowder

OPTIONAL TOPPING

½ cup sour cream

1. Preheat the oven to 400°F. Spritz a large rectangular or square cake rack with nonstick cooking spray, then stand in a large, shallow roasting pan.

2. Arrange the bacon slices in a single layer on the cake rack, then slide the pan onto the middle shelf of the preheated oven and roast the bacon for about 20 minutes or until crisp and brown. Using tongs, lift the bacon to paper toweling and reserve. Pour the bacon drippings into a heat-resistant glass measuring cup and reserve.

3. Remove the rack from the roasting pan, add the potatoes and 1½ tablespoons of the reserved bacon drippings, and turn until nicely coated.

4. Return the pan to the middle shelf, and roast the potatoes for about 10 minutes, stirring now and then, until they begin to soften, then scoop onto a plate and reserve.

5. Spoon the remaining reserved bacon drippings into a large, heavy nonreactive Dutch oven or stew pot, add 1 tablespoon of the vegetable oil, and set over moderately high heat. After about 1½ minutes, ripples will appear on the pan bottom, so begin browning the chicken in batches, allowing about 4 minutes per batch. Lift the browned chicken to a paper-towel-lined pie pan, and reserve.

6. If the fat in the pot seems skimpy, add another tablespoon of the oil. Reduce the heat to moderate, add the next 6 ingredients (onion through garlic), and sauté, stirring often, for 8 to 10 minutes or until the onion is translucent and the peppers softening.

7. Increase the burner heat to moderately high, add the sausage, breaking it up as you add, then mix in all 6 seasonings (cumin through cayenne). Cook, stirring now and then, for 5 to 7 minutes or until the sausage is nicely browned.

8. Add the heavy cream slowly, stirring all the while, then continue to cook and stir for about 5 minutes or until slightly reduced.

9. Add the corn and, if it's fresh corn, cook and stir for 5 minutes. If frozen, add while stirring in the great northern beans, chicken broth, reserved potatoes, and chicken. Finally, crumble in the reserved bacon. *Note*: If the chili seems too thick, thin with a little additional chicken broth.

10. Reduce the burner heat to low, set the lid on the pot askew, and simmer gently for about 10 minutes or until the flavors meld. Taste for salt, and adjust as needed.

11. Ladle at once into pottery soup bowls, and if you like, drift each portion with sour cream. *Note*: Sandy Gluck, a New York friend who tried this recipe, pronounced it "deliciously rich," then added that topping with "dollops of sour cream is gilding the lily."

5

East Fork:

Alex Matisse

FOR MORE INFORMATION:

eastfork.com

. . . .

"East is East, and West is West, and never the twain shall meet" (Rudyard Kipling).

Wrong. New Englander Alex met Angeleno Connie Coady (the future Mrs. M) at a roller-rink-turned-antique-store in Mars Hill. A Berkeley lit major, Connie was selling chèvres from a dairy in the Blue Ridge where she'd retreated "on a whim" after bouncing from New York to L.A. to Montana.

Like Connie, Alex was new to North Carolina, but he knew exactly what he wanted: his own pottery. With Connie beside him, mission accomplished in 2010 on the tired thirty-acre tobacco farm he'd bought near Marshall in mountainous Madison County. Then with children another move, this time to Biltmore Village in Asheville.

The scion of an artistic family (mother and father both artists, not to mention a great-granddad named Henri), Alex made his first pot in the seventh grade and for the first time felt the thrill of creating something all his own—but only briefly. The three Rs came first.

Craving anonymity as well as an academic education, Alex enrolled at Guilford, a small Quaker College in Greensboro, utterly unaware that he'd landed in a state made of clay. He'd no sooner wandered into the school's pottery studio than the old urge to create surfaced, so he talked his way into Charlie Tefft's ceramics class.

Now committed, Alex dropped out of college after two years to apprentice with mountain potter Matt Jones, whose slip trailing on earthen jugs (lacy designs piped on in a glaze the color of country cream) intrigued him. Then, still eager to learn, he moved to the Piedmont to work with master potter Mark Hewitt, whose unique ash-glazed garden urns are as tall as a man.

Now known for the artistry of his own slip-trailed pots as well for his colorful palette of tableware, Alex considers himself lucky to live where the quality of one's work is what counts. "It's wonderful," he admits, "to be recognized for something that's yours alone."

East Fork Morel and Green Pea Tartine

To quote East Fork's headnote for this unusual tartine recipe, "Spring is such an exciting time in the kitchen. As warm weather rolls in, eager little shoots with bright, sweet, vegetal flavor poke their heads through the chilly soil."

Note: If morels are unavailable, substitute small cremini or shiitake mushrooms, both supermarket staples.

GREEN PEA PURÉE

½ cup cooked and drained fresh or frozen green peas

2 tablespoons unsalted butter, at room temperature

¼ cup heavy cream (about)

½ teaspoon salt, or to taste

⅛ teaspoon freshly ground black pepper, or to taste

MOREL MIXTURE

3 tablespoons unsalted butter

1 medium-size leek, trimmed, halved lengthwise, carefully washed, and thinly sliced (white and pale green parts only)

16 fresh small morel mushrooms, halved lengthwise and carefully cleaned in cool water (see *Note* above)

¼ teaspoon salt, or to taste

⅛ teaspoon freshly ground black pepper, or to taste

TO ASSEMBLE THE TARTINES

1 cup ricotta cheese

4 lightly toasted slices good country bread about ¾ inch thick and 3½ to 4 inches long

GARNISHES (CHOOSE ONE OR ALL)

¼ cup fresh green pea shoots or, if you prefer, ¼ teaspoon coarsely shredded lemon zest

1 tablespoon extra-virgin olive oil

¼ teaspoon coarse sea salt

1. *For the green pea purée*: Pulse the peas and butter in a food processor equipped with the metal chopping blade until smooth, then with the motor running, trickle just enough heavy cream down the feed tube for a purée the consistency of sour cream.

2. Remove the processor blade, then scoop the pea purée into a small bowl, season to taste with salt and pepper, and set aside.

3. *For the morel mixture*: Melt 2 tablespoons of the butter in a heavy, medium-size skillet over moderate heat, add the leek and sauté, stirring often, about 2 to 3 minutes until limp and translucent.

4. Add the morels and cook, stirring often, for about 4 minutes or until they are tender, have released their juices, and most of these have evaporated. Mix in the remaining 1 tablespoon butter, then season to taste with salt and pepper.

5. *To assemble the tartines*: Spread each slice of toast with the ricotta cheese, dividing the total amount evenly, spread the pea purée on top, then spoon on the morel mixture. Finally, garnish with whatever you fancy.

6. Serve the tartines as the main course of a casual lunch and accompany with a compatible wine. Alex and Connie Matisse like a "fresh wine with good acid" and suggest either a Grüner Veltliner or a Muscadet.

Connie Matisse's Southern Shrimp Rolls

Makes 8 servings

"When the weather's warm," Connie says, "we're all about beach-vacation meals." Like these shrimp rolls that can be "thrown together" in less than half an hour. She insists on ocean-fresh shrimp, not farmed or, heaven forbid, frozen. For special occasions, substitute lobster.

Tip: You can cook and refrigerate the shrimp a day ahead of time.

Note: This recipe and the one for the tartine that precedes it are adapted from those that appear in the *East Fork Journal*, an online newsletter that describes itself as "a collection of musings, interviews, recipes, and special features on products, collaborations and beautiful objects we stumble across on our journey." To subscribe, visit eastfork.com, click on "Read," scroll to the bottom of the page, and enter your e-mail address in the subscription box.

SHRIMP SALAD

1½ pounds fresh shelled and deveined raw North Carolina shrimp (see *Tip* above)

1 cup firmly packed mayonnaise or ½ cup each firmly packed mayo and plain yogurt

3 large celery ribs, trimmed and finely chopped (include a few leaves)

1 large shallot, finely minced

2 tablespoons finely minced fresh Italian parsley

1½ tablespoons fresh lemon juice

1 tablespoon finely minced fresh chives

1 tablespoon finely minced fresh dill

1½ teaspoons hot red pepper sauce

½ teaspoon finely grated lemon zest

½ teaspoon salt, or to taste

¼ teaspoon freshly ground black pepper, or to taste

BUNS

5 tablespoons unsalted butter

8 hotdog buns, split lengthwise

1. *For the shrimp salad*: Cook the shrimp in a large pot of boiling water for about 2 minutes or just until they turn pink, then drain and quick-chill in ice water.

2. Meanwhile, combine the next 11 ingredients (mayonnaise through black pepper) in a medium-size nonreactive bowl, whisking until smooth.

3. Drain the shrimp well, pat dry on paper toweling, then cut into ½-inch dice. Add to the mayonnaise sauce, toss until well coated, and reserve.

4. *For the buns*: Melt the butter in a heavy 12-inch skillet over moderate heat, then spritz the buns lightly with cold water. Working in 2 batches, lay the buns cut-side down in the butter, cover, and toast for about 1 minute or until

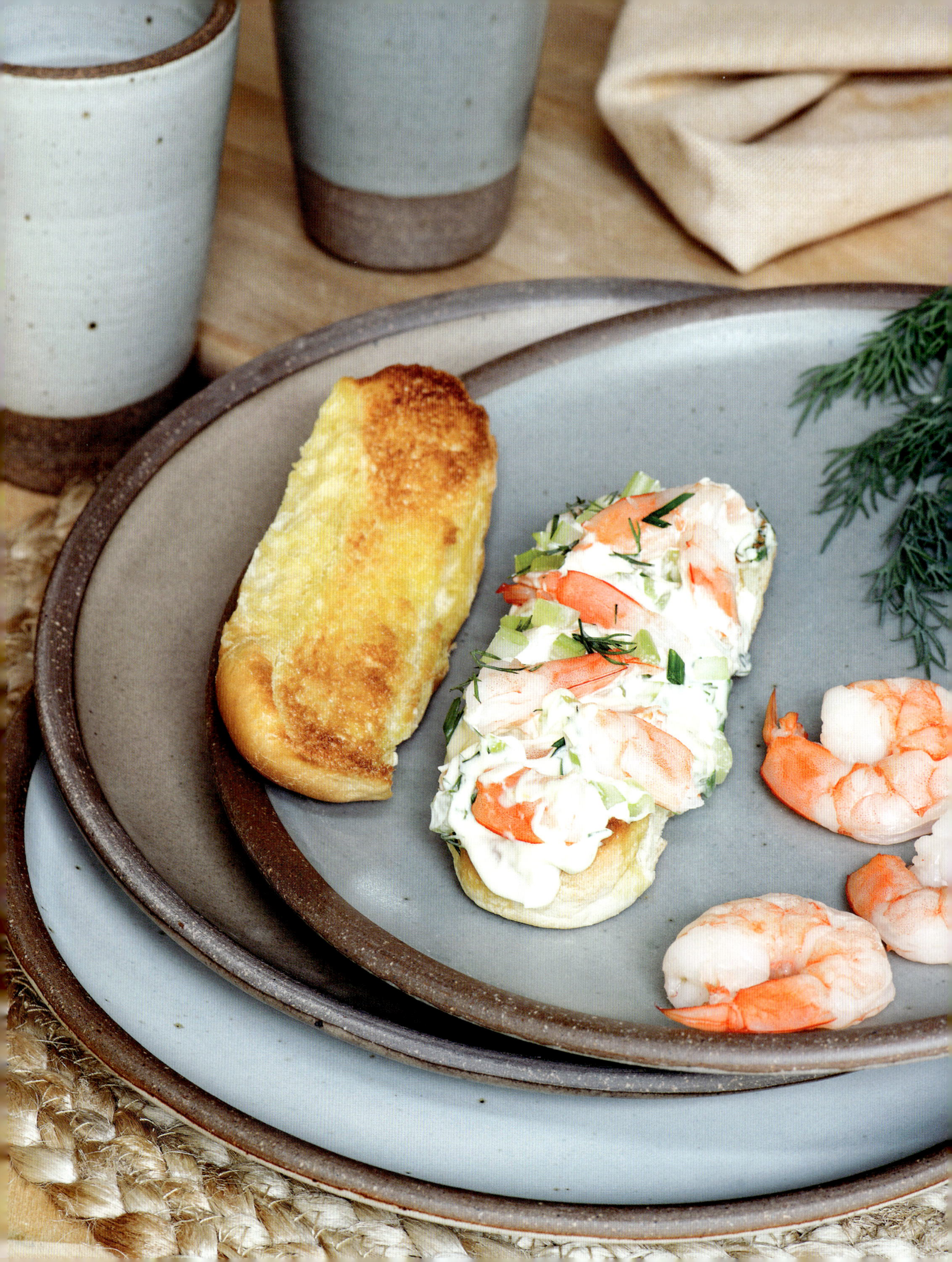

golden brown. Drain the buns on paper toweling and cool to room temperature.

5. To assemble, mound about ⅔ cup of the shrimp salad on each bun bottom, dividing the amount as evenly as possible, then add the bun tops, and serve. Accompaniment? Connie Matisse recommends a local craft pilsner or a good German Riesling.

Steamed Green Tea and Rose Cake with Sesame Whipped Cream

Makes one 7- to 7¾-inch cake
(6 to 8 servings)

"This cake's so easy to make," Connie says, "and it stays moist and delicious for days." She steams the cake in husband Alex's 7¾-inch, 3-cup shallow soup and salad bowl, "the most versatile personal bowl we make."

Notes: Matcha, if you don't know it, is a Japanese green tea powder. If not sold in your area, order it online (see Sources, page 164). To my surprise, coarse salt works in this steamed cake, but I still don't recommend it for baked cakes because the salt may not dissolve. Tahini (sesame seed paste) in whipped cream? What a good idea!

Tip: If you don't have that shallow soup and salad bowl, you'll find that a heat-resistant glass bowl 7 inches across and 3 inches deep works equally well.

CAKE

¾ cup sifted unbleached all-purpose flour

⅓ cup raw sugar

2 tablespoons matcha (see *Notes* above)

1 teaspoon baking powder

¼ teaspoon flaky Maldon or other coarse sea salt (see *Notes* above)

⅓ cup heavy cream blended with ¼ teaspoon rose water (see Sources, page 164)

¼ cup (½ stick) unsalted butter, melted

1 large egg, at room temperature

SESAME WHIPPED CREAM

1 cup heavy cream

1 tablespoon honey (not too dark)

1 tablespoon tahini (see *Notes* above)

1. *For the cake*: Combine the flour, sugar, matcha, baking powder, and salt in a large mixing bowl and make a well in the center.

2. Whisk the heavy cream mixture, melted butter, and egg together in a small mixing bowl, pour into the well in the dry ingredients, and gently fold the two together—takes about a minute, 12 strokes. Don't overmix or your cake may be tough.

3. Scoop the batter into a well-buttered 7- to 7¾-inch, 3- to 3½-cup heatproof pottery, other ceramic, or heat-resistant glass bowl, leaving 1½ to 2 inches at the top (see *Tip* above). Cover snugly with buttered aluminum foil.

4. Set the pudding in a steamer basket over 1½ to 2 inches of simmering water and steam for about 1 hour and 10 minutes or until a cake tester, inserted midway between the rim and the center, comes out clean. *Note*: After 30 minutes, check the level of the water in the steamer, and add more, if necessary.

5. *Meanwhile, prepare the sesame whipped cream*: Using a hand electric mixer at medium speed, beat the cream in a small bowl for about 2 minutes or until it begins to thicken. Then with the mixer at low speed, slowly add the honey, then the tahini, and continue beating for about 1½ minutes or until the cream mounds softly. Don't overbeat.

6. Remove the cake from the steamer and cool right-side up for about 15 minutes on a wire rack. Remove the foil covering, then carefully loosen the cake around the edges with a small thin-blade spatula, and invert on a large plate.

7. To serve, cut the cake into 6 to 8 wedges, and drift each with some of the sesame whipped cream.

6

Rutkowsky Pottery:

Michael Rutkowsky and

Ruth Fischer Rutkowsky

FOR MORE INFORMATION:

rutkowskypottery.com

"Making pottery is like cooking," Michael says. "There is room for experimentation and the process is enjoyable no matter what your level of expertise."

Yet becoming a potter was a fluke for Pennsylvania-born Michael, who grew up in Florida and earned a degree in economics at the University of Central Florida.

"To defer my college debt," Michael explains, "I began taking art courses that interested me with no intention of getting a degree in art." As it happened, he passed the ceramics studio en route to the dark room he used for his photography class. "I liked what I saw there, so I enrolled in Ceramics 201." Talk about a game changer.

The next steps fell quickly, almost automatically, into place: earning an MFA in ceramics at the University of South Carolina while serving as a graduate teaching assistant, becoming a full-time studio potter, first in South Carolina, then in the North Carolina mountains where he and his family had often camped in summer.

"We found genuine people and affordable living in Yancey County," Michael adds. Moreover, he could join the Southern Highlands Craft Guild, a major outlet for his work.

In 1985, Michael bought twelve acres of land, "built a house and studio while living in a seventeen-foot camper and studio loft." Today, he and his wife, clay sculptor Ruth Fischer Rutkowsky, share his studio with a standard poodle. Though Michael makes "a few decorative pieces," he focuses on nontoxic microwave-, oven-, and dishwasher-safe stoneware. Because he's the family cook? "I mainly cook out of necessity because we live in a rural area," he says.

Given the recipes that follow, not to mention the relish with which he writes about food, I think that Michael Rutkowsky finds cookery and pottery equally creative arts.

Chicken Baked in My Handmade Lidded Bowl

Makes 4 to 6 servings

"When we finally gave up on the pan and the baking bags," Michael says, "we found that the 2½-quart lidded stoneware bowl I have been making for years is the easiest and most delicious way to bake a chicken."

Note: You'll find coconut oil at specialty groceries as well as online (see Sources, page 164). Ditto Herbes de Provence, an herb and lavender blend popular in the south of France.

Tip: Remove the giblets from the chicken and from their packet. Slip into a small plastic zipper bag, press out all the air, then label and date and store in the freezer. Use within three months when making stock, soup, or gravy.

1 (5- to 6½-pound) oven-ready chicken
   (see *Tip* above)
2 tablespoons coconut cooking oil (see *Note* above)
2 teaspoons finely crumbled Herbes de Provence
   (see *Note* above)
½ teaspoon salt
¼ teaspoon freshly ground black pepper

1. Rub the chicken generously inside and out with the coconut oil, then with the Herbes de Provence, salt, and pepper.

2. Place the chicken in a large, lidded, shallow oval ovenproof stoneware, other pottery, ceramic, or heat-resistant glass casserole that's 9 to 10 inches long (or if the bird's a bit smaller, in the Rutkowsky Pottery lidded bowl Michael makes). Cover, slide onto the middle shelf of a cold oven, and set the thermostat at 350°F.

3. Bake the chicken for about 2 hours. Remove the lid, then bake uncovered for 15 to 20 minutes or until the chicken is nicely browned and an instant-read thermometer, inserted in the meatiest part of a thigh not touching bone, registers 165°F.

4. Remove the chicken from the oven and let it rest on the counter for 20 minutes to give the juices time to settle.

5. Carve the bird at the table and accompany with a sauceboat of pan drippings and simply seasoned steamed broccoli (Michael's favorite) or, if you prefer, fresh asparagus.

Sausage Grits

Makes 4 to 6 servings

"Breakfast is the most important meal of the day," Michael says. "It energizes us, sets the pace and mood for the day." But this recipe is a brunch favorite, too.

Notes: Michael likes organic yellow grits, but regular grits are fine as long as they're not the instant or quick-cooking variety. And the sausage? Swaggerty's from the Tennessee side of the Smokies is Michael's choice, but any good country sausage will do. Like Neese's of Greensboro.

1 tablespoon vegetable oil

1 small yellow onion, coarsely chopped

1 small red or yellow bell pepper, cored, seeded, and diced

½ pound mild or spicy sausage patties or sausage meat (see *Notes* above)

1 cup regular grits, cooked by package directions (see *Notes* above)

½ cup half-and-half

Salt and freshly ground black pepper to taste

½ cup coarsely shredded sharp white Cheddar or Monterey Jack cheese

1. Spritz a 9-inch ovenproof stoneware, other pottery, ceramic, or heat-resistant glass pie pan with nonstick cooking spray and set aside.

2. Heat the vegetable oil in a deep, heavy, medium-size skillet over moderately high heat for about 1 minute, then add the onion and bell pepper, and cook and stir for 3 to 4 minutes or until limp.

3. Add the sausage, breaking it up with a large spoon, and brown for 5 to 7 minutes, forking all the while until crumbly and cooked through.

4. Mix in the grits, half-and-half, and salt and pepper to taste. Scoop into the prepared pie pan, pushing to the edge, then scatter the shredded cheese evenly on top.

5. Slide the pie pan onto the middle shelf of a cold oven, set the thermostat at 350°F, and bake uncovered for 30 to 35 minutes or until the cheese has melted.

6. Serve at once for breakfast or brunch.

Rutkowsky Apple Cobbler with Walnut Crust

Makes 8 to 10 servings

"This is not a low-calorie dessert," Michael admits, "and, whenever possible, contains no processed ingredients." Michael harvests his own apples, an heirloom variety called Black Twig. "They're on the tart side," he adds, "desirable for any apple dessert."

Note: If Black Twigs are unavailable, substitute Rhode Island Greenings, Winesaps, or Rome Beauties. Michael bakes the cobbler in his 10-inch round stoneware baking dish greased with unrefined coconut oil (see Sources, page 164)—"a great releasing agent."

Tips: He also uses a high butterfat European-style unsalted butter "because it has less water." And organic light spelt flour, a primitive variety of wheat that contains less gluten than regular flour, but make a note, it is not gluten-free. For a gluten-free dessert, substitute rice flour for the spelt; see the information on flours on page 8. Finally, Michael uses an organic raw vinegar (Bragg is the brand); it's available at health food stores.

WALNUT CRUST

1¾ cups walnut halves

3 tablespoons refrigerator-cold unsalted butter, diced (see *Tips* above)

2 tablespoons granulated sugar

OATMEAL CRUMBLE TOPPING

5 tablespoons plus 1 teaspoon unsalted butter, cut up and at room temperature

1 cup light brown sugar (do not pack)

¾ cup unsifted organic light spelt flour (see *Tips* above)

¾ cup old-fashioned rolled oats (oatmeal)

½ teaspoon ground cinnamon

¼ teaspoon fine sea salt

APPLE FILLING

2 pounds medium-size tart, juicy apples, peeled, cored, and sliced ¼-inch thick (see *Note* above)

2 tablespoons fresh lemon juice

2 to 4 tablespoons filtered water, depending on how dry the apples are

2 tablespoons raw organic cider vinegar (see *Tips* above)

2 tablespoons organic light spelt flour (see *Tips* above)

2 tablespoons cornstarch

1 teaspoon ground cinnamon

¼ teaspoon fine sea salt

⅛ teaspoon freshly grated nutmeg

1. *For the walnut crust*: Pulse the nuts in a food processor fitted with the metal chopping blade for about 1 minute or until the texture of coarse sugar crystals. Add the diced butter and the sugar and pulse quickly about 10 times or until the mixture sticks together.

2. Grease a 10-inch round stoneware, other pottery, ceramic, or heat-resistant glass baking dish with unrefined coconut oil, then line the bottom and sides with baking parchment. Scoop the walnut mixture into the prepared baking dish, and pat firmly over the bottom and about

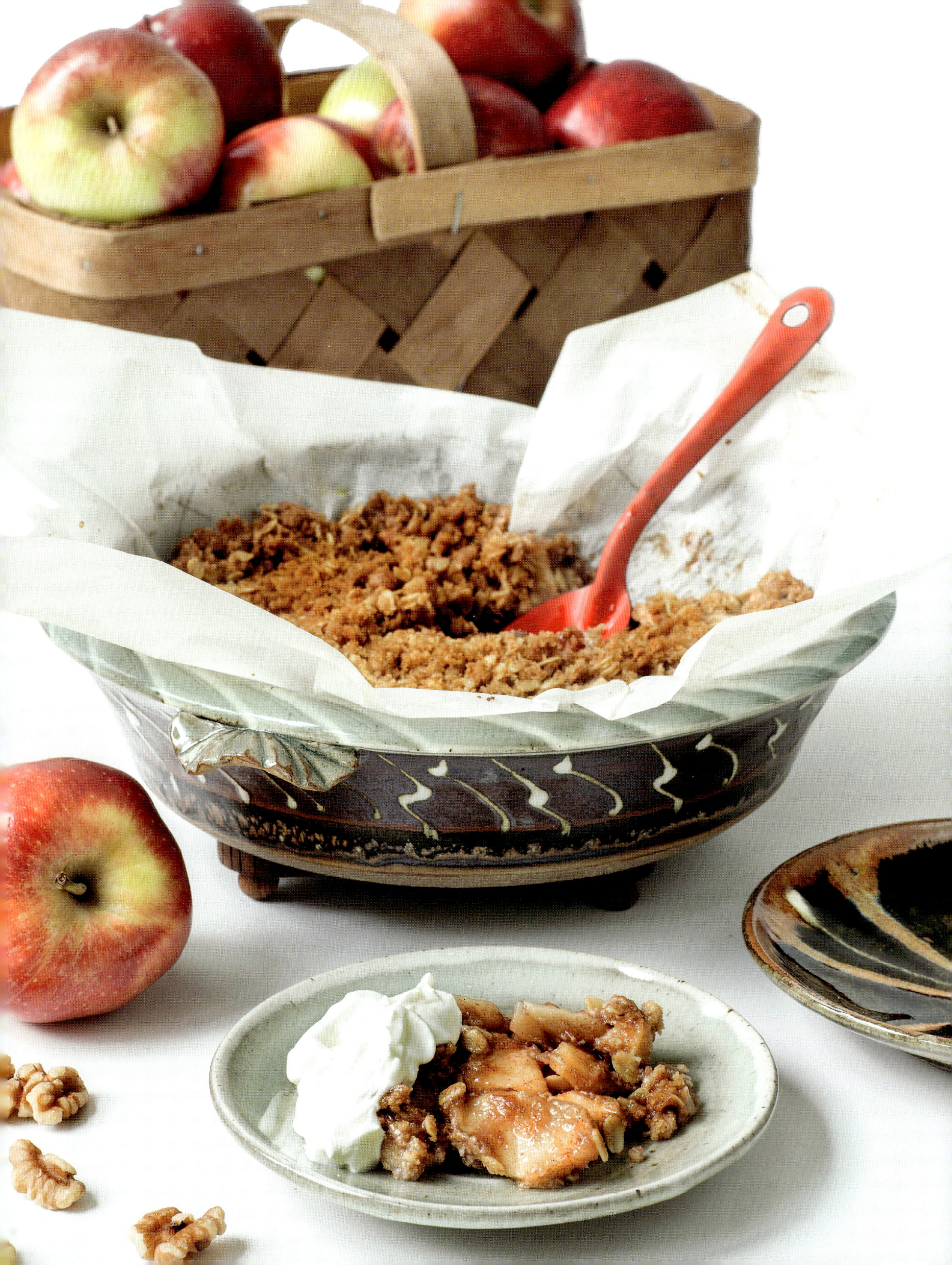

halfway up the sides, making the crust as thin as possible, then set aside while you proceed with the recipe.

3. *For the oatmeal crumble topping*: Place all ingredients in a large mixing bowl, then fork together until uniformly crumbly, and reserve.

4. *For the apple filling*: Place the apples, lemon juice, 2 tablespoons of the water, and the vinegar in a large mixing bowl and toss well. Place the remaining ingredients (spelt flour through nutmeg) in a small bowl and whisk until well blended. Add to the apple mixture, and toss until the apples are nicely coated. If the mixture seems a little dry, add 1 to 2 tablespoons more water and mix well.

5. Scoop the apple filling into the walnut crust, smoothing the top, spreading to the edge, and patting with the back of a large spoon to release any air pockets.

6. Add the oatmeal crumble, distributing as evenly as possible, but do not pat down.

7. Slide the cobbler onto the middle shelf of a cold oven, set the thermostat at 375°F, and bake for 15 minutes. Reduce the oven temperature to 350°F, and bake for 25 to 30 minutes or until bubbling and lightly browned. *Note*: If at any point the cobbler seems to be browning too fast, cover loosely with foil, but remove for the final 10 minutes so that the cobbler browns nicely.

8. Set the baked cobbler on a baking rack and cool for 30 minutes.

9. Dish the cobbler up at table and, if you like, add scoops of vanilla ice cream or blob with whipped cream. "Yes," Michael says, "a little cream of some sort" makes the cobbler even more "enjoyable."

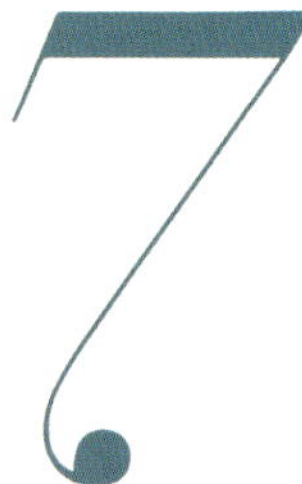

Barking Spider Pottery:

Jon Ellenbogen and

Rebecca Plummer

FOR MORE INFORMATION:

barkingspiderpottery.com

The Penland Potters? Nine full-time clay artists living within a three-mile radius of Penland.

And Penland? It's the famous crafts school about an hour northeast of Asheville that's been teaching everything from metalworking to jewelry making for nearly one hundred years. My mother studied weaving here, a Santa Fe friend bookbinding, and Jon and Rebecca ceramics, though neither had considered pottery as a profession.

Jon, weary of his job as a professor of engineering, enrolled in Cynthia Bringle's pottery course, never dreaming that he'd get hooked, let alone meet Becky, the classmate who'd become his wife, his partner, and the mother of twin sons.

To this day, Jon credits Bringle for showing him "the light." It was possible to leave his New York engineering degrees behind and find fulfillment as a potter in the North Carolina Blue Ridge. The same applies to philosopher Rebecca, who grew up near Andrew Wyeth country.

Finishing their Penland courses in the mid-1970s, these two founded the Barking Spider Pottery and work in a passive solar studio above the Toe River surrounded by yellow poplar, black locust, white pine, and hemlock. Believing that "handmade objects in everyday use bring pleasure and meaning to our lives," they've focused on turning their special clay and exclusive glazes into functional stoneware that accommodate Jon's—and others'—passion for cooking.

Everything they make is nontoxic and durable enough to withstand repeated trips to the oven, microwave, and dishwasher—though never the thermal shock of stovetop heat.

There's an adjective missing in the descriptions above. I find my Barking Spider bakeware so beautiful I keep it out on display for others to admire. And admire, they do.

Asopao
(Puerto Rican Seafood Stew)

Makes 8 to 10 servings

Of all the Puerto Rican dishes Jon cooked during his four years as an engineering professor
at the university in Mayaguez, this shrimp and
sausage dinner-in-a-dish is a favorite. "Spicier,"
Jon admits, "than what you'd find in PR and a
great way to use up leftovers."

Note: Barking Spider stoneware can go into
a hot oven. "We've designed a clay formula to
resist thermal-shock, and as long as the pot and
its contents are room temperature or warmer,
Becky and I put things directly into a 325° to
350°F oven. If a recipe calls for higher temps,
we just add more time."

¼ cup extra-virgin olive oil

1 large yellow onion, coarsely chopped

1 large red or yellow bell pepper, cored, seeded,
   and coarsely chopped

1 large celery rib, coarsely chopped (include a
   few leaves)

2 large garlic cloves, minced

½ pound smoked chorizo or kielbasa, cut into
   ¼-inch dice

1½ cups uncooked long-grain white rice (preferably
   California rice; see page 9)

5½ cups chicken broth or stock (homemade or
   canned), divided

1 tablespoon plus 1 teaspoon Asian fish sauce
   (see Sources, page 164)

2½ cups canned diced tomatoes, with their liquid

¼ cup canned diced green chilies, with their liquid

1½ cups (¼-inch) diced leftover cooked chicken
   (dark and/or light meat)

1 cup small pimiento-stuffed green olives, drained
   and halved crosswise

2 teaspoons crumbled dried leaf oregano

½ teaspoon salt, or to taste

½ teaspoon freshly ground black pepper, or to taste

1 pound medium-size fresh raw shrimp, shelled and
   deveined

1. Preheat the oven to 350°F. Spritz a lidded
4-quart Barking Spider stoneware casserole (or
same-size ovenproof stoneware, other pottery,
ceramic, or heat-resistant glass casserole that
can go into a preheated oven) with nonstick
cooking spray and set aside.

2. Heat the olive oil in a heavy, deep 12-inch
skillet over moderately high heat 2 to 2½
minutes until ripples appear on the pan bottom.
Add the onion, bell pepper, and celery, and stir-
fry for about 5 minutes or until the onion begins
to soften.

3. Add the garlic and chorizo and stir-fry 1 to
2 minutes. Reduce the heat to moderate, mix in

the rice, and stir until all the grains are nicely coated. Add 4 cups of the chicken broth and the fish sauce, bring to a boil, and cook uncovered for 6 to 8 minutes, stirring occasionally, until the rice begins to soften.

4. Add the canned diced tomatoes and green chilies, chicken, and olives along with the remaining chicken broth, oregano, salt, and black pepper to taste.

5. Transfer all to the prepared casserole, cover, slide onto the middle shelf of the preheated oven, and bake for 20 minutes. Uncover and add the shrimp along with bits of leftover cooked vegetables (green peas, beans, diced sweet potato, etc.).

6. Stir well, set the lid in place, and bake about 20 minutes longer or until the rice is tender and the stew resembles, in Jon's words, "a soupy paella."

7. To serve, carry the casserole to the table, and ladle the Asopao into Barking Spider's white- or rust-glazed soup bowls.

Quick Pasta Carbonara

Makes 4 servings

While on a semester-abroad program, Becky and Jon spent a month in Tuscany and fell in love with Italian food. Back home, Jon streamlined his favorites, turning them into short-cut versions of Italian classics that didn't require all day in the kitchen, among them this crowd pleaser. "It's very quick," Jon says, "very easy, very delicious, not really carbonara at all." And he serves it in one of the low, wide stoneware bowls he calls a "pasta server."

½ pound thickly sliced lean smoked bacon

1½ pounds cremini or shiitake mushrooms, stemmed, wiped clean, and thinly sliced

½ tablespoon extra-virgin olive oil

1 large red bell pepper, cored, seeded, and coarsely chopped

1 large garlic clove, finely minced

2 cups heavy cream, at room temperature, divided

½ pound linguini, cooked and drained by package directions

¼ teaspoon salt, or to season

2 tablespoons coarsely chopped fresh Italian parsley

Freshly grated Parmigiano-Reggiano cheese (accompaniment)

1. Cook the bacon in a large, heavy skillet over moderately high for about 8 to 10 minutes or until crisp. Lift to paper toweling to drain, then dice—you should have about ½ cup—and set aside.

2. Raise the heat to high and brown the mushrooms in 2 batches using half the bacon drippings and about 4 minutes for each or until lightly browned. Once all of the mushrooms are browned, add to the reserved bacon, and set aside.

3. If there are no drippings in the skillet, add the olive oil and stir-fry the red pepper for about 2 minutes or until beginning to soften. Reduce the heat to moderate, mix in the garlic, and cook and stir 1 minute more. Add 1 cup of the cream and simmer for about 5 minutes or until lightly thickened.

4. Add the reserved bacon and mushrooms along with the remaining cream, then simmer, stirring occasionally, for about 5 minutes or until the consistency of café au lait, remembering that the pasta will absorb much of the liquid.

5. Add the cooked and drained linguini and toss until nicely coated. Taste for salt and adjust as needed.

6. To serve, scoop into a low, wide bowl, scatter the chopped parsley on top, and set on the dinner table along with a bowl of freshly grated Parmigiano-Reggiano.

Banana-Nut Bread with Raisins

Makes one 9 × 5 × 3-inch loaf (6 to 8 servings)

Jon Ellenbogen likes to serve whipped cream cheese with this banana bread, inspired by a recipe in *Beard on Bread* (Random House, 1973), which he bakes in Barking Spider's stoneware loaf pan. "The bread freezes well," Jon says, "and I usually have one in the freezer."

Note: Unlike mass-produced metal pans, pottery ones are individually shaped and thus their dimensions vary slightly from pan to pan but fortunately not enough to affect baking times.

2 cups sifted all-purpose flour

1½ teaspoons baking soda

½ teaspoon baking powder

½ teaspoon salt

¾ cup granulated sugar

¼ cup raw sugar

¾ cup coarsely chopped pecans, walnuts, or black walnuts

½ cup golden raisins or, if you prefer, seedless brown raisins

3 medium-size overripe bananas (about 1 pound), peeled and mashed

⅓ cup buttermilk (or more as needed)

⅓ cup melted unsalted butter

2 large eggs

1 tablespoon fresh lemon juice

1. Preheat the oven to 350°F. Stand a 9 × 5 × 3-inch ovenproof stoneware, other pottery, ceramic, or heat-resistant glass loaf pan on a small sheet of aluminum foil, and trace around the bottom of the pan. Using scissors, cut around the traced lines, then place the foil liner shiny-side down in the bottom of the pan. Now spray the foil and the sides of the pan liberally with nonstick cooking spray, and set the pan aside.

2. Whisk the flour, baking soda, baking powder, and salt together in a large bowl, add the granulated and raw sugars, and whisk well to combine. Mix in the pecans and raisins, then make a well in the middle of the dry ingredients, and set aside.

3. Using a hand electric mixer at high speed, beat the remaining ingredients (mashed bananas through lemon juice) 1 to 2 minutes in a medium-size bowl until smooth.

4. Pour the liquid ingredients into the well in the dry ingredients and fold in—gently, gently. *Note*: If the batter is too stiff to pour, mix in another 2 to 3 tablespoons buttermilk.

5. Scoop the batter into the prepared pan, smoothing the top and spreading to the corners.

6. Slide the pan onto the middle shelf of the preheated oven and bake for about 1 hour or until the bread begins to pull from the sides of the pan, is springy to the touch, and a cake tester inserted in the center of the loaf comes out clean.

7. Transfer the pan to a wire rack, setting right-side up, and cool the bread in the pan for 15 minutes.

8. Carefully run a small thin-blade spatula around the edge of the bread to loosen it, invert on the wire rack, and quickly peel off the foil liner. Turn the loaf right side up—easy does it—and cool to room temperature before cutting.

9. To serve, cut the banana bread into slices about ½ inch thick using your sharpest serrated knife. And don't forget to follow Jon's lead by putting out a bowl of whipped cream cheese.

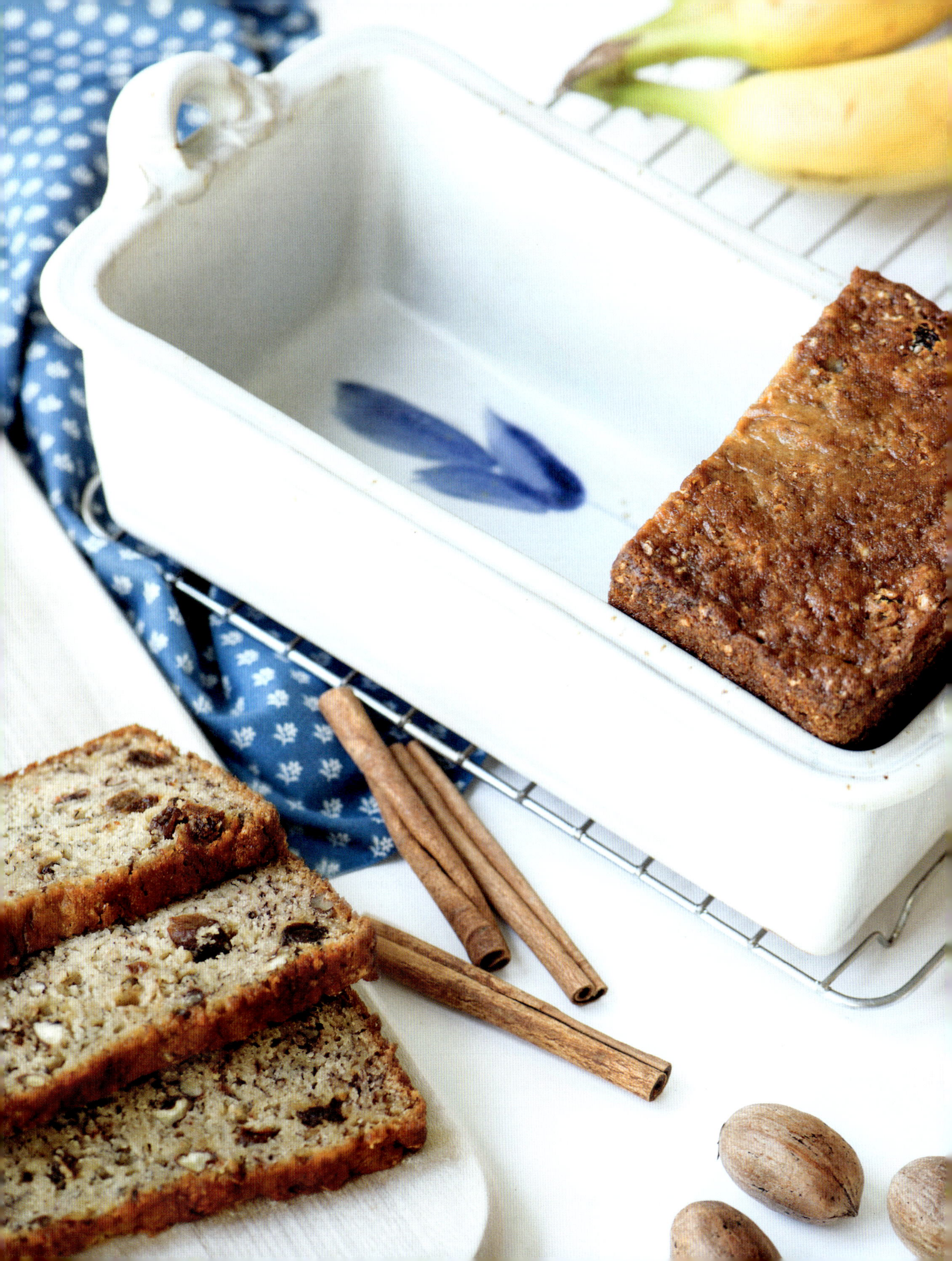

Pear Crumble with Crystallized Ginger

Makes 8 servings

"Perfect pears are hard to come by," Jon says. "In the supermarket they're hard as rocks and seem to be ripe for only a few hours before they're mushy. On those occasions when you get the timing right, this dessert is hard to beat." He bakes it in Barking Spider's 11-inch, 6-cup stoneware au gratin dish and serves it with heavy cream "whipped with a little dark rum."

Note: We used Bartletts in testing this recipe, but if Anjous or Boscs are in season, by all means substitute one of these. They're sweeter and blessed with deep pear flavor.

1 tablespoon unsalted butter, at room temperature

CRUMBLE

1 cup sifted all-purpose flour

2/3 cup old-fashioned rolled oats (oatmeal)

2/3 cup firmly packed light brown sugar

1 teaspoon ground cinnamon

1/8 teaspoon salt

1/2 cup (1 stick) refrigerator-cold unsalted butter,
    cut into 1/2-inch dice

FRUIT FILLING

3 pounds firm-ripe pears, peeled, cored, and cut into
    1/2- to 3/4-inch dice (see *Note* above)

2 tablespoons fresh lemon juice

1/3 cup granulated sugar

2 tablespoons finely minced crystallized ginger

1 1/2 tablespoons all-purpose flour, 2 tablespoons
    if your pears seem overly juicy

TOPPING

1 cup heavy cream whipped with 1 tablespoon each
    dark rum and confectioners' (10X) sugar until soft
    and billowing

1. Butter an 11-inch, 6-cup stoneware au gratin dish or similar-size ovenproof stoneware, other pottery, ceramic, or heat-resistant glass baking dish that can go into a preheated oven, and set aside. Preheat the oven to 350°F.

2. *For the crumble*: Place all but the last ingredient (diced butter) in a medium-size mixing bowl and toss well to mix. Scatter the diced butter on top, then using a pastry blender, cut in until the texture of lentils, and reserve.

3. *For the filling*: Place all ingredients in a second medium-size bowl, toss well to mix, then scoop into the prepared baking dish, spreading to the edge.

4. Scatter the crumble evenly over all, slide the baking dish onto the middle shelf of the preheated oven, and bake for about 45 minutes or just bubbling and tipped with brown.

5. Remove the crumble from the oven, set on a wire baking rack, and cool for 15 to 30 minutes.

6. To serve, spoon the crumble into decorative dessert bowls, and drift each portion with some of the whipped cream topping.

8

Bandana Pottery:

Michael Hunt and

Naomi Dalglish

FOR MORE INFORMATION:

bandanapottery.com

"Plates are such a great canvas for creativity that happens in the kitchen," say Michael and Naomi, "and of course we are often dreaming of those possibilities as we move clay on the wheel."

Their recipes prove that these two clearly know their way around a kitchen as well as around the old barn among the boulders near Bakersville they've given new life as a pottery.

Michael and Naomi both felt the magic of clay early—Ohio-born Michael as an Orlando teenager blessed with a high school pottery class. And Naomi at the age of five. Growing up in an artistic Indiana family (her father's a famous musician—www.oooliticmusic .com). She spent summers shaping and firing pots with her Pittsburgh grandmother, a high school art teacher.

So it's not surprising that Naomi studied ceramics at Earlham, a small Quaker college in Richmond, Indiana, or that she spent a semester with a family of Mexican potters before heading to Penland in the Carolina Blue Ridge to study kiln-building. Michael, having dropped out of ceramics at the University of Florida, was immersed in the core course at Penland and, when Naomi arrived, was building his own kiln.

In short order they discovered their "similar passion and approach to making pottery." Michael's trips to the Far East give his work a dramatic Asian accent, not only the giant onggi storage jars he learned to make while apprenticing in Korea but also his utilitarian mugs, plates, and bowls. Naomi collaborates on Bandana's functional items but also finds time to shape clay into little figurines inspired by the pre-Columbian ones that had caught her eye in Mexico.

"We feel lucky to live in a place where there are so many native clays," they say. "And in such a great community of potters that share with each other."

Gambas al Ajillo

We know this as shrimp scampi, but Hunt and Dalglish make it a bit differently. They sauté the garlic in olive oil until crisp, then sprinkle it over the sautéed shrimp just before serving on one of their dark green platters.

¼ cup extra-virgin olive oil

8 medium-size garlic cloves, thinly sliced

1 teaspoon sweet paprika

½ teaspoon salt, or to taste

⅛ teaspoon freshly ground black pepper, or to taste

1½ pounds fresh large raw shrimp, shelled and
   deveined

3 tablespoons fresh lemon juice

3 tablespoons coarsely chopped fresh Italian parsley

1 medium-size lemon, quartered lengthwise

1. Heat the olive oil in a large, heavy skillet over moderate heat for about 1½ minutes or until ripples appear on the pan bottom.

2. Add the garlic, and stir-fry quickly for about 2 minutes or until pale tan and crisp. Using a slotted spoon, lift the garlic to paper toweling to drain, and reserve.

3. Sprinkle the paprika, salt, and pepper over the shrimp and toss until evenly coated.

4. Reduce the heat under the skillet to moderately low, add the shrimp, and sauté, stirring often, for 2 to 3 minutes or just until the shrimp turn pink.

5. Using a spider or mesh skimmer, lift the shrimp to a large heated platter, sprinkle with the lemon juice, chopped parsley, and reserved garlic, then for a final flourish, garnish with the lemon wedges.

6. Serve at once accompanied by steamed fresh asparagus, broccoli, or, even easier, lightly sautéed cherry or grape tomatoes.

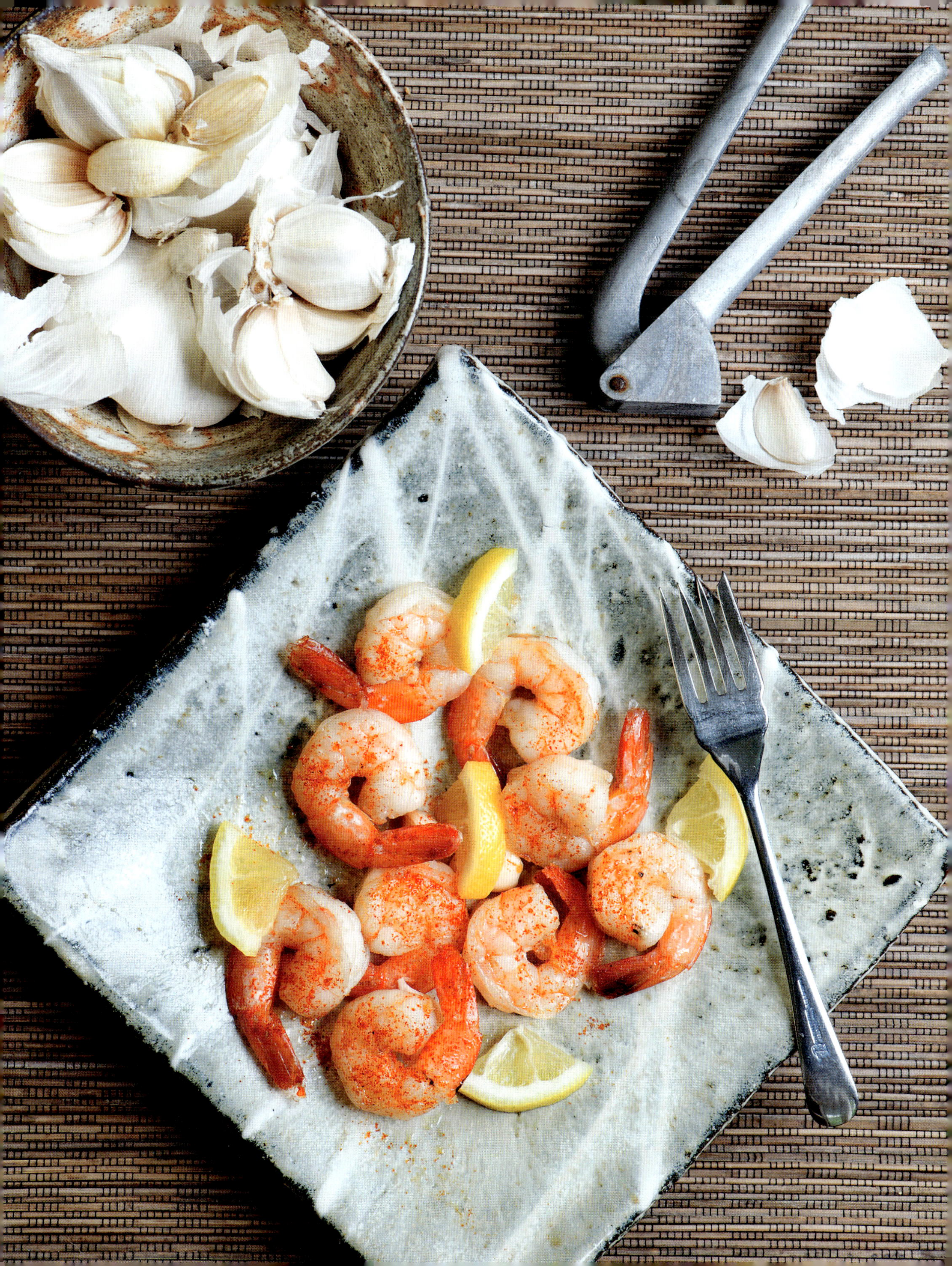

Butternut-Coconut Soup

"We've enjoyed making this soup," says Naomi, "with the overabundance of butternut squash coming from the volunteer plants growing out of our compost pile these past few summers. However, I'm sure any dense, slightly sweet winter squash would work well."

Note: Though neither Naomi nor husband Michael suggests this, try chilling this nutritious soup, then freeze to enjoy on hot summer days.

1 medium-size butternut squash (about 2 to 2¼ pounds), halved and seeds removed

1 large yellow onion, peeled and quartered

1 (13- to 14-ounce) can unsweetened coconut milk

4 cups canned vegetable broth, preferably unsalted

1½ tablespoons fresh lemon juice

1½ teaspoons salt, or to taste

¼ teaspoon freshly ground black pepper, or to taste

¾ teaspoon chili oil

1. Preheat the oven to 375°F. Spritz a large, shallow roasting pan with nonstick cooking spray.

2. Place the squash halves cut-side down toward each end of the roasting pan, then arrange the onion quarters in the middle.

3. Slide the pan onto the middle shelf of the preheated oven and roast uncovered for about 1 hour or until the squash is soft. *Note*: Stir the onion quarters occasionally as they roast to prevent overbrowning, and if the outer layers toughen, remove and discard.

4. Scoop the soft squash flesh into an electric blender, add the roasted onions and half the coconut milk, and whiz for 1 to 1½ minutes or until smooth.

5. Pour the puréed soup into a large non-reactive saucepan, then blend in the remaining coconut milk and just enough of the 4 cups vegetable broth to give the soup the consistency of vichyssoise.

6. Set over moderately low heat, and bring just to serving temperature—this will take 6 to 7 minutes. The soup should steam, not boil.

7. Set off the heat, stir in the lemon juice, then salt and pepper to season.

8. Pour into a heated tureen or large bowl, drizzle in the chili oil, then carry to the table and ladle into individual pottery bowls, mugs, or cups—Bandanas are worth ordering just for this 24-carat soup.

Black Sesame Seed Cake with Orange and Almond

Makes one 9-inch cake (8 to 10 servings)

"Our family is gluten- and dairy-free," says Michael Hunt, "and this cake fulfills those requirements. Gluten-free flour makes for a more tender cake, and the almond flour creates a lovely richness. We like the contrast of the slightly mysterious dark nuttiness of the black sesame seeds [see Sources, page 164] with the brightness of the citrus."

Tip: Michael grinds the sesame seeds in a little coffee and spice grinder.

¾ cup granulated sugar

¾ cup unsifted almond flour (see information on flours on page 8)

½ cup unsifted gluten-free rice flour (see information on flours on page 8)

¼ cup black sesame seeds, finely ground (see *Tip* above)

1½ teaspoons baking powder

1 teaspoon salt

½ cup extra-virgin olive oil

½ cup fresh orange juice

3 large eggs

1 teaspoon grated orange zest

¼ teaspoon almond extract

1 tablespoon confectioners' (10X) sugar (topping)

1. Preheat the oven to 350°F. Spritz a 9-inch springform pan well with nonstick cooking spray, then line the bottom with baking parchment, and set aside.

2. Place the first six ingredients (granulated sugar through salt) in a large mixing bowl, whisk until thoroughly mixed, then make a well in the middle of the dry ingredients.

3. Whisk the olive oil, orange juice, eggs, orange zest, and almond extract until smooth in a medium-size mixing bowl, then pour into the well in the dry ingredients, and fold together until well blended.

4. Scoop the batter into the prepared pan, smoothing the top and spreading to the edge.

5. Slide the cake onto the middle shelf of the preheated oven, and bake for about 35 minutes or until springy to the touch and a cake tester, inserted midway between the rim and the center, comes out clean.

6. Transfer the cake to a wire cake rack and cool right-side up for 20 minutes. Loosen and remove the springform pan sides, then cool the cake—still on the pan bottom and rack—to room temperature. *Note*: Being gluten-free, the cake will sink somewhat in the middle as it cools. No problem. It cuts beautifully.

7. Sift the confectioners' sugar over the cooled cake, then carefully ease it from the pan bottom onto one of your prettiest round pottery plates. Michael and Naomi would use one of their own one-of-a-kind.

8. To serve, cut the cake into wedges and accompany with mugs of freshly brewed coffee.

Address Book

Bandana Pottery (Michael Hunt and Naomi Dalglish), 3385 N.C. 80, Bakersville; bandanapottery.com

Barking Spider Pottery (Jon Ellenbogen and Rebecca Plummer), 1446 Conley Ridge Road, Penland; barkingspiderpottery.com

Beckett Pottery (Robin Beckett), 1884 Fonta Flora Drive, Nebo; beckettpottery.blogspot.com

Ben Owen Pottery, 105 Ben's Place, Seagrove; benowenpottery.com

Brad Tucker Pottery, Cedar Creek Gallery, 1150 Fleming Road, Creedmoor; bradtuckerpottery.blogspot.com

B. R. Hilton Pottery (Bob Hilton, Heather Hilton, and Linda Hilton Long), 4026 Old State Road, Newton; hiltonpottery.com

Bulldog Pottery (Bruce Gholson and Samantha Henneke), 3306 U.S. 220 N., Seagrove; bulldogpottery.com

Cady Clay Works (Beth Gore and John Mellage), 3883 Busbee Road, Seagrove; cadyclayworks.com

Cape Fear Pottery (Reuben and Ann York), 3309 U.S. 401 N., Lillington; info@ncpotterycenter.org

Doug Dotson Pottery, 326 Mockernut Road, Pittsboro; dougdotsonpottery.com

East Fork (Alex Matisse), 82 N. Lexington Avenue, Asheville; eastfork.com

Ellington Pottery (Kim Ellington), 7110 W. N.C. 10, Vale; ellingtonpottery.com

Falcon Lane Pottery (Susan Kern), 108 Falcon Lane, Mebane; falconlanepottery.com

Goathouse Gallery (Siglinda Scarpa), 680 Alton Alston Road, Pittsboro; siglindascarpa.com

Hickory Hill Pottery (Daniel Marley), 4539 Busbee Road, Seagrove; hickoryhillpottery.blogspot.com

Jugtown Pottery (Vernon and Pamela Owens), 330 Jugtown Road, Seagrove; jugtownware.com

Julie Jones Pottery, 119 W. Seeman Street, Durham; juliejonespottery.com

Latham's Pottery (Bruce and Janice Latham), 7297 U.S. 220 Alt., just north of Seagrove; lathamspottery.com

Lyn Morrow Pottery, 3449 U.S. 15-501, Pittsboro; lynmorrowpottery.com

Mark Hewitt Pottery, 424 Johnny Burke Road, Pittsboro; hewittpottery.com

Melting Mountain Pottery (Joey Sheehan), Phil Mechanic Studios, 109 Roberts Street, Asheville; meltingmountainpottery.com

New Salem Pottery (Hal Pugh and Eleanor Minnock-Pugh), 789 New Salem Road, Randleman; newsalempottery.com

Rutkowsky Pottery (Michael Rutkowsky and Ruth Fischer Rutkowsky), 1489 Cane Branch Road, Burnsville; rutkowskypottery.com

Westmoore Pottery (Mary Farrell), 4622 Busbee Road, Seagrove; westmoorepottery.com

For more information about North Carolina pottery and North Carolina potters, contact the North Carolina Pottery Center, 233 East Avenue, Seagrove; ncpotterycenter.org. The museum here displays some ancient Cherokee and Catawba pots. Though the Cherokees are better known today for basketry, they also have a pottery tradition that's very much alive. Check out the Cherokee potters at http://www.blueridgeheritage.com/directory/artist/206.

Sources

EXOTIC SEASONINGS

Asian (Thai) fish sauce: importfood.com

Chili pequins: wholespice.com

Gochugaru (Korean chili flakes): spicejungle.com

Gochujang (spicy Korean chili sauce):
    gochujangsauce.com

Herbes de Provence: penzeys.com

Matcha (green tea powder): vitacost.com

Penang (red) curry paste: posharpstore.com

Peruvian chili lime seasoning: savoryspiceshop.com

Rose water: kalustyans.com

FLOURS, GRAINS, AND MEALS

Banana flour: nuts.com

California long-grain white rice (low arsenic):
    lundberg.com

Cornmeal (stone-ground): oldmillofguilford.com

Grits (stone-ground): ansonmills.com

Potato flour: ener-g.com

Rice flour: bobsredmill.com

Soy flour: bobsredmill.com

MEAT

Andouille sausage: www.cajungrocer.com;
    also dartagnan.com

Country-style southern sausage meat:
    neesesausage.com; also swaggertys.com

NUTS AND SEEDS

Black walnuts (shelled): heartlandnutsnmore.com

Black sesame seeds: webstaurantstore.com

Chia seeds: iherb.com

Hickory nuts (shelled): rayshickorynuts.com

VEGETABLES

Dried porcini mushrooms: olivenation.com

Fooled-you jalapeño peppers (seeds):
    downrightnatural.com

Purple Japanese eggplant (Yasakanaga hybrid
    seeds): kitazawaseed.com

MISCELLANEOUS

Coconut oil: healthytraditions.com

Maple syrup (deep-flavored Grade B):
    vermontpuremaplesyrup.com; also
    piecesofvermont.com

Wild persimmon purée:
    indianapersimmonstore.com

Recipe Index

General Index

All potteries, galleries, and schools are in North Carolina unless otherwise noted.